Diary of a Creeper King

An Unofficial Minecraft Series

Books 1-4
FULL QUADRILOGY

Diary of a Creeper King – Book 1
Diary of a Creeper King – Book 2
Diary of a Creeper King – Book 3
Diary of a Creeper King – Book 4

Skeleton Steve

www.SkeletonSteve.com

D1519362

Copyright

"Diary of a Creeper King Box Set 1"

"Diary of a Creeper King – Book 1"

"Diary of a Creeper King – Book 2"

"Diary of a Creeper King – Book 3"

"Diary of a Creeper King – Book 4"

Published in the United States of America by Lightbringer Media LLC, 2017

To join Skeleton Steve's free mailing list, for updates about new Minecraft Fanfiction titles:

www.SkeletonSteve.com

Table of Contents

Contents

Book Introduction by Skeleton Steve

Love MINECRAFT? ****Over 74,000 words of kid-friendly fun!****

This high-quality fan fiction fantasy diary book is for kids, teens, and nerdy grown-ups who love to read epic stories about their favorite game!

Thank you to <u>all</u> of you who are buying and reading my books and helping me grow as a writer. I put many hours into writing and preparing this for you. I *love* Minecraft, and writing about it is almost as much fun as playing it. It's because of *you*, reader, that I'm able to keep writing these books for you and others to enjoy.

This book is dedicated to *you*. Enjoy!!

After you read this book, please take a minute to leave a simple review. I really appreciate the feedback from my readers, and love to read your reactions to my stories, good or bad. If you ever want to see your name/handle featured in one of my stories, leave a review and *tell me about it* in there! And if you ever want to ask me any questions, or tell me your idea for a cool Minecraft story, you can email me at steve@skeletonsteve.com.

Are you on my **Amazing Reader List**? Find out at the end of the book!

December the 5th, 2016

For those of you who love Mighty Cth'ka the Creeper King, and like a good deal, enjoy this Box Set! If you'd like to see me continue the adventures of Cth'ka and his friends, please let me know in the comments!

- Skeleton Steve

P.S. - Have you joined the Skeleton Steve Club and my Mailing List?? *Check online to learn how!*

You found one of my diaries!!

This is a BUNDLE OF STORIES of one of my friends, Cth'ka the creeper—a *true hero* of Diamodia. You are holding the first *box set* collection of diary entries from his journey of becoming a great king of *creeperkind!*

Be warned—this is an *epic book!* You're going to *care* about these characters. You'll be scared for them, feel good for them, and feel bad for them! It's my hope that you'll be *sucked up* into the story, and the adventure and danger will be so intense, you'll forget we started this journey with a *video game!*

So with that, dear reader, I present to you the tale of **Cth'ka the Creeper King**, the **Box Set**...

Box Set Book 1 - Diary of a Creeper King

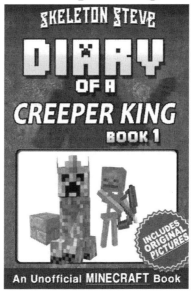

Ever heard of the Creeper King, mighty Cth'ka?

Read the adventure diary of a young creeper who was looking for a way to protect himself without blowing up!

When Cth'ka the Creeper and Skeleton Steve leave the forest to ask a local witch for help, they are soon on a long and dangerous journey to find a

5

secret artifact that will allow Cth'ka the power to move blocks with his mind! But will the difficulty of traveling across the Minecraft world, coming across a village under attack, hiding from a fully-armored killer hero, and finding the way to a hidden stronghold be too much for a creeper and his skeleton companion to handle?

Day 1

Let's see … is this *'Night* 1' or *'Day* 1'? I figure I'll write these entries in terms of *days*, since I never sleep. I will try to ignore the fact that, since I don't have hands that I can write with, I'm sitting under a tree right now *dictating*, saying my story out loud, to my good friend, Skeleton Steve.

He says that I should just tell the story like I'm writing it. I'll give this a try.

My name is Cth'ka. I'm a creeper. I don't know if that's the *real* name of my race, but that's what everyone calls us, so it works.

Other creepers would probably say that I'm a weird guy. An oddball.

But other creepers don't say much.

That's what's different about me. I don't know very much about where we came from. Heck, I don't even remember much about a year or so ago.

How did I get here? As far as I know, I've always lived in this forest. Skeleton Steve calls it "Darkwood Forest". He says that there are hundreds—*thousands* of other forests, so he likes to give names to places.

I do love this place.

The hills rise and fall, and the trees are thick, tall, and dark. *Dark oak*, Steve says. It's a very large forest too. I've never felt much of an urge to leave.

On one side of the forest, where the hills slope down, there's a thick jungle where the trees are different. On another side, the hills rise higher and higher until the trees stop, and snowy peaks reach into the sky.

I never go there, to the cold mountains. Hardly ever, really. I prefer to be in warmer places.

The jungle is nice and warm, but it's also full of water and rivers, and I don't care for water—not at all.

On the other sides of Darkwood forest, the hills continue for quite a ways with tall, dark oak trees, until they wind down into some grassy plains full of flowers and horses.

I love this forest, but I'm getting side-tracked.

Creepers are very solitary. I've seen many creatures in this world, living in and passing through my forest. Some creatures have moms and dads. Most of them are babies and then grow up. The zombies and skeletons don't. I don't know where *they* come from. Where Skeleton Steve came from. I think he was something else before he became who he is today.

I don't know much about my past. Or where my race came from.

I don't remember having a mom or dad. And I don't remember being smaller, or growing up in any way. I hope to find out about these things in time.

Creepers don't exactly have a library of their race's past. There's nothing to study. Nothing we can learn from our elders. I can't even tell the difference between a young creeper and an old creeper! I assume that I'm young, but maybe we just don't have very good memories. Who knows?

And the creepers I see while I walk around my forest don't have much to say either.

Earlier today, I was in my favorite part of Darkwood. My *clearing*. Near the very middle of this forest is a large clearing, a place where the trees break, and a wide valley of grass stretches out a long way. Red and yellow flowers pepper the open expanse. I love to go there during the day and watch the flowers sway in the breeze, feel the sun on my skin, and watch the clouds roll by.

At the time, Skeleton Steve was back in the forest. He doesn't sleep either, but he can't explore with me during the day. If Skeleton Steve steps into the sunlight ... *foom*! He'd catch on fire. I've only seen it happen once before—he's pretty careful. But I guess that's just part of being undead.

So Skeleton Steve was back in the thickest part of the forest, waiting out the day in the shadow of a large dark oak tree, and I was watching another creeper walk across the clearing.

Whenever I see another creeper, I always try to make conversation, to learn about them. It's always my hope to learn more about my people, and to make friends who are like me.

"Hi there," I said.

The other creeper noticed me, said nothing, then turned to continue moving away. I followed.

"My name is Cth'ka. What's yoursss?"

The other creeper stopped, and turned to face me. "What you wantsss?"

"I don't sssee othersss like me very often. Where did you come from? Where are you going?"

"What doesss it matter to you?" he said in a gravelly voice. He turned, and continued walking through the valley.

"I jussst want to be friendsss," I said to his back. "Pleassse tell me about yoursssself!"

I stopped.

The other creeper kept moving, without speaking again, and I stood in the sun and watched until he disappeared into the shadows of the dark oak trees.

Later that day, when the sun went down, I walked back to where I knew Skeleton Steve was waiting for me. In the shadows of the darkening forest, I could see the glowing red dots of his eyes, hovering in the middle of his empty black eye sockets, watching me approach.

"Why do you always try to talk to the other creepers?" Skeleton Steve asked after I told him about my day. "They always act the same way."

We were walking along a ridge, watching the moon rise into the sky. Skeleton Steve's face was silver in the fading light. I could see in the darkness just fine, but when the light faded away, the colors of the world disappeared too. I did love the daylight, when everything was bold and colorful. It was too bad that Skeleton Steve always had to hide in the dark.

"I've got to try," I said. "There have to be more creepersss out there like me. I want to know more about why we're here. How we creepersss *get* here."

"So many creepers are just … grumpy, it seems," Skeleton Steve said.

We walked in silence for a while.

"I wonder if we're ssstuck like thisss, or if there will ever be sssomeone to bring usss together. If there are other creepersss, sssmart like me, I'm sure we can do *great* thingsss."

"Why are you so interested in other creepers?" Skeleton Steve said.

"I think … it would be a good thing for usss to come together," I said. I wasn't quite sure what I was getting at, but I knew that I wanted creepers, as a *people*, to find strength together somehow. To have a real race, a real history. Something unique that we could pass down to whatever it meant to be the next generation. I didn't even know if creepers had children, or how more creepers came to be. "We could maybe be—I don't know—a *real race*. Develop oursssselvesss instead of jussst being like animalsss wandering around all alone."

"You mean like creeper cities? A creeper nation?" Skeleton Steve said, smirking.

"I don't know," I said. "I jussst feel like, we could be … more."

Day 2

I stayed with Skeleton Steve in the dark during the day. We were close to the jungle, and I thought it might be fun to walk along the border when the sun went down. We might even see some areas of the jungle that were dry enough to let us walk down into it for a while without having to cross any *water*.

It would be nice to feel the warmth of the tropical forest. I hadn't visited the jungle in a long time.

Another creeper passed by, and I was at least able to get his name. Car'nuk. But we didn't talk about much else. I tried to find out how old Car'nuk was, and where he lived, but, like all of the others, he scowled at me, and went on his way.

It was a little sad, how difficult it was to communicate with my people. It's like we creepers were designed to never have anything to do with each other. And that was a pity. Creepers are natural-born explorers. We walk, all day and all night, and I'm sure there would be *plenty* to talk about if the others like me weren't so grumpy about having conversations.

When the sun went down, Skeleton Steve and I walked to the next ridge over, where we could look down into the jungle. Even in the fading light, I was surprised at how *green* the area was.

Some of the trees were squat and so thick that it made it hard to see the ground beneath them, and they were covered with vines that descended like green, ropy sheets from the treetops. Other trees were massive and tall, popping out of the canopy with large clumps of leaves extending in multiple directions.

I bet it rained a lot here.

It was hard to see through the trees, but I could see water here and there, down below. There must be rivers and pools *all over*.

I could never live in the jungle. I don't like the water. Never have. I've always had a hard time with the idea of floating in the water, even though I've seen other creepers swim before—I don't know how to ssswim, and didn't know if I'd ever be able to figure it out.

With my little legs, the idea of not being able to keep my head out of water, the idea of sssplashing and ssstruggling to get back to sssolid ground …. my lungsss filling up with water …. Sssssssssss … sssssssssplashing, sssssssstruggling …

No thanksss. Just the *thought* of being stuck in water gets me all … excited. I've always thought it would be better to avoid water altogether.

As Skeleton Steve and I walked along the ridge, we looked out over the expanse of trees into the dense jungle below. The ridge descended gently into an area of jungle that wasn't as thick.

I hesitated.

"It's okay," Skeleton Steve said. "I don't see anything bad in there. It's just *part* jungle. Do you want to see what it looks like inside?"

I walked with him down into the tree-line. Darkwood Forest was behind us now, just on the other side of the ridge. There were no rivers or pools in the immediate area. No water.

We stood, peering into the depths of the jungle, and I was thinking about heading back to the forest when I saw movement! Green.

Another *creeper*!

I saw the distinct shape, its head turn, a face like mine looking back at us from the darkness for just a moment before it turned again.

"Hey!" I shouted. "Hello there!"

The creeper stood still, then turned to look at us again.

"Let'sss go in!" I said.

Skeleton Steve shrugged, and followed me deeper into the jungle.

We approached the creeper, and I called out to him again from a distance. "Hi there, fellow creeper! I'm Cth'ka! Do you live here in the jungle?"

As we continued making our way to my new friend through the heavy underbrush, I saw the creeper suddenly snap his attention to one side, then stagger back a few steps. I could hear him *hiss*, unsure at first, then again—intensely! The creeper fell back again, and I saw something on its chest—a *blur* of a creature, dim without color, but ... *spots*?

The creeper was under attack?!

I was suddenly afraid, and faintly heard Skeleton Steve, at my side, pull out his bow and nock an arrow. The creeper hissed again, a continual, rising, sputtering sound! It was definitely an animal of some kind, a spotted creature, small, clawing and biting at my intended friend.

"Ocelot!" Skeleton Steve said.

Expanding and shaking, hissing even louder, the creeper suddenly *exploded* with a thunderous *boom!*

What?! *How*?

How did that ...?

Shocked, I stood, staring at the spot where the creeper and the ocelot were fighting, now a crater of raw dirt and shredded plants, and I felt fear wash over me again when I saw two white and

21

yellow forms darting through the bushes ... straight at *me*.

Two more ocelots! Little greens eyes, focused on me.

"Run!" Skeleton Steve yelled, and I stumbled backwards as an arrow suddenly struck one of the cats. It turned and sprinted off to Steve.

As I focused on the ocelot about to attack me, trying to force my body turn and run away back up the hill, my *hearing* seemed to tighten around my heartbeat, my vision darkened around the edges, and Skeleton Steve's shouted warnings suddenly seemed very far away...

The ocelot leapt through the air at me, and I felt its claws and teeth sink into my body. I tried to turn and run, but it was hanging onto me. My hearing, now weird and hollow like I was in a deep cave, was focusing more and more on a ... hissing sound ... I ssscrambled, tried to essscape, tried to call for Sssskeleton Sssteve ... Sssssssss ...

"Sssteve!   Ssssssssssssssssssssssssssssssave me!"

An arrow appeared out of nowhere sssticking out of the ocelot'sss ssside, and the cat fell. I turned and sssaw Ssskeleton Sssteve nocking another arrow, aiming past me.

I ran up the hill. Turned. Sssaw Ssskeleton Sssteve kill the ocelot. He ran to catch up to me, his bonesss rattling.

We ran back up the hill out of the jungle together, back up to the ridge.

"Are you okay?" Skeleton Steve said.

I could suddenly hear again, see again, like normal!

"Yesss," I said. "What ... sssssssssss .... What happened?"

Skeleton Steve sat on the ridge, looking out over the jungle, his bow still in his hand.

"Those were ocelots," he said. "Mostly harmless animals. Strange that they attacked. Usually they mind their own business. I know they don't like creepers, but I've never seen them *attack* one before."

24

"What happened to the creeper?" I asked. "It *blew up!*"

Skeleton Steve looked at me. "You don't know?" he asked.

I shook my head.

Skeleton Steve's glowing red dots of eyes looked me over. "That—blowing up—that's what creepers *do*. They explode. In self-defense, and also when they're attacking a *Steve*."

"When they're attacking *you?*"

"No," Skeleton Steve said. "A *Steve*." He looked off at the moon. "My name is Steve, yes, but there is another creature on this world named 'Steve' as well. He's different than us."

"But why *explode?*" I said.

"That's all that the creeper *could* do," Skeleton Steve said. "When the ocelot attacked him, he exploded in self-defense, and killed it."

I was so confused. Why would he defend himself ... by killing himself?

"It doesn't make sssenssse," I said.

Skeleton Steve looked at me. "No one knows why creepers explode, Cth'ka. There's no other way for them to defend themselves, really. And I've never seen a creeper really *care*. I've seen creepers launch themselves at Steve and happily blow up in his face!" He regarded me for a moment. "*You* were about to explode too, you know. When that ocelot attacked you? I'm surprised you didn't, actually."

I looked down at my body, at the wounds where the cat had ripped at me.

So *that's* what that was—when I was losing concentration, when my vision and my hearing changed. Was I preparing to blow myself up?

"Why didn't I explode?" I asked.

"I don't know," Skeleton Steve said. "Maybe you're a little different? Maybe with how *smart* you are, compared to other creepers I've seen, you're able to control yourself better? We'll have to look into that some more—so you can survive longer. I'd hate to lose you as my friend, if you ever

26

get attacked again and blow up, or if we run into the *Steve*."

What a twist to my pleasant little life, roaming around in my forest! I had never seen a creeper explode before. I didn't even know it was possible. And now, there was a way that, if I was freaked out enough, I could lose control of my mind and blow myself up, too?

No way! That's crazy. I had a life to live. I wanted to bring 'creeperkind' together and learn more about our race. To learn more about our past and our culture … if there was one. Surely there was more to the creeper race than random solitary creatures that avoid having friends and then eventually blow themselves up?

What could I do?

I was defenseless. If Skeleton Steve wasn't with me, I would have been helpless, and killed by those ocelots. Or turned myself into a living bomb and ended up *dead* just the same.

"How can I defend mysssself?" I muttered.

We sat quietly for a few moments. The tall grass swayed in the night breeze.

"I have an idea," Skeleton Steve said. He was watching me as I sat, thinking. "*You* are special, Cth'ka. I'd like to see you learn to control your 'defense mechanism' and be able to defend yourself properly, but you can't use weapons like me, and you can't run very fast. We should go and talk to the witch! Maybe she'll have an idea."

"Witch?" I asked.

"Yes," Steve said. "There's a witch not too far from here, named Worla. I've dealt with her in the past, and she's very clever. She might be able to figure out why you're different. Maybe she'll have an idea about how to make it *easier* for you to survive without blowing yourself up one day."

For the rest of the night, Skeleton Steve and I traveled to the edge of the forest that was closest to the swamp. Before the sun came up, we found a small cave, and decided to wait out the day in there.

Day 3

When the sun went down, and undead could walk around outside safely again, we departed for the witch.

Standing at the edge of the forest, I could feel Darkwood behind me like a warm, safe hug, and the plains stretching out ahead of us, the empty rolling hills in the distance were … unknown.

We struck out, down from the shadows of the dark oak trees, into green and yellow fields. A group of horses of different colors stood quietly in the grass far off to the left, staying still in the night. A couple of zombies roamed aimlessly in the valley nearby.

"So, over those hills ahead," Skeleton Steve said, "is a swamp where Worla lives."

"A ssswamp?" I said. "Like, full of … water?"

Skeleton Steve laughed.

"Yes," he said. "Swamps are full of water. But that's where *witches* live."

"Can't we just have her come to usss?"

Skeleton Steve looked back at me while we walked. "Cth'ka, sometimes, to get good things, you have to take *risks*."

We walked across the great, open valley, then up into some sparse hills, as the wind whistled across the plain and the moon slowly moved across the sky. The hills were mostly devoid of trees at first, then started sprouting white trees here and there. Skeleton Steve called them 'Birch' trees. The hills rolled on, with more and more trees, until we seemed to be heading downhill all the time, and the trees turned darker.

Eventually, vines started growing from the trees, then further on, thick *sheets* of vines cascaded down their sides, a lot like the trees we saw in the jungle. The ground flattened out, and we were suddenly standing at the edge of a huge swamp, with random dirt and mud and water alternating as far as I could see, full of weeping trees. The air was hot and wet, and large lily pads spotted the surface of the water.

"That'sss a *lot* of water," I said.

"It's okay," Skeleton Steve said. "We'll stay on land where we can, and you can use the lily pads when you need to."

Lily pads? A sssaucer of *plant stuff* being the only thing keeping me from drowning in the murky water of this dreadful place?

"Where'sss the witch?" I said.

"Worla's hut is a little ways past that outcropping of rock over there," Skeleton Steve said, pointing to a spire of rock sticking out of a small hill, deep in the swamp.

Over the next few hours, we traveled across the bog. There was a *lot* of water, but Skeleton Steve was right! He was careful in planning where to walk, and planning ahead, and we stayed on dry ground most of the time. There were a few places where I had to cross water, but we were able to avoid swimming by finding areas where the land was close together, and joined with lily pads.

Once we reached the spire landmark, Skeleton Steve pointed deeper into the swamp, and I saw, in the fog, a small, dark dwelling standing on wooden stilts. The light of a fire inside made the hut stand out in the darkness.

"I've never ssseen a witch before," I said.

"Just be respectful, and certainly stay calm!" Skeleton Steve said with a smile.

When we approached the little building, I was relieved to see that it was mostly on land. I was afraid that I would have to cross more lily pads or even try to cross open water to get there. A rickety wooden ladder was lashed to one of the stilts, and it led to the deck on the front of the little house, and standing on the deck...

"Who goes there?" a woman's twisted and sharp-edged voice rang out in the quiet, dark night.

I saw a strange creature standing on the deck, just outside the doorway, her body wrapped in a dark purple robe, her hands hidden inside, and a black cowl hid most of her face. Her features were angry, and a hook-like nose curled down in front of a scowling mouth.

"Reveal your intentions," she said, "or I'll set you on *fire*!"

32

"Worla!" my bony friend said, "It is I, Skeleton Steve, and my companion, Cth'ka, come to consult your wisdom!"

She seemed to think for a moment.

"Skeleton Steve," she said, her voice suddenly much more friendly. "*You* are welcome, but I cannot risk your creeper companion destroying my home! I'll be down directly. Have a seat." She disappeared back into her doorway.

Skeleton Steve smirked at me. He looked around the clearing where we stood, and walked over to a circle of fallen logs. He sat on a log.

I followed.

A few minutes later, the witch descended her ladder with ease, and approached us. She sat on a log opposite Skeleton Steve so that we could all speak. A torch stuck out of the ground in the middle of our circle, which I didn't notice before, and it *flared* to life, casting fiery reflections and dancing shadows all around us.

"I am Worla," she said to me, "the witch of Lurkmire Swamp."

"I am Cth'ka," I said, "creeper ... of Darkwood Foressst?"

Skeleton Steve laughed. Worla laughed. I relaxed.

"What can *my wisdom* do for you tonight, Skeleton Steve?" she said.

"We've come because of my creeper friend here, Cth'ka," he said. "He is on a quest to learn more about his race, and to bring his people together, but is in need of a way to *defend* himself without blowing himself up."

Worla cackled. "A creeper trying to *avoid* blowing himself up?"

"Why isss that ssso funny?" I asked, my tone a little harsher than I intended. Skeleton Steve flinched a little.

"Because," the witch said, "creepers are quite *happy* to blow themselves up. It's their *destiny*. It's how they make *more* creepers."

What?

34

"Ssssss ... *More* creepersss?" I said. That was absurd!

"Look into my eyes, young creeper. Let me look into your *destiny*." She leaned forward toward me.

I looked at Skeleton Steve. He shrugged. Looking back at Worla the witch, I took a deep breath, steadied my fear, and held still, looking right into her beady, black eyes. In the flickering flames of the torchlight, I saw my frowning, green face reflected back at me in her eyes. Worla's face was still and passive, then it transformed in surprise!

"Oh my," she said, her black eyes unmoving but her face animating around them. "My, my. What an *interesting* path you have, mighty Cth'ka..."

Mighty?

She continued. "I can see what lies ahead for you, most interesting creeper. Interesting, indeed!"

"What isss?" I asked.

"Yeah," Skeleton Steve said. "What's so interesting?"

Worla laughed, breaking her eyes out of the dark and stony stare that held my own eyes in a tight grip. My attention to the swamp around me suddenly snapped back into focus.

"Cth'ka the creeper," she said. "I *will* help you, yes. I will tell you the location of an ... *artifact* of sorts, something that will allow you the ability to act with *hands unseen*, strong hands that will let you *smash* your enemies and defend yourself without using your ... last resort. Is this idea to your liking?"

I had no idea what she meant by all of that. Hands unseen? Some kind of weird magic?

"What do you mean?" I said. "Handsss unssseen?"

"Yes," she replied. "A magical item that will let you manipulate the world around you with your *mind*. The only possible defense for someone of your kind, assuming you don't want to destroy yourself."

She waved her hand, and the torch snuffed out like magic. A snap of her long, spindly fingers, and it flared to life again.

"I will give you items to assist in your journey as well. I only ask a small price in return..."

"What price?" I said.

"I am … building my interest here in Lurkmire still, and will require your assistance in the future. I ask for three favors upon your return with the artifact, and in exchange, I will give you the knowledge and ability to attain the power to fulfill your destiny and *lead your people*."

Everything I wanted.

But at what price?

What could the witch possible ask of me that I wouldn't be able to give her, especially once I had the power to manipulate the world with my mind and bring my people together in a nation of creeperkind?

I looked to Skeleton Steve. He returned my gaze without emotion.

He wasn't going to help me with *this* decision.

Wasn't this kind of idea what we traveled here for in the first place? Could I trust Worla the witch? If I asked Steve for his opinion, I would basically be asking him whether or not he thought I could trust the witch. I might offend her, and she might change her mind about the whole thing!

"Okay, I'll do it!" I said. "I'll get the artifact, then help you with your three favors."

She instantly pulled her hands out of her robe, her fingers like white spider legs in the darkness, tipped with thin claws. "Say it again," she commanded. "Repeat—I, Cth'ka the creeper, in exchange for assistance in finding the *Crown of Ender*, will perform three favors for Worla the Witch when she requires in the future."

I repeated her words, and she traced patterns in the darkness with her fingertips as I did. When I completed the sentence, she lashed out with her index finger, and touched my forehead. I flinched in surprise, caught control of my hisssssssss,

38

and felt a warm sensation bloom between my eyes then disappear.

Some sort of magic?

"You are unique, creeper," she said. "You will learn to control your *last resort* with your willpower. I can sense that already you can calm yourself back down. In time, you will be able to fight your enemies while keeping your mind calm, and not have to worry about exploding at all!"

Her hands disappeared back into her robes, then she produced three greenish-blue and yellow spheres. When she held out her palm to show us, the three spheres floated above her hand, throwing off purple motes of light. In the center of each sphere was a black slit of a pupil. They were *eyes*. Weird, magical eyeballs.

"These are eyes of Ender." She looked to Skeleton Steve. "Use them wisely. They will show you the way to the underground stronghold where you will find the Crown of Ender. Use one at a time, and *only* when you need to find the way. They will burn out in time. Follow the eyes to the location of the stronghold."

39

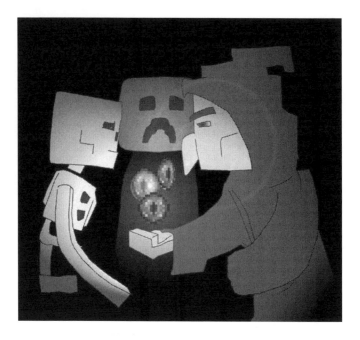

"Thank you," he said. Skeleton Steve took the eyes and put them into his pack.

"Remember," she said. "Only use them when you need to. Don't squander them!" She stood, pulling her robes about her. "And take care crossing the desert, my skeleton friend!" Worla laughed, and pulled the black cowl over her face again. The torch went out. "Good luck, mighty Cth'ka. Return to me once you have obtained the *crown.*" She looked at the sky. "The night will soon be over..."

With that, Worla turned, and moved back to her hut with a speed and dangerous grace that I wouldn't have imagined.

I looked at Skeleton Steve. "I guesss we're ssstaying out of Darkwood Foressst for a while?"

He nodded, and we traveled back the way we came, stopping to spend the day under a large tree at the edge of the swamp.

Day 4

When the sun set, Skeleton Steve and I stepped out of the swamp.

"Do you think Worla can sssee the future?" I asked.

Skeleton Steve stood in the fading light, and pulled one of the Ender Eyes from his pack. He held it in his bony fingers, turning it around and looking it over. It reminded me of the eyes of the ocelots, except larger. There were lots of colors—blue, green, and yellow. I was surprised that I *remembered* the cats' green eyes. But this eye was the size of an apple!

"Worla is a *witch*, Cth'ka," Skeleton Steve said. "I've seen her perform magic, and she's very smart. I don't how powerful she really is." He shrugged. "Maybe."

The Ender Eye in Steve's hand seemed to jitter with a life of its own suddenly, and my friend *released* it into the air. Bolting through the sky like a glowing arrow, the eye flew across the grassy plain for a while, then paused in the air. It left purple motes of light behind it, a softly falling path of magic *dust* for us to follow.

After floating in the air far away for a little while, the Ender Eye flashed, then fell lifeless to the ground.

"Come on!" Skeleton Steve said, and his bones clattered as he ran after it.

"I guesss we go thisss way!" I said, hurrying after him.

We found the eye of Ender lying in the grass.

Skeleton Steve picked it up, regarded it for a moment, then *launched* it into the air again!

"How are you doing that?" I said. We watched as the eye bolted across the sky in the same direction as before, leaving a trail of drifting purple motes of light. It traveled the same distance, up and away, paused, flashed, then fell to the ground.

"Hard to say," Skeleton Steve said. "When I hold it, it kind of *buzzes* with energy and feels like it *wants* to get away. I just *let* it."

We ran after the eye, and picked it up again.

Off in the distance, I saw the glowing red eyes of a couple of spiders wandering around on a hill. On another hill were a couple of zombies and another skeleton, doing their own thing, silhouettes against the sky.

Skeleton Steve picked up the eye, thought to himself for a moment, clenched it in his bony fingers.

"You know," he said, "Worla said not to squander them. Maybe they can only do this so many times. We should just keep walking in this direction, and only use the eyes every once and a while to make sure we're still on track."

"That'sss a good idea," I said. "Who knowsss how far away thisss ssstronghold isss?"

I glanced back at the way we came. The purple light that had dusted our path was gone.

45

Looking ahead, I saw that the grasslands continued for miles, with a hill veering into our way here and there, until the dark form of another forest swallowed up the horizon ahead of us.

A single hill on the horizon cast a crooked, black form against the sky.

"I think," I said, "if we walk ssstraight to *that* hill, we'll go the right way, and when we get there, we can find another hill or sssomething elssse far away on the other ssside to walk to next."

"Good idea," said Skeleton Steve. "I've done a lot of traveling myself, and using landmarks like that is a good way to keep going in the same direction."

We walked.

Over the course of a few hours, we crossed the lowlands, and made our way into a *birch* forest as we neared our 'landmark hill' on the horizon. Across the landscape, we watched other mobs wandering the night. We saw the usual zombies, skeletons, and spiders. Once, I saw another creeper, and was tempted to go off course to try and talk to him, but I didn't want to lose our way.

Once we reached the strange-shaped hill, we had already been walking among short birch trees for a while. The land ahead of us rose higher, and became more varied.

The birch trees stopped on the other end of the hill after about a mile, so we continued in the same direction until we were out of the trees. Skeleton Steve was planning to use the Ender Eye again from the crooked hill itself, but we didn't want to risk the eye falling out of the sky onto the top of a tree, or otherwise getting lost.

The two of us cast the Ender Eye once more. The yellow sphere flew across the valley ahead of us, going in the same direction we had been walking all night, before flashing and falling down into the grass.

So far, so good.

Up ahead, in the darkness of the night, the land turned into a black wall. It looked like we were approaching some extremely hilly and steeply-cut terrain.

Using the eye again once we crossed the flat space and ventured into the hills, we chose a new landmark—a bizarre floating island of rock, *hovering in the air* next to a sheer cliff. The only thing that connected the weird, floating island to the world around it was the constant stream of a small waterfall.

How in the world did that little island even produce a waterfall without just running out of water? I thought.

As the night went on, and the moon moved across the sky, we struggled over the bizarre and sharp landscape. Staying focused on our strange landmark, the floating island, was more difficult than we thought it would be.

Not long before dawn, we crossed most of the hilly terrain, and found ourselves standing under the floating island. It wasn't very big—about as big as Worla's hut. And I couldn't figure out where the water was *coming from* that created a constant waterfall, filling a pool on the ground up ahead of us.

It felt like we were doing well. We covered a lot of ground.

"How far do you think thisss ssstronghold isss?" I said.

Skeleton Steve shrugged, and walked off to the left of our path, to a small cave, cut into the side of a hill. I followed, and we holed up for the coming day.

Day 5

The sun was bright and hot in the extreme hills.

Skeleton Steve stayed back in the darkness of his cave, and I wandered around the immediate area under the floating island.

I approached the large pool of clear, blue water at the base of the floating island's waterfall.

It wasn't very deep. I was sure that I could keep my feet on the ground if I went into the water—probably across the entire small pond. This area was nice and hot, but it was also dry. It would feel so good to get wet.

"*But what if I fell?*" I thought. What if I slipped on the stone under the water, and my face went under? I could still drown! Even if the water only went up to my waist, I could *still* drown.

… Probably.

I approached the water's edge. The sound of the cascading waterfall was relaxing. I looked back for a moment to where Skeleton Steve was hidden in the darkness, then I *slowly* dipped one clawed foot into the pool.

"Sssssssssssssss," I said, and pulled my foot back out again.

I spent the rest of the day sitting by the mouth of Steve's cave, watching the mobs come and go. There were chickens somewhere—up above me on the hill, or around a corner. I could hear them, but I couldn't see them.

When the sun finally went down, Skeleton Steve emerged from the darkness, and we continued on our journey, following the eye once again.

Within the first hour, the crazy hills came to an end, and we looked out over a vast expanse of *tall* pine trees and twisting hills and ridges. We chose a tall ridge with three massive trees as a landmark, and set out into the huge taiga forest.

It was difficult to stay on course in this forest. Easy enough when we were going up a ridge, then back down again. Up and down. But sometimes, the direction of the ridges changed, and we were suddenly walking in a different direction.

One time, we lost track of our three-tree landmark entirely, and had to use the eye again.

The Ender Eye launched into the air and flew off in a direction we weren't expecting—we were so turned around—and it disappeared into the trees over a ridge.

"Great," Skeleton Steve said, and we ran over the ridge after it.

We searched for almost an hour. The trees were thick and tall, the ground steep, and moss-covered boulders lined the landscape. Eventually, we went down a ridge, and saw the yellow glint of the Ender Eye sitting on the other side of a winding stream.

"There it is!" Skeleton Steve exclaimed. "Let's go. Man, I thought we lost it for sure..."

He stepped down to the edge of the rushing water, and turned back to me when I didn't follow.

"I ..." I said. "I can't."

My friend stroked his bony jaw and thought for a moment, then said, "It's not deep, Cth'ka. We're going to have to cross it eventually. The path to the stronghold continues on the other side." He stepped into the water. The cold, rushing stream split around his bony legs and continued through the gulch until disappearing around a corner.

I stepped down to the water's edge. Touched the stream with my foot. It was cold. I pulled back.

"Sssssssssss ... I can't ... sssssssssssssssss..."

Skeleton Steve sighed. He crossed the stream, picked up the Ender Eye, then crossed the stream again back to me. His legs dripped. Skeleton Steve was undead. I'm sure he wasn't bothered at all by how cold the water was.

"Well," he said, trying to be patient with me, "we'll probably have to cross this stream *eventually*." He looked upstream, to where the water was flowing from. "But maybe you'll get lucky! Maybe it'll wind around and we can keep going without crossing it. Let's go *this way*, I guess."

We followed the stream in the direction of its source, winding through the bottom of a gulch through the forest. The little river continued out of our way for quite a while, then turned back.

I *did* get lucky.

There was a point, following the stream, where we felt like we had doubled back onto our course. Maybe we wouldn't have to cross the stream after all!

Skeleton Steve took out the Ender Eye to make sure we were back on our path. The sphere launched into the air and continued *away* from the stream like I hoped it would.

Yes!

I smiled. I looked at Skeleton Steve, thinking that he'd be annoyed with me, but he was smiling too. We were back on course!

The Ender Eye floated through the forest across the night sky, flashed ... and then *disintegrated*! Instead of falling back to the ground, the magic sphere *shattered* into dust and bits of purple light, then was gone!

"Oh no! Sssss! What?!" I said.

"I guess that's what Worla meant when she said that they would *burn out*." Steve said. "It's a good thing we have two more! Hopefully they last until we reach the stronghold."

We continued our journey with the *second* Ender Eye.

Fortunately, the huge, confusing forest didn't last much longer. Before dawn, we could see the end of it. When the trees started thinning out, the hills and ridges tapered and smoothed together, leading downhill to a great, open valley that stretched as far as I could see! There were huge, open lowlands of dirt, and strange, creeper-shaped plants. I was sure that we'd get a better look at the strange environment when we made it down there tomorrow.

We found a hole in a gulley of boulders that lead to a shallow cave, and Skeleton Steve got himself situated inside just in time for morning.

Day 6

Looking down the hill from the great, pine forest, I could now see, in the blinding light of day, that the huge open area ahead of us was not dirt. It was *sand*.

This was a desert.

Skeleton Steve would later point out to me that the weird plants that looked a little bit like me were called *Cacti*.

As I waited through the hot morning, another creeper passed by.

"Hello!" I said, approaching.

"Ssssssss," it answered. "What you want?"

At least it stopped walking. It stood, facing me.

"Do you live here?" I asked.

"Yesss." Its voice was harsh and slithery.

"I'm Cth'ka. What'sss your name?"

"Cho'thosss. Why do you asssk questionsss?" Cho'thos turned clearly thought about moving on, but turned back to me again.

"I ..." I began, but realized that I had never thought far enough ahead to get past *hello!* "Have you ever tried to explode, Cho'thosss?"

Dumb question.

I finally found another creeper willing to talk to me past *hello*, and I started with something stupid!

"Yesss," Cho'thos replied.

"Really?" I said. "Why?"

"I sssaw Ssssteve, once. Tried to sssneak up to him and *kill*, but he ssstruck me and got away." The creeper turned his body to show me his side, and I saw a scar slicing across his green midsection.

"Ssssteve?" I asked. As in *the* Steve? The *other* Steve?

"Yesss. He livesss near here."

"Why ... um—?"

My mind was a flurry of questions. Of course he must have meant Steve the *other Steve*. The same Steve that Skeleton Steve referred to back by the jungle. But where was this *Steve*? The *dangerous* Steve? Did he live in the forest? In the desert down below? And how this Cho'thos know to try and use his *last resort* as a weapon in the first place? Did he already know about creepers exploding and do it on purpose? Or did it just kind of *happen* in the moment? And how did he get away? Why would the Steve have 'struck' him and not finished him off?

Cho'thos turned away and continued on his path.

"Wait! I have questionsss!" I said.

"I mussst go," the creeper said, navigating across the boulders. "Ssso long, Cth'ka."

"Uh ... bye?" I said, then I returned to the cave to wait for Skeleton Steve.

Well, that was *something* at least.

Better than nothing.

61

I was suddenly sure that if I traveled like this a lot, I would encounter *many* different creepers. Who knows what I might learn?

"Hey!" a dull, deep voice called from around the corner. That's where Cho'thos had just passed, but that wasn't the creeper's voice! "Hey, hey!" the voice repeated.

"Sssssssss," I heard from over there. Probably Cho'thos responding.

"Hey, *help me!*" the deep voice said. Dull and thick, like talking with a mouth full of cotton. "Come on … come … back!"

Such a sad, dull voice.

I looked back at the cave where Skeleton Steve was waiting in the dark.

"Sounds like a zombie," Skeleton Steve said, his voice surprising me. He'd been watching everything from the safety of the shadows the entire time. "Be careful."

I looked back to the voices around the corner, and approached slowly, my soft-padded feet quiet in the grass and gravel.

Around the corner was another small field, a gulley in between ridges, full of moss-covered boulders, and in the middle, a hole. It wasn't a very *deep* hole, but it was too much of a hole for me to climb out of if I were to accidentally fall inside.

And inside the hole was a creature that *had* fallen inside!

He was a large man, wearing disheveled blue clothing, and I could tell from the green, rotting skin that he was a zombie. Undead, like Skeleton Steve. But the interesting thing about him was that he was dressed in metal armor, from head to toe—protection that covered most of his body, and a helmet sitting on his head. The armor was brilliant, and gleamed in the sunlight.

Gold.

The zombie wore a full suit of armor made of *gold*.

The armored man was looking off at where Cho'thos must have gone and left him behind. I didn't see the creeper now. After a moment, the undead brute looked down at his feet, sighed, then looked up at the sky. I wondered how long he had been stuck in that hole. Suddenly, the zombie startled to attention when he noticed me watching him.

"Hey!" he said. "You!" His eyes were black and dead, and his mouth was slow like mud. His voice sounded so strange, because his *vocal cords* must be rotting away.

I'd never gotten to know a *zombie* before.

"Yesss?" I said. "Hi there!"

"Hey, will you help me?" the zombie asked. "Please? Get me out of this hole?"

I looked around the area, but couldn't think of any possible way that I could help. I had *no hands* to move sticks and blocks with. I had no tools for digging, and no way to use them if I had. There was no way I could push any dirt or boulders into the hole that he could use to climb out.

"I would, zombie, but there'sss nothing I think I can do …"

The zombie let out a disappointed moan, and looked down again. "I don't know what to do…"

"How long have you been in thisss hole?" I asked.

"I don't know," the zombie said. "Days and nights … and days and nights. Long, long time."

The zombie and I chatted for a while. I was very careful not to get too close to the hole myself—there would be no way out! He told me that his name was Zarek. He was a warrior.

When night fell, Skeleton Steve joined me, and we all talked for a while, but even Skeleton Steve, as smart as he was, could not figure out a way to get Zarek out of that hole.

"Only the *Steve* would be able to dig you out of the hole," my skeleton friend said, "or maybe he could *build something* that would let you climb out."

"No!" Zarek said. "Not *Steve!* He would try to kill me for sure…"

We promised Zarek that we would give it some thought and help him if we could, but we needed to continue on our journey.

Over the first half of the night, we walked across the desert. Skeleton Steve had to use the second Ender Eye multiple times, because there weren't really any landmarks we could use to stay on track.

After several hours, we came across something I had never seen before.

In the middle of the desert was a collection of buildings. Houses. Skeleton Steve called it a *village.*

And it was *directly* in our path.

There was clearly a commotion going on in the little town, so we tried to keep our distance and veer around it. The village had several houses, a tower, a structure in the middle that my friend called a 'well', and several fields of plants that, apparently, the villagers used for *food*.

I could hear the creatures that resided in the community, the *villagers*, crying out and

67

scrambling to defend their little town from a growing horde of undead and spiders that were attacking from all sides.

The village was under siege!

We watched from a distance as groups of zombies and skeletons (more zombies than anything else) ransacked the town, stumbling through the narrow cobblestone streets, beating on the doors of the little houses. Villagers cried and screamed and barricaded their doors.

Skeleton Steve threw the Ender Eye to confirm our path past the village, and it flew through the air, indifferent to the battle going on beneath it. We watched the trail of purple light motes and the flash of the eye stopping in the sky, then hurried around the edge of the village to grab the magical sphere and get back to our path.

And then the *Steve* appeared!

As we ran across a small field of crops on the edge of the village, our path was cut off by a quick-moving man in *full iron armor*, charging from one group of mobs to another. He raised a large, blue shield, and *bashed* into the nearest zombie, sending the mob flying back. A wicked metal sword in his other hand moved like lightning, and he struck the next-closest zombie once, twice, then cut him down! Another zombie fell under Steve's blade as a skeleton in the group of mobs raise its bow and fired. The Steve deftly caught the arrow on his shield—*thunk*— then cut down the archer as well.

Looking for his next foe, the Steve turned his attention to us. His blue eyes regarded us impassively from under his iron helmet, like he was looking at a couple of harmless *bugs*.

"Run!" Skeleton Steve cried, and his bones clattered as he dove into the streets of the village.

I followed my friend as fast as I could on my little creeper legs, not daring to look back at the armored monster that was *just* behind us!

We turned a corner on a cobblestone street, ran past another house, then turned around another corner.

"Wait, Ssskeleton Sssteve!" I called out. "Can't you shoot him? *Kill the Sssteve!*"

"I can't!" my friend yelled. "Not like this! Steves are *very powerful!* We've got to hide!"

We turned around another corner, and found a building where the door was broken. Pieces of wood were scattered on the floor and all over the stairs leading up to the doorway. Skeleton Steve and I ducked inside.

It was a very small place, with a ladder leading up through a hole in the roof. Looking back at the doorway to the street, I saw a blur of blue and grey, and I knew that the Steve had just sprinted by. Just outside, we heard the sounds of a sword sinking into flesh, and a zombie crying out.

"Up!" Skeleton Steve said, then climbed the ladder quickly, his scrabbly bone fingers and feet scraping on the wood. My friend disappeared into the hole, then moved aside so that I could follow.

I don't know how, but I managed to get up that ladder too, and we were suddenly on the roof of a very basic watch tower under an open sky. I heard the sounds of battle all around me.

Looking out over the village, I saw a couple of spiders on other roofs, and watched the chaos below of zombies and skeletons trying to get through wooden doors at the villagers who were barricaded inside, and the *Steve* was darting around the entire town slaying any mobs he found.

Sssssssssssssssssss ... *boom!*

A creeper blew up somewhere suddenly, but I couldn't tell where. I heard bricks and pieces of cobblestone clattering to the ground. The unseen creeper, dead and gone now, must have tried to attack the Steve next to one of the buildings. I realized that my vision was dim around the edges again, and the sounds around me were muddled, but everything was returning to normal.

"Oh no," Skeleton Steve said. "The Ender Eye!" He pointed with a long bony finger down to the ground just past a farm field. The magical eye sat all alone in the dirt, surrounded by battle. "What are we going to do?"

"We have to go get it, sssssss!" I said.

"No, not yet!" Skeleton Steve said. "We can't! *Steve* would get us."

"But it'sss just sssitting out there!" I said. "Sssomeone will *take* it!"

"I know," my friend said. "We have to wait, and hope that no one finds it."

"Sssssssssssss ..." I sighed. "Sssssssssssssssssssss..."

"Calm down," said Skeleton Steve. "You're doing really great at keeping calm, by the way. How did you not blow up when Steve attacked us?"

"Sssssssssssssssss ... I don't know?"

"You were hissing the whole time he was chasing us."

Really?

"I was?" I asked. I never noticed.

73

We waited for a while, and hid from sight around the edges of the roof. Unless the Steve bothered to come up the ladder, or saw us from another roof, we'd be safe here until he left.

If he left.

The Steve was still down there, killing mobs. And they kept coming. But the 'horde' was definitely thinning out now. We watched the Ender Eye. It sat lifeless on the ground, staring up at the sky. Shiny. I was afraid that Steve or one of the villagers would find it. The torches lighting up the town cast a yellow, flickering light all around the village, and the Eye of Ender sparkled like a jewel.

"No..." Skeleton Steve said, his voice low. "Oh, no, no, no..." I looked where he was peering over the edge, and saw the *Steve*. He emerged from an alley at the edge of the village, looked in the direction of the Ender Eye for a moment, then ran up and snatched it from the ground. Right away, he was back around another corner killing another zombie. He was so *fast* and casual!

"Oh, no!" I said. "Now we jussst have *one left!*"

74

We were getting worried. Morning was coming, and the Steve was still in the village, roaming the streets and killing mobs.

The moon went down, casting a few minutes of silvery light over the world.

The sun began to rise on the opposite end of the sky...

Skeleton Steve was completely exposed!

"Oh, man," my friend said. "This is bad!"

"Isss the Sssteve gone yet?" I cried, panic growing in me. "What are we going to do?!"

"I don't know, I don't ..." Skeleton Steve began to stammer. "This is a tight spot. We're in a tight spot. It's—"

He burst into flames. *Foom!*

"Sssssssssssss!" I said. "What—?!" I looked at my friend. What could I do? I couldn't.... He was not ssscreaming, he ssseemed to be trying to ssstay calm and put the flamesss out, but ...

Ssssssssssssstay calm...

75

My vision wasss a tunnel. Dark around the edgesss. I could hear the crackling of the flamesss, and his bonesss clattering as he rolled around on the roof…

I pushed Ssskeleton Sssteve down the ladder hole, and dove in after him! We collapsed into the sssmall room below. Sssomehow, I didn't catch on fire. Somehow … I calmed myself down.

My vision returned to normal. I could hear the flames, and the squawking words of the villagers outside of this broken building. I couldn't understand them. Not a word.

Skeleton Steve tried to douse the flames on his body, and eventually, the fire was gone.

We sat in silence for quite a while, Steve looking over his charred body, his bones blackened, his skull streaked with soot. With our backs to the front wall of the structure, we remained still, hoping that the Steve or villagers wouldn't find us.

"Thanks," Skeleton Steve said. "That was some quick thinking, Cth'ka."

"Let'sss hope we can ssstay hidden and make it worth sssomething," I whispered.

Day 7

In an amazing stroke of luck, we managed to pass the entire day without being discovered.

We heard the villagers bustling around us, maybe fixing up the village from the night's attack. But for some reason, they never came to the watchtower.

The *Steve* must have left just before we jumped down the hole, because we didn't see him again.

Over the course of the day, Skeleton Steve wiped at his bones with a strip of leather, and some of the charring flaked off, but he was still streaked with proof of his burns by the time the sun went down.

"Are you okay, Sssteve?" I said.

"I'll be okay," he replied. "I'll heal from this … in time."

By nightfall, we heard the villagers all shutting themselves in their houses again, slamming the doors behind them. We also heard the zombies when they returned.

Emerging carefully from our broken watchtower, we snuck down the streets quietly, just in case the *Steve* was around. One of the houses was missing most of a wall, and a large crater disrupted the street. There were no villagers in that house anymore.

Sneaking back to where we remembered the second Eye of Ender had fallen (and was snatched up by Steve the night before), we both stopped for a moment to gape at the spectacle in the middle of town.

The village well was *overrun* with zombies. The undead were emerging from the town's water supply, climbing out of the cobblestone structure, and spreading through town looking for victims.

The mobs ignored us.

Was this something that happened *every* night here?

"Let's go," Skeleton Steve said.

Standing next to the crop field where we lost the second Ender Eye, Skeleton Steve pulled the last remaining magical eye from his pack, and released it into the night sky.

Our path continued away from the village, of course.

We followed.

After hours of walking through the desert, the village was long behind us. I thought back to the creeper I met in the taiga forest, Cho'thos, about how he had mentioned that Steve (*the* Steve) lived nearby. The iron-clad killing machine must not live too far from the village, and probably goes there fairly often for some reason. Why else would he be at the village last night?

If zombies always come out of the village's well to attack every night, then the Steve must go there regularly to help them, right? Do zombies come out *every* night? Maybe it was just a coincidence. Who knows?

Eventually, our horizon of desert sand changed, and I saw another magnificent, new sight.

In the distance, past the edge of the sand, was a spread of *endless water*, glittering in the moonlight.

Skeleton Steve called it *the ocean*. A whole *world* of water.

Amazing.

And terrifying.

And it was in our way.

Would we have to cross the water, or go around it somehow? Was this the end of the journey?

As we approached the ocean, Skeleton Steve stopped, far enough away to avoid landing the Eye of Ender in the water after its flight. He looked at me, trying to be hopeful, holding the magical eye. We were surrounded by sand on one side, and ocean on the other. Some areas of the beach were pocketed with caves, and we could see the dangerous, red glow of what I would learn was called 'lava' emitting from some of the holes in the ground.

"What if it goes across the ocean?" Skeleton Steve asked. "What will you do?"

"Sssssss," I said, and looked away.

He released the Ender Eye.

It flew up into the air like it did every time, but instead of flying off away from us, it seemed to *stall*, then fell back to the ground. Purple motes of light drifted down around us.

"What the—?" Skeleton Steve said. He walked the short distance, picked up the eye, and looked it over.

"What'sss the matter?" I asked. "Isss it … broken?"

"Maybe it can't cross the water?" Skeleton Steve said. He shrugged, and released it into the air again.

Our last Eye of Ender flew up into the air over our heads, flashed, then *exploded* into dust and purple motes of light.

"No!" we both cried.

"What happened?" I said.

"I don't know," said Skeleton Steve. "That's not how the other eyes acted!"

We looked around the area for any hints about what to do next.

I heard the lava bubbling in the distance, and the constant *whoosh* of the ocean lapping back and forth on the shore, the waves folding over each other again and again all the way to the horizon.

"What do we do now?" I asked. I hissed in frustration. "Sssssssssss..."

Steve stood and thought for a while. He looked at the ground where he last retrieved the eye. He looked at the pockets of caves and lava.

"Maybe..." he said, "the stronghold is *under* us!"

"The cavesss?" I asked. "We can go inssside the cavesss and maybe find it?"

My friend pondered this for a moment. "Well," he said, "It's worth a try. What else are we going to do?"

We crossed the beach to the nearest collection of holes in the earth. What a strange place! Wherever the sand ended, there was sandstone, and there were holes, here and there, leading into darkness below. Two of the caves led to a single, large pool of lava, burning brightly under the surface close to the shore. Very hot.

Choosing the largest cave opening that didn't lead to a fiery death, we descended into the underworld.

Day 8

We didn't stop to rest.

The sun must have risen by now up on the surface, but underground, it didn't matter. The adventure did not have to wait until sundown to continue.

The cave tunnel was bumpy, random, and treacherous at times, but we moved slowly, descending deeper and deeper underground.

At times, our cave was joined by other caves, and I was sure that this complicated network of tunnels would make it hard to find our way *back out* later. But the end of our journey was close at hand—I *knew* it—so we pressed on.

We ran into bats most frequently. The little creatures fluttered around the cave, spooked out of their resting places when we passed by. Sometimes I could hear zombies and other skeletons making noises through the walls. At one point, I looked down a side tunnel, and saw another creeper staring back at me.

"Hi there," I said. My voice was louder than I expected, and my words echoed around us.

Hi there, hi there, hi there...

The creeper didn't respond. Instead, he turned and disappeared into the darkness.

I looked at my companion.

"Weirdo," Skeleton Steve said, and we moved on.

The deeper we explored into the cave, the more we were certain that we'd have a hard time getting back. It looked like finding the stronghold would be the only option. Hopefully the magical crown inside would help us find a way to get home.

Eventually, wandering through the unending tunnels, we came across a strange and out-of-place room made of *cobblestone*. We entered the odd room through a break in the wall on one side, and saw that the way out was through a similar hole on the *other* side.

In the middle of the room was a small cage with a fire burning inside.

Two zombies stood still near a small, wooden container. The zombies turned their heads and watched us enter, but did not say hello or seem to care.

"Huh," Skeleton Steve said, considering the zombies, shrugged, then walked around the burning cage to the wooden chest. He casually popped open the lid.

"Don't touch that!" said one of the zombies.

Skeleton Steve paused, looking at them, then looked back at me.

My skeleton friend then continued opening the chest, watching the zombie who spoke. The zombies watched him, but neither of them moved to stop him.

Satisfied, Skeleton Steve turned his attention to the wooden box, and rifled around through its contents, items that I couldn't see from where I was standing.

"Let's see," he said. "Some bread, a piece of iron, a ... saddle? That's interesting." He put the saddle in his pack.

The zombies watched us, but didn't say anything else.

I passed through the room behind Steve, and we left through the hole in the other wall.

"Well, if I ever need a *horse* in the future, I guess I've got a saddle," Skeleton Steve said, laughing.

We continued deeper into the world, following winding paths, occasionally climbing, but mostly going *down*. Or so it seemed. I lost track of all feeling of *time* eventually. Surely we hadn't been down here for more than a *day*, but, at this point, I had no idea whether it was day or night up above!

Eventually, our path led to an opening into a large cavern full of lava. The brightness of the molten earth was startling, and it became clear that there was no way to go forward. It was a dead end.

"I don't know about thisss, Ssskeleton Ssssteve," I said. "We've been going down for a *long* time, and we haven't ssseen any sssign of the ssstronghold."

"Yeah, I agree," he said. "We don't even know if it's *down* here, or if we're just wandering around in some huge, random cave!"

We turned around and went back.

When we found a joining tunnel, we changed direction to try a new way. For another hour or so, we followed the next cave, the tunnels tight, climbing down pits, following the tunnel when the only way to go was *up* … and we ended up cut off again by a river of burning lava.

Another dead end.

Skeleton Steve hit the stone wall of the cave with his bony fist.

"What are we going to do?" I asked.

"Let's go back and try *another* way," he said.

Day 9

We followed another tunnel even deeper.

Found more lava. Went back.

After spending hours more, we broke out into a large cavern that we hadn't seen before. There were several more tunnels leading in random directions from here.

"Great," said Skeleton Steve. "I guess we can pick the one that seems to go ... the deepest?"

I noticed that one of the tunnels looked easier to navigate than the others. Maybe it would give us more room to move around in while we descended. It did go *down* at least.

"Thisss one," I said.

Skeleton Steve shrugged and followed.

We went on for what seemed like another couple of hours, then saw the tunnel climb up into another strange, cobblestone room.

So weird. Just a random room in the middle of the world.

We climbed up into the room.

It was small, just like the other room we saw before.

A small cage with a fire inside sat in the middle. A single zombie stood near a wooden chest.

"No…" Skeleton Steve said, walking into the room. "Don't tell me. No way…"

"What isss it?" I said, climbing up into the room to catch up.

Skeleton Steve reached down to open the chest.

"Stop that!" the zombie standing next to it said. Skeleton Steve froze, and we looked up at him. "Don't touch that!" the zombie said.

Skeleton Steve looked over at me, then back to the chest. Opened it.

The zombie didn't object.

94

"Bread, and a piece of iron." My friend sighed and looked up at me. "We are, *somehow*, back in the same dungeon that we passed through *hours* ago."

"But," I said, "how is that posssible? We've been going *down!*"

"Have we?" Skeleton Steve said, his tone annoyed. "We've been going all *kinds* of ways. I can't believe it! We circled back to this room."

The zombie watched us passively.

"Then," I said, "... what now?"

"I don't know," Skeleton said, then sighed. "I don't even know if the stronghold is *down* here." He looked at the zombie. "Is there a stronghold down here?"

The zombie shrugged.

"Let's go *down* again, I guess," Skeleton Steve said.

I followed.

We followed the tunnel again as it wound down, ever down. When the cave turned, we turned with it. When it rose, we climbed. I'd like to say that I remembered which way we went the *last* time we went down from the dungeon room, but I didn't. I don't think Skeleton Steve remembered either.

Somehow though, we ended up on a new path.

We made our way through another cavern, one I don't believe we had already seen. A handful of bats flew around us, and a couple of zombies and a single skeleton ambled around.

"Excuse me," Skeleton Steve said to the bony stranger.

The other skeleton glared. "What do *you* want?"

"Have you guys seen a *stronghold* around here?"

"No," one of the zombies said.

"Yep, that way," the skeleton said, raising a bony finger toward a dark hole in the cavern wall.

"Really?" I said.

Skeleton Steve was also surprised.

The other skeleton turned and walked away.

We rushed to the hole, the entrance to yet another tunnel, and continued our journey.

The path wound down and around, like all of the other tunnels that came before it, then it dumped us into another huge, deep cavern featuring a massive lava pool. This time, at least, there was a stone ledge continuing past the burning, molten rock, and we were able to continue into the darkness of another tunnel.

I felt that *finally*, for some reason, we were getting somewhere! Skeleton Steve seemed determined, but had a faint smile on his bony face.

And then we hit another dead end.

Tunnel. Blocked by lava.

"No!" I cried. "Sssssssss."

With the tunnel ending in lava, the only possible path (without going back) was a small but fast river of water that emerged from one side of the tunnel, crossed our path, then disappeared into a dark hole on the other side.

The water and lava passed right next to each other. The lava tried to *ooze* its way to where we were standing, but the water was in the way. The two fluids warred against each other, hissing and spitting, cooling the edges of the lava flow into stone.

"Cth'ka," Skeleton Steve said, "I don't think there's a stronghold down here..."

I crumpled and leaned against the stone wall.

We had come so far.

What a crazy adventure this had been, only to end with us stuck at the bottom of a cave, deep underground, without even a sure way to get back to the surface.

"Unless," Steve said, looking at the stream.

I knew what he was thinking. I looked at the deep, dark hole, full of water. No way!

"Are you nutsss?" I said. "That'sss water. *Deep* water. And we don't even know where it'sss going!"

"That's it," said Skeleton Steve. "I mean, it could go ... nowhere! But it has to go somewhere! *All* of that water is going somewhere."

I hissed.

"It's either that, or we go back up, and wander around here for *days* trying to find the way out!" Skeleton Steve secured his bow, and double-checked his pack. "You know, my creeper friend, I have a good feeling about this! I want to see where this water goes. You'll have to get over being scared of the water, be brave, and see this through to the other side."

"Insssane!" I said. "No way, Sssteve!" My vision dimmed around the edges. "We jussst need to go back and find another way!"

"I'm *tired* of going back, Cth'ka. Come with me, good buddy."

With that, Skeleton Steve took a step away from me, smiled, turned to the stream, and leapt into the water. The strong current pulled him instantly toward the dark watery hole.

"Wait!" I cried. I heard hissing, and wondered if it was me, or the water cooling the lava...

In a moment, Skeleton Steve was zipped under the surface of the water.

Then he was gone. Down the hole. Flushed down the hole.

"Easssy for you, Sssteve!" I sssaid. "You don't have to breathe!"

I wasss all alone. The water gurgled as it rushed into the hole. The lava bubbled and frothed and hissssssssssssssssed as it tried to ooze past the sssssssssstream.

Calm down, Cth'ka...

I could hear Skeleton Steve's words in my mind.

I focused on the water. The stream rushed past, flowing, ever moving, ever *down* into the hole. The brilliant light of the lava glittered and reflected on the river's surface and lit up the tunnel.

My vision cleared. I heard myself hissing, and stopped.

Edging closer to the water, I watched it disappear down the hole. Constant, flushing, sucking … down the hole.

I held my breath, and walked into the water.

Day 10

After an intense moment of fear and darkness, having my head underwater, and feeling myself moving *much faster* than I normally do, I finally broke through the surface of the water and took a gasping breath!

It was dark, but I could see. I was still rushing down a river of water, but I was floating on top!

I could float!

The tiny tunnel I rushed down suddenly broke open into an *enormous* cavern—a ravine—a deep cut through the world, and I was dumped into a pool.

The ravine was massive, and went as far as I could see in either direction, slicing through the underground realm, and I was at the *bottom* of it. The ceiling of the ravine stretched up into darkness farther than I could see. Bats chirped and echoed all around.

"Hey!" Skeleton Steve's voice rang out, echoing across the black space.

I looked over, and saw my friend sitting on a rock.

"Sssteve!" I said. My voice echoed too. "I can float!" I sat, floating in the pool, my feet not touching bottom, with no danger of sinking.

"Of course you can float!" he said. "You're a creeper."

"Why didn't you *tell* me?"

"Would you have believed me?" Skeleton Steve asked. "You were afraid of water! You had to deal with that *yourself*."

I moved my legs, flailing around, trying to paddle to the edge of the pool. When I reached the edge, I climbed up onto the cool, stone floor. Looking ahead of me, up the ravine past Skeleton Steve, I could see ledges winding up and across, higher and higher, strange rocks and ores glittering in stone walls. I could see a couple of water falls, and a *lava* fall, lighting up the entire area far ahead with its fiery glare.

"But where are we going to go now?" I asked.

"Look behind you," said Skeleton Steve.

I turned, and looked down other direction of the ravine. It was a lot like what I'd already seen—ledges, ores, water, lava, light and shadows, but there was also something very different...

There was a *structure* was built in the stone ahead.

The walls were stone and brick, and I saw walls of wood inside as well, but it was as if the ravine *cut* straight through it. Like the structure was there first, and a great earthquake or something had split a rift through the world, and sliced right through the building, from one side to the other, cutting it in half.

What we were looking at seemed to be some sort of .... library? A *large* library, full of wood and shelves, books, and cobwebs—an amazing amount of cobwebs. The ravine cut a rift right through the walls and floor, then the massive cavern continued out the other side.

Now that I had calmed down from my ride through the water, I could actually hear the mobs inside, moaning, clattering, spiders hissing and chattering. Their voices and noises echoed through the ravine.

"Are you ready to go into the stronghold?" Skeleton Steve asked, a smile on his face.

"Let'sss go!" I said.

I shook myself from head to toe, spraying water onto the rocks, and headed to the break in the library wall.

We stepped carefully through the yawning crack in the wall, and climbed up the rubble to the library floor. The shelves and books around me had a strange smell. Everything was dusty, and very old. A wooden chandelier hung in the center of the library, suspended from the ceiling of a second floor, also lined with bookshelves.

"Remember," said Skeleton Steve, "we're mainly here for the crown!"

"Ssssss … right."

I heard an echoing *creak*, and turned to see Skeleton Steve peering into a wooden chest that he found on top of a short bookcase.

"*Mainly* here for the crown," he said, looking back at me with a smirk.

Skeleton Steve pulled several old books out of the old chest, gently stacking them on the next shelf, then smiled to himself.

"A compass," he said. "And … a map?" He took the 'compass' and scrutinized it. I saw a black disc about the size of an Ender Eye with glass on top. He took a scroll of paper from the chest, and stuffed it into his pack.

Hopping down, Skeleton Steve moved ahead of me, watching his newfound compass in his bony hand.

"Well," he said, "this isn't very helpful *down here*, but it should help us get home when we get back to the surface!"

The idle sounds of the mobs grew louder, and I looked up to the second level of the library. *Dozens* of glowing red eyes looked back down at me. Chittering and chattering sounds, lots and lots of legs scrambling around on the wood. Spiders. And they were *not* ignoring us.

"Uh .... Sssssteve?" I said.

"What is it?" he said, approaching another wooden chest.

"Maybe … sssssssss … maybe we should *keep moving…*"

Skeleton Steve opened the second chest, and paused to look back at me. My friend saw me looking up, and his red dot eyes looked up as well.

"Yeah … okay," Skeleton Steve said, "*That's* weird. We'd better find the crown and get out of here."

He ventured another quick look into the chest, then reached inside and pulled out a book, shaking off all of the other books and junk stacked on top of it. The book he chose glowed in his bony hand, and it emitted a faint purple glow. Wisps of gentle, pink light lashed to and fro over its surface.

"What'sss *that* book?" I asked.

"Magic book," Steve replied, and put it into his pack.

I hurried to catch up and get away from the spiders watching us. "What'sss it do?"

"Don't know yet," Skeleton Steve said, looking ahead. "There's a door. Let's go."

We left the library through a thick, old wooden door, and stepped into a stone-bricked hall. Two zombies stood in the hall, and turned to face us.

Walking past the zombies, I watched as one of them ignored us, but the other turned and followed. We approached a metal door. The zombie following us seemed torn between the idea of keeping up with us, and the idea of going back to standing still.

"How do we—?" Steve said, pressing on the metal door.

"Isss that a button?" I asked. There was a stone push-switch of some kind on the wall next to the door.

Steve looked at it. Smiled. "Yes, good!" He pressed the button, and the door quickly and noisily sprung open.

Ca-chung ...

"Smart, Cth'ka," my friend said.

Ca-chunk.

The door closed again.

"Ready?" Skeleton Steve asked.

I nodded.

He pushed the button again, and we ran through the door before it closed. A moment later, we heard one of the zombies in the room behind us bang against the door. I guess it tried to follow us after all.

"What?" said Steve, asking the zombie through the bars of the door's little window. "What do you want?"

The zombie groaned, and turned away.

"Thisss is weird," I said.

"Yeah, there's something different about these guys, I agree," said Skeleton Steve. "We'd better get what we came for and get going..."

Up ahead was a hallway, leading to a *well* in the center of a small room.

Three other halls split off from the room. Four paths going away from the well. As we approached, a couple more zombies and a skeleton, bow in hand, approached from the other halls.

"Hey, you there!" said the skeleton. "You're not supposed to be here!"

"What do *you* care?" Skeleton Steve said. "We're just wandering around here just like you."

"Not like me," said the strange skeleton. His voice was raspy and mean. "We're protecting something important here, and you're not a part of that. Leave now, or you'll be destroyed!"

The zombies began moving toward us. The skeleton pulled an arrow from his back and made ready to fire.

Skeleton Steve looked at me, then looked back at the guards.

"Um, okay," Steve said. "We'll leave." He turned to me. "Come on, Cth'ka."

We began walking past the skeleton. Where was Skeleton Steve taking us? He must have been thinking of *something*.

"The exit is … *this way*, right?" Skeleton Steve said. We walked past the skeleton, and started heading in a hurry to the door in another hallway. "Thanks, goodbye!"

The enemy skeleton cried out. "Intruders!" He raised his bow and fired, just as Skeleton Steve dodged to the side. An arrow struck the stone-brick wall. The zombies changed direction and came after us with a purpose.

"Uh oh," Skeleton Steve said. "Get to that door!"

Skeleton Steve whipped his bow off of his back, nocked an arrow, and fired back at the other skeleton, hitting it in the shoulder and forcing it to back away, seeking cover. The zombies advanced into the hall after us. Skeleton Steve fired off another shot, hitting a zombie square between the eyes.

It kept coming.

"Huh," Skeleton Steve remarked, then shot the zombie again. That time, he fell.

I reached the iron door, and saw that there was a button on the wall, just like with the other, but I couldn't figure out a way to push it! The other zombie was still advancing on us, and I was sure that the other skeleton would be firing back soon. Skeleton Steve ran to me.

"Let's go!" he said, and pushed the button. The door sprang open.

Ca-chung!

We rushed into the next room.

Ca-chunk!

The door shut.

We were in a hallway, extending two directions, and a zombie we encountered in the new area was already heading toward us. Skeleton

Steve took quick aim, and shot it in the chest. The zombie staggered backwards. Steve put another shot into its head, and it fell with a groan. The remaining zombie in the room behind us banged on the metal door.

"Sssssssssssssss..." I hissed quietly under the sound of the mobs around us getting riled up.

"Calm down! Don't worry," Skeleton Steve said. "I don't think the zombies are smart enough to open the doors."

Ca-Chung!

Just then, the metal door we stood next to sprang open. The zombie stood in the doorway, but I saw the skeleton's long, bony arm reaching around him. The *skeleton* had pressed the button.

"Uh-oh," Skeleton Steve said, and promptly shot a quick arrow into the zombie's gut before the door closed again.

Ca-chunk!

"Let's go."

We hurried down the hall to the right until we passed through an open doorway into another brick-walled room.

Thunk!

"Aagh!" Skeleton Steve cried out, and I saw an arrow sticking out of the back of his shoulder bone.

Looking past him, I saw the zombie and the skeleton through the door behind us, and the skeleton took aim again.

We ducked around the corner into the room to take cover. I heard a faint hiss. Assumed it was just me. Saw *another* zombie in *this* room.

Not good.

There were two more metal doors leading out of this room, and a stone archway leading to a staircase going *down*. Something suddenly *bit my foot*, and I leapt back in surprise!

"Sssssssss!"

A small, grey snake-like creature was attacking me from the floor. It had tiny red eyes. Or maybe it was more like a worm than a snake? A frill of spines stuck out from behind its head. Maybe it was a huge bug. Whatever it was, it was *fast*, and trying to bite me again!

"Sssssssssssteve!" I cried.

Another arrow flew past us from the hall we just left. The zombie in this room approached. The silver creature lunged at me, and I could see tiny, silver teeth! I tried to get away.

Skeleton Steve launched an arrow at the zombie in the room, hitting it in the chest and staggering it for a moment. Then, he ran over to me, and kicked the silver creature away with a bony foot. It hissed in pain and flew back into the wall! The tiny creature fell, turned back at us again, then hissed a cry of defiance into the air as it slithered toward us once more.

Two stone blocks in the wall suddenly *crumbled open*, and *two more* of the silver creatures joined the fight! The little monster wasn't hissing at us—it hissed for help!

"Silverfish..." Skeleton Steve said.

"The ssstairsss!" I exclaimed.

Skeleton Steve and I rushed across the room as another arrow whizzed through the air, and we fled down the stairs, deeper into the stronghold.

By now, there must have been at least a couple of zombies, that mean skeleton, and three silver bug creatures chasing us!

On the next level down, we arrived into another room that led to a metal door.

Hitting the button and running through the door, we were suddenly in another one of those four-way 'hubs' with the well in the center. Two zombies joined the pursuit. We ran past the well to a random door, and hit the button. I heard the door at the bottom of the stairs open again. They were behind us. We tried to rush through the open door, but it closed in our faces.

Ca-chunk!

Skeleton Steve hit the button again, and the metal door sprung open another time. We were surprised by a zombie waiting *directly* on the other side!

The undead man swung at us with his fist, and *smashed* Steve in the chest! My friend staggered back, and shot the zombie with his bow. The zombie fell, and we pushed our way past it into another long hall.

As we were halfway down the hall, the door behind us opened again—*Ca-Chung!*—and the skeleton and a large number of zombies *poured* through.

"You know," Skeleton Steve said as we ran, "I never anticipated the mobs inside the stronghold turning against us! That's definitely a weird thing!"

He fired his bow off ahead of us as he spoke, and I saw a skeleton that was waiting up ahead take an arrow in the skull. The injured skeleton fired back, and hit *me*! An arrow appeared stuck in my midsection. My vision darkened, the sound of the room grew muddled, and I was suddenly aware that I was hissssssing!

"No, Cth'ka!" Steve said. "Calm down!"

Skeleton Steve fired again, and hit the skeleton a second time, sending it crashing into the upcoming room, bones flying!

I managed to calm my *last resort* yet again, and my vision and hearing returned to normal. An arrow flew past us from behind. There was a horde of undead chasing us now, several of them with Steve's arrows sticking out of their bodies.

We turned into the next room, scattering the bones of the fallen skeleton underfoot. I saw another metal door on the left, and as I looked to the right, I was suddenly face to face with another creeper.

Thank goodness!

"Sssave us, brother!" I said with a smile.

It approached, a vicious hiss emanating from its core. I turned to look at Skeleton Steve and saw him under attack by a couple of zombies, right in his face! How did they get there? The hissing creeper approached us, hissing louder, shaking.

A zombie smashed Skeleton Steve again, and I was horrified to see one of his *arms* knocked out of its socket! The arm went flying, clattering to the floor, the bony hand still holding Steve's bow.

"Sssssteve!" I cried. "Hit the button!"

Skeleton Steve, not paying attention to his lost arm, backed away from the zombies, hit the button to the metal door, and we pushed through it as it opened, into a room unknown. The shaking, hissing creeper and the zombies tried to follow. The door closed.

Ca-chunk!

BOOM!

The creeper exploded in the next room, taking out several zombies with it.

Another silver creature … a *silverfish* … approached us from the darkness of the new room. Skeleton Steve, now without his bow, and missing an *arm*, kicked it once, then stomped on the creature with his bony foot before it could recover.

Splat.

"Sorry, Cth'ka," Steve said. "I don't know if we'll make it out of this one…"

I looked through the barred window of the door into the next room, where the creeper had exploded, to assess the situation.

The door still stood.

Pieces of zombie were all over! Some of the zombies were just wounded, and were getting back to their feet. The original skeleton we encountered was probably still approaching. *Who knows* what happened to the silver creatures...

The creeper's explosion had formed a crater in the room, and blocks of the stone slab floor were scattered everywhere! Steve's bony arm, still holding his bow, was on the floor in a corner of the room.

Skeleton Steve slumped down to the floor.

My own injuries caught up to me suddenly. I realized that one of my legs was wounded from the bite of the silver creature, and I still had an arrow sticking out of my abdomen.

The room was dark.

"Hello in there," said a menacing voice from the other side of the door.

I looked out of the window. It was the enemy skeleton.

"Sssssss," I said. "What do *you* want?"

The skeleton laughed. I looked down to Skeleton Steve. My friend sat with his back against the wall, downcast and still. He didn't look up.

"Intruders," the mean skeleton said, "I think you'll be happy to know that this is almost over! You're at a *dead end*. There's nowhere to go from here."

"Ssso what are you waiting for?" I said. "Come on in and finish usss off!"

He laughed again. "Well, the creeper destroyed the door switch, but I'm sure the one on *your* side still works. Press the button! You'll have to come out *eventually!*"

I looked around. We were in a small room like all of the others, but it was a dead end. There was only the one door we used to come in, and some sort of *altar thing* at the other end. Stone slabs, and ... a chest?

"Sssteve!" I said. "Ssskeleton Sssteve, look!"

Skeleton Steve stayed where he was, looking at the floor, defeated.

The skeleton on the other side of the door spoke again. "Hey, little creeper, I can see that your friend has been ... *disarmed*!" He stopped and cackled. What a jerk. "Why don't you *open the door* and let us finish the job, eh? We'll be quick! I promise!"

I walked over to the altar. Definitely a chest. But I had no hands with which to open it.

"Sssteve!" I said again. "Pleassse get up! Come here!"

Skeleton Steve raised his head. He looked at the other skeleton sneering at him through the window of the door, then looked at me. "What is it, Cth'ka?" He sounded so tired.

"A chest!" I said.

Skeleton Steve rose to his feet slowly, obviously very damaged. He shambled over to me, reached out with his remaining hand, and opened the chest.

Looking into the wooden box, I saw a variety of stuff. There was a metal helmet. A sword. Some food … apples and bread. And … a crown!

Skeleton Steve immediately straightened up and looked at me, the red dots in his eye sockets dancing lively. He reached into the chest and pulled the crown out from all of the other items.

The crown in Steve's hand was thin and modest, not chunky and gaudy like I expected it would be. It was made of gold, with a strange, blue sheen of color. In the front of the crown were three gems in a triad. The two smaller gems were like chiseled, frosty, blue glass. Steve would later tell me that they were *diamonds*. And the third gem, the one on the peak of the crown, was a cloudy and mysterious greenish-blue orb, similar to the Eyes of Ender we had before.

The green orb *swirled* inside, light and shadow. Power. I could feel the energy radiating off of the artifact.

We'd found the *Crown of Ender*.

"What are you doing in there?" the skeleton at the door yelled. "Get away from that altar! That's not for you!"

Skeleton Steve turned to me, the Crown of Ender in his bony hand.

"You ready?" he said.

"Yesss," I replied.

My friend raised the crown, and set it onto my head. The artifact surprised me when it cinched around me suddenly, tightening down *just enough*.

And then ... I could *feel*.

Suddenly, I could feel everything around me!

It was as if the whole world around me was my hand. My hands! And I had a *thousand* hands. Invisible, magic hands!

127

I could feel the edges of the chest. The smooth, cool stone of the altar's surface. I could feel the helmet sitting in the chest as if I had hands like Skeleton Steve. I felt that I could run my fingers along the edges of the helmet, and pass an invisible palm over the cold, curved metal of its dome.

I felt that I could pick it up.

So I did.

Skeleton Steve gasped as the helmet floated out of the chest on its own, hovering in midair.

Holding the helmet with my mind, I turned to my friend, and placed it on his head.

Skeleton Steve stood and allowed the helmet to be placed onto his skull, then beamed back at me with a huge skeleton grin.

"Thisss," I said, "thisss is amazing!"

"You're right about that, Cth'ka!" Steve shouted. He was grinning from ear-hole to ear-hole, excited and ready to take on the world!

I picked up an apple, holding it in front of my face. I turned it around. It floated in midair before me, but it felt like I was holding it firmly with hands that I didn't really have.

Magical, invisible hands. Hands controlled by my mind.

Using my new power, I threw the apple across the room, and it exploded into a mushy mess against the stone wall!

It was time to get out of here.

"Take the sssword, Sssteve," I said.

Skeleton Steve reached into the chest with his one good arm, and hefted the iron sword.

I walked back to the metal door, and looked through the window at the group of mobs waiting on the other side to kill me. With my new power, I could feel them all with my mind through the window! I felt their skin, their shirts, the feathers of the skeleton's arrows sticking out of the quiver. I could feel the chunks of stone and blocks laying around the room from the creeper explosion. I could feel the edges of the bricks in the walls.

"What the—?!" the enemy skeleton said, when he saw me through the door. "What are you doing with that? You can't have *that!*"

He was afraid.

"Don't worry," I said. "It'll be quick. I promise..."

I picked up a stone block from the floor inside there and *smashed* his skull!

The mean skeleton clattered into a pile of bones against the wall.

The iron door separated us from the hostile mobs in the ruined room, but the door wasn't in *my* way. I could feel everything in the room full of enemies, even through just that tiny, barred window!

Suddenly, I sent blocks flying around the group. I made the room a tornado of stone! The zombies scattered as I focused on picking up a chunk of stone, throwing it at one of them, then releasing my grip on it. Picking up another piece of rubble, I bashed it into a zombie's head! Picking up a stone slab, I flung it across the room to crush another.

I tried, with my invisible magic hands, to pick up an actual zombie, but in a weird way, the undead enemy was too hard to hold onto.

No matter. I smashed it's head with a block of stone.

Within a few minutes, through a flurry of flying blocks and stones, zombie screams, and bodies smashing, our enemies were all dead. I dropped the block of stone I was holding up in the middle of the room. It fell to the floor of the quiet room with a crash!

Using my new power, I pressed the button to open the door.

Ca-chung!

It was easy.

We stepped out, Skeleton Steve holding his new sword with his good arm. He gaped at the destruction.

Ca-chunk!

The door closed.

"Holy … cow … Cth'ka …" he said.

"Thisss isss amazing, Sssskeleton Sssteve," I replied.

"Worla sure wasn't kidding about the crown giving you the ability to defend yourself!"

"No," I said. "Guesss not." We looked about the room. "Let'sss get out of here."

I picked up one of the big stone blocks with my mind. The chunk of chiseled stone hovered in the air in front of me.

Skeleton Steve carefully stepped around the bodies to the corner of the room, and retrieved his bow. And his lost arm. He slung his bow around his good shoulder, and stashed the arm as best he could in his pack. He could still use his new sword with the remaining good arm.

Day 11

Leaving the stronghold was effortless.

We didn't bother exploring the rest of it. True, there would be treasure. But for now, since I had the crown, and especially since Skeleton Steve was ... *broken*, I wanted to get us home.

I found that I had to put down my stone block before I could push the door buttons with my power. I could *almost* push the button while holding the block, but not quite. Maybe I could only do one thing at a time ... for now.

Of course, after juggling block and buttons for a few doors, I realized that I could just push the button *with* the block.

Going back the way we came was pretty easy. We just had to follow the bodies. And using my block of chiseled *stronghold stone*, I *smushed* any bad guys we ran into along the way, including the multiple *silverfish* that lingered and came at us from the walls.

"One day, we'll have to come back here," said Skeleton Steve. "Look at how much cool stuff we found in such a short time! I bet there's *a lot more*."

"Well," I said, "Now that you have that map, you can mark thisss location!"

Once we found our way back to the library, as I feared, the spiders *did* attack. But by taking it slow, I was able to kill the majority of them with my *block*, and Skeleton Steve killed a couple with his sword. It became obvious that we'd have to be careful, though. Skeleton Steve was clearly very wounded.

Upon returning to the ravine, it must have been daytime up on the surface, because, through the rift of darkness, past the lava and waterfalls, we saw a single column of light piercing the ceiling of the long cavern, far away.

We approached the other random mobs in the cave with caution, my floating block ready to destroy them if they attacked us, but it looked like things were back to normal. Apparently, the only unfriendly mobs were in the *stronghold*.

Traveling across the bottom of the ravine, I found that I wasn't afraid to cross water anymore. We walked along the dark cavern floor, climbing here, descending there, following ridges to get to higher areas when we could. We climbed and hiked higher and higher, until the hole showing daylight was close.

We navigated ledges and inclines until we were just below the surface world once again. Eventually, Skeleton Steve and I found ourselves sitting in the dark *just outside* the sunlight.

And, just like with any other day, we decided to wait until dark to go out into the open.

Steve sat, waiting, pondering his dismembered arm, watching me play with the crown.

I spent the time focusing on my new power, feeling the world with the Crown of Ender, and experimenting with the limits of my new *invisible hands.*

With ease, I could lift blocks and other things that were just sitting around. I still had my block of chiseled stronghold stone that I brought with us all the way from the stronghold room outside where we found the crown. I hadn't tried lifting anything bigger or heavier, but there wasn't really anything around that I could practice on.

Of course, a solid block of stone was pretty darned heavy.

I learned that if Skeleton Steve threw an arrow *on the ground*, I could pick it up with my power easily. Of course—that was just like a block. But if my friend *held* the arrow, it became a lot harder to manipulate. I could pull it around a little while Skeleton Steve struggled against me, but I couldn't just rip the arrow out of his hand.

Not yet, anyway.

I also found that I could pull blocks out of the wall. *Pop!* Just straight out of the wall.

That was a lot more difficult, depending on what it was.

Pulling a block of the *raw stone* out of the cliff's wall was difficult. I had to try *really* hard, and try for a long time, but I could do it!

Dirt was *a lot* easier.

And, while we were waiting for the sun to go down, I pulled a lot of dirt out of the ground around us. I tried to build the dirt up into structures of my own. I built little *walls* of dirt. A tiny, little *hut* of dirt.

"Dirt village!" I said, looking out from inside a little dirt building I stacked up.

Skeleton Steve laughed.

By the time night rolled around, I was skilled enough with the basics of moving easy blocks, that I was able to move dirt, one block at a time, to build a crude staircase out of the hole, to lead us back to the surface.

Skeleton Steve watched with interest, and I believe he was truly impressed.

Over the night, after locating the ocean nearby and figuring out where we lost the last Eye of Ender, we were able to figure out the direction back to the village.

"South," Skeleton Steve said, looking at his compass. "Pretty much, exactly, South. It looks like we were walking directly *North* this whole time!"

We reached the village eventually, and passed around it with care. If this was close to where the *Steve* lived, we sure didn't want to run into *him* again!

I noticed, when we passed the community of houses, that the home partially blown up by the creeper last time we were here was now patched up with cobblestone. The crater in the street was full of dirt.

Either the villagers repaired the town, or *Steve* did.

The town was under attack again, the villagers barricaded inside, and zombies pounding on the doors.

Before the sun came up, we made it to the large pine forest. Skeleton Steve found a little hideaway from the sun, and we stopped for the day.

Day 12

While Skeleton Steve hid in the shadows from the sunlight, I practiced with blocks.

Feeling the forest with my power, I practiced moving dirt blocks around, just like I did in the ravine. I could pull a block of dirt *right* out of the ground, with grass still attached on top, and put it down somewhere else. Approaching the moss-covered boulders, I learned that I could *not* pick up an *entire* boulder, but I could break a piece of it off, and move a block of boulder-stone just like a block of anything else.

Moving dirt and boulder blocks around in the taiga forest suddenly made me remember...

Zarek!

Zarek the Zombie in the gold armor! With my new powers, I could help him now! *We must be close to him*, I thought.

For a little while, I wandered around, staying pretty close to Skeleton Steve's hideout, searching for the poor zombie, stuck in his hole. Eventually, I found him. He was still in the same predicament as when I found him days ago.

"Hi, Zarek!" I said, approaching the edge of his hole.

"Hey … creeper!" He looked up at me in the sunlight, his golden helmet gleaming. "You help me out?"

"Yesss," I said. "I *can* help you out."

Lowering my block of stronghold stone, I felt around the edge of the hole with my mind. I felt the dirt around it. After assessing the situation, I pulled out blocks of dirt (*pop!*) and placed them down, until Zarek had a crude staircase of earth he could use to climb out of the hole.

The large zombie climbed with care and shuffled up the block stairs until he once again had grass beneath his feet. He looked up at the sun, smiled, then looked down at me. He was a *big* zombie.

"Creeper," he said, his voice thick and heavy. "Thank you."

"You're welcome, Zarek."

"Pretty crown," he said. "What is your name, creeper?"

"My name is Cth'ka."

The large zombie, his golden armor shining in the sun, dropped to a knee and looked up at me.

"Mighty Cth'ka," he said, "creeper who can move the earth with ... magic. I am the zombie warrior, Zarek. You have my .... thanks ... for saving me, and I ... am *yours* to command."

Zarek and I made our way back to where Skeleton Steve was waiting, and we chatted for the rest of the day until the sun set. It turned out that Zarek was a bit of an adventurer himself. Skeleton Steve joined us when darkness fell, and learned about the events that led him back to us.

The three of us traveled through the night, following Skeleton Steve and his compass, through the taiga, past the floating island, through the extreme hills, across the plains and forests, past Worla's *Lurkmire swamp*, all the way home.

When the sun's rays started poking through the horizon again, we had made it back to Darkwood.

My home.

Day 13

I was very happy to be back in my forest. It was a long journey, and Skeleton Steve and I saw many interesting places. What a real adventure it was! I supposed that I was an 'adventurer' now, just like Skeleton Steve. Over the course of the day, while waiting for Skeleton Steve to come out of the darkness, I brought Zarek the Zombie to my clearing.

My favorite part of Darkwood forest, my *clearing*, was as peaceful and beautiful as ever. Zarek thought it was nice too.

When the sun set, I met up with Skeleton Steve again, and we walked across the grassland to Lurkmire swamp once more to visit Worla the witch, just as she requested.

"Who's this?" Worla asked in her edgy voice, meeting us in the clearing outside of her hut. She pointed at the zombie in our group with a long, clawed finger.

"This is Zarek the Zombie," Skeleton Steve said. "He … ah … swore his fealty to the *mighty Cth'ka* yesterday."

Worla cackled, pulling her purple robes around her. "Pretty smart for a zombie, I should say!" the witch said. "So it begins. Zombie also smart enough to wear a helmet, eh?"

"Why do you sssay *that*?" I asked.

Laughing, Worla replied, "Ask your friend, Skeleton Steve, young Cth'ka! I'm sure he knows. It looks like old *Bones* here claimed a helmet of his own!"

Skeleton Steve seemed perplexed. "Why, Worla? Why is a helmet so interesting?" he said.

"Silly skeleton," the witch replied. "So you don't *burn*, dummy!" She laughed.

It suddenly occurred to me that every time I saw Zarek, standing in the hole, it was *daytime*! I never saw him catch on fire. Why didn't the zombie burn like the other undead? Like Skeleton Steve did? Was it because he wore a helmet?

"Really?" Skeleton Steve asked. "A helmet will keep me from *burning?*"

Worla smirked at him, her hook-nose crinkling. She turned to me. "So I see you found the Crown of Ender," she said. "Very serious stuff, this is. *Very powerful*."

"Yesss," I said. "We found it when we needed it the mossst."

"Do you know how to use it?" Worla asked.

"I'm learning," I said. "Trying to learn ssstill."

Worla laughed. "Yes, Cth'ka, and I'm sure you'll be learning more and more for a long time! Are you ready to do your first favor for me, young one?"

I looked at Skeleton Steve. He shrugged. I felt confident.

"Yesss," I said. "What do you need of me, witch?"

The witch smiled, but there was no joy in it. The good hearted laughter in our conversation suddenly died out, and her eyes were as black as coal.

"Return to me in a week, Cth'ka, and I will send you on your first errand."

I *knew* that I could not disobey. Beyond the shadow of a doubt. For a moment, a cold spot of dread grew inside of me, but then it disappeared in a flash. I felt uneasy, but I didn't know why.

"Worla," Skeleton Steve said, "I got beat up pretty bad in there. Do you think you could ... uh ... *heal* me? Please?"

The witch laughed again. "Ha ha ... *yes*, Steve! It seems you're not quite the *man you once were* before you left on your journey, eh?" She cackled. "Or, the *skeleton* anyway. Give me your arm."

She extended a hand and spread out her long fingers, tipped with thin claws.

Skeleton Steve pulled his dismembered arm out of his pack, unfolded it, and handed it to the witch.

Worla threw the arm onto the muddy ground, then produced two glass vials from her robes. She threw one down at the lonely bone arm, and the glass shattered! The liquid inside coated the bones and wrapped around the arm as if the magical goo-stuff was alive.

The witch then threw the other potion directly at Skeleton Steve, hitting him in the bony chest! The second vial also shattered, and Skeleton Steve gasped as the liquid coated his body.

With surprising quickness, Worla then picked up the arm, and *jammed* it into Skeleton Steve's empty shoulder socket. My friend gasped again, there was a *crack* and a *pop*, and then his arm began moving! Skeleton Steve moved the arm on his own once again, flexing his long, bony fingers, then rubbed his shoulder. The blackened charring on his bones from when he almost burned to death in the village also disappeared.

"You should be *all* better now," Worla said. "And not just the arm..."

"Thank you, witch," he said.

She smiled, then looked back at me.

"One week, mighty Cth'ka! Be back in *one week*. Be gone with you now."

With that, Worla turned and zipped back up her ladder and into the hut.

We turned and returned to Darkwood forest.

Day 14

After meeting with Worla, I knew I had plenty of time to practice my mind moving skills.

Skeleton Steve learned, from that conversation, that wearing a helmet would protect him from burning in the sunlight. That would change a lot for him. That would change a lot for our next adventure, too! Of course, a *lot* had changed.

I would have never *imagined* being granted this power like I had now.

And now, with Skeleton Steve, and my new friend, Zarek the Zombie, I felt that through adventuring, I might be able to start bringing creeperkind together. To learn more about my people. To *make something great*.

In several days, I would have to report back to Worla to see what deed she wanted me to do. I didn't feel very good about that, but a deal's a deal! I just hoped that it wouldn't be anything *too* unpleasant.

I decided to start building a home with my new powers in my favorite place—right at the edge of my clearing. That way, I could look out from my home, and see the sunlight on the red and yellow flowers *every day*. When I wasn't out adventuring with Steve and Zarek, I could live here, in the middle of my forest, *my* Darkwood.

Sure, I didn't know how to make doors, or tools, or windows, like I saw in the desert village. And I couldn't make stairs, or torches, or a *well*. But building out of dirt and stone was a start! And who knows what I might accomplish later?

Over the day, as Zarek sat in the flowers, watching the rabbits play and the clouds go by, I moved blocks.

I didn't want to mess up my pretty clearing and all of the flowers and grass of my forest, so I decided to use my powers to cut into a hill farther away. After I pulled out many dirt blocks, making a stack of them to use later, I was able to reach the *raw stone* underneath.

And then I started building a cobblestone *foundation* for my new home.

154

Once I had the beginning of a foundation set, I started building a stone column for one corner of the house, and that was when another creeper came by.

"What isss thisss?" it asked, its voice raspy like dry grass. "What are you doing?" The creeper looked at me, then the structure. It shook in excitement.

"Oh, hi!" I said. "I'm building." Zarek watched with interest. I had the feeling that he would jump to defend me at the drop of a hat.

"Where'sss Sssteve?" the creeper asked. "Sssteve'sss houssse?"

"No," I said. "There'sss no Sssteve. Thisss isss *my* home."

The creeper thought about that for a moment. "Sssteve," it said. "We explode Sssteve'sss houssse."

"Yesss," I said. "But thisss isn't hisss. It'sss mine. There isss no Sssteve here!"

155

The newcomer contemplated this for a while.

"I'm Cro'asss," it said. "What'sss your name?"

"I am Cth'ka," I said.

"I will ssstay with you, Cth'ka," it said.

"Okay," I said. "You are welcome. Welcome to Darkwood."

Box Set Book 2 - Diary of a Creeper King

What does Worla the Witch have in store for Cth'ka the Creeper King??

Now that he has the Crown of Ender, Cth'ka feels like he can take on the world! But at what cost?? Now, building a home for himself and his new friends in his favorite part of the forest, he can't help but wonder what dreadful errand the witch will require him to do first...

With the help of Skeleton Steve and his new followers, will Cth'ka be up to the task? Or will he try to take the easy way out? And, as always, when Minecraft Steve gets involved, everything is headed for trouble...

Day 15

What a beautiful day it was today!

The sun was warm and the breeze was gentle in 'my clearing' in Darkwood Forest. The yellow and red flowers waves and winked at me in the breeze while I worked on my new house of stone, and the dark oak trees stood tall and green against a lovely blue sky!

I do love this forest.

It's only been a few days since Skeleton Steve and I returned home, and I've been working hard on the new house. But in the calm air of my clearing, I can already feel the stress and excitement of our adventure to find the *Crown of Ender* washed away from my mind.

Man, it's been a busy last two days!

Ever since we got back from Worla's swamp, I've been working on this house. And I've been so excited about it, so amped up about using my *new powers* to pull stone out of the hill and actually build something cool, that I've hardly slept!

When we returned yesterday, and I started working on this super-cool structure, and it was a good thing that I decided to make what is essentially a *mine* a little ways away from the clearing, tucked away in the side of a hill.

Working with a stone quarry like this is a lot of work.

But is it *actually* stone quarry? Maybe it's just a *mine*. Skeleton Steve mentioned the term 'stone quarry', but he mentioned that term off-hand when talking about an area he saw once, cut into a mountain out in the open.

I'm definitely not getting my stone from out in the open! I wouldn't want to make *any part* of Darkwood Forest less pretty than it is.

Nope. It's a *mine*. For sure.

Using my new powers from the Crown of Ender, I made a tunnel of dirt into the side of a hill, pulling out one block of dirt at a time, until the dark corridor led me to the raw stone beneath, and

I've been pulling *stone* out of the ground ever since.

In fact, instead of just pulling stone, block by block, and creating a big, fake *cave*, I started digging *down*. At an angle. Like a long, dark staircase extending deeper and deeper into the ground...

I figured that there might be more interesting stone down there, the farther down I went. And I was right.

But I'm losing track of where I was going with this entry!

Let me tell you about the house!

So exciting.

I started off by building a stone foundation in the middle of my clearing. At first, I thought I'd make it into a little *house*, like the ones Skeleton Steve and I saw in the village we found on our adventure.

But then, I realized that I would need space for Zarek the zombie (who has been hanging out around me all this time), and maybe a room for Skeleton Steve, too! I know that Skeleton Steve is a busy guy and goes on lots of adventures—more than just doing stuff with *little old me*—but he may as well have his own room here for whenever he's visiting me at Darkwood, right?

And then, the deeper I went into the hill, farther and farther underground, I started running into weird blocks of stone that held shiny strips of metal chunks of different colors.

It was *ore*, Skeleton Steve said.

Apparently, that's where swords and helmets and stuff come from. Skeleton Steve told me about a villager he knows who can take ore like this, and make it into metal. Then, this villager can *build metal things* with it, like armor, weapons, tools—even doors and other pieces of houses and such!

To think that just over two weeks ago, I was just a simple creeper that never wanted to leave my forest...

Now I'm learning about such a larger world.

And in time, I hope that I can bring *many* creepers together to learn more and get smarter together ... as a people.

What great things we could accomplish if we tried to better ourselves as a whole!

Anyway...

I started to come across these *ore blocks* down in the mine, so I decided to build *another* room in the house where I could keep all of this ore stuff.

So now, I have a large stone room where I've got stacks of iron ore, a couple of pieces of gold ore, and lots of coal ore, which I had actually *seen* before on the surface, but never knew what it was up until now. I realized that the 'gold ore' was gold, because Zarek recognized it. It's the same metal that all of his armor is made out of.

Would I ever be able to do anything with any of this stuff?

Who knows?

But in the meantime, I figured that it was worth hanging on to. Maybe one day I'll learn how to do something with it. It would be nice if I could figure out how to build things other than just moving blocks around with my powers. Heck—it would be nice if I could figure out how to make things out of wood. It'd be nice to have a *door*...

My other creeper friend, Cro'as, wasn't able to help much with the mining and the building, so he just hung around near me most of the time and chatted with me here and there.

It was so nice to talk with another creeper at length for a change.

"Ssso where did you come from?" he asked me at some point.

"Here in Darkwood," I replied. "I don't remember ever living anywhere elssse."

"Sssame here," he said.

"Do you remember your mom or dad?" I asked. "I don't."

"No," Cro'as said. "I don't either..."

I wondered why we didn't remember any further back than living in this forest. Where did we *come from?* Did creepers even *have* parents?

Today, Cro'as has been gone. He left this morning to explore more of the forest. He said that he wanted to find more creepers and bring them here.

I wished him luck, but I could definitely remember how hard it was to find other creepers that would even bother to stop to talk with.

Skeleton Steve has also been away. Yesterday, he told me that he had business to attend to, and would be back before it was time to visit Worla to help her with my first obligated task.

Now, as I write this, I'm taking a break, sitting in the main room of my house and watching Zarek do sword-fighting drills in the clearing. He looks splendid in his golden armor, moving slowly, swinging his sword around and pausing here and there in his positions, surrounded by a field of green grass and yellow and red flowers.

I love this forest.

So now the house has a solid foundation, a main room, *my* bedroom, Skeleton Steve's bedroom, Zarek's bedroom, and a large store room. And I can still see the sky from all of the rooms—there's no roof! Not yet, anyway. But all of the rooms have walls, and I even left some spaces for windows—if I can ever figure out how to make them.

Well, back to work.

I've gotta say, though, working *all* of yesterday, through some of the night, and all day today, I've gotten a *lot* of practice at pulling blocks out of the ground with my powers. It's getting a lot easier. Even stone.

Back when Skeleton Steve and I were waiting for nighttime at the top of the ravine outside the stronghold, I remember experimenting with dirt and stone, feeling my invisible hands reach around a block, pass through, and *pop* it out of the ground … dirt was easy, but stone was very difficult.

Now, it's like my new weird powers to *feel* the world around me were like invisible, magic

168

arms ... or *hands* ... and they had invisible, magic *muscles*. And those muscles were getting stronger.

Just an hour ago, I was in the deepest part of my mine. The crude, stone stairs led ever downward into the darkness of the underworld. The further down I cut into the ground, the darker it became—impossibly so! Every time I thought it couldn't get any darker, the deeper I went into the ground, the darker it became!

Anyway ... I didn't think about it at the time, but looking back now, I was amazed at how easily I could pull a block of stone out of the bottom of my tunnel staircase now.

Pop.

My invisible feelers—hands, whatever— glided along the surface of the stone, then slipped into the weak points, enveloped the entire block like a ghostly net, then ... *pop!* The stone block would be out and floating in the air in front of me with little effort.

After a few hundred stone blocks and chunks of various ores, it was getting pretty easy.

Then, it was a matter of heading back up to the surface, the stone block floating in front of me, until I emerged in the sunlight again.

So many times now, I had gone down into the depths and emerged with a floating block of stone, and Zarek and Cro'as still stared in wonder as I guided the block through the air and joined it in its new place as part of my home...

Heck—I could write about this forever. I'd better get back to work.

Day 16

Today was another bright and sunny day.

It hardly ever rained in my clearing!

On the other side of the clearing, through a bend in the forest, there is a small, blue creek. In the past, before I overcame my fear of the water at the stronghold, I was always afraid to go near it. But now, since I've been back home, I've taken to having a quick dip in the cold mountain water every morning.

A quick bath in the stream this morning felt great, and was pretty much necessary, since I was so covered in stone dust from working solidly in the mine and on the house these last few days.

Later this morning, I realized that I hadn't made a place for any creepers that decided to join us. There was Cro'as, of course, but he was only *one* creeper, and I figured he could just stay with me in my room.

I didn't count on him bringing back another two creepers with him when he returned!

After chatting with the newcomers for a little while, I decided we would need a *second* house—a large and open place where many creepers could live, if any more kept coming later.

"Cth'ka!" Cro'as cried out as I was deep in the mine. I heard his sibilant voice echo down the stairway when I was half-way up, heading back to the surface with another block of stone.

Emerging into the late morning sun, a block of stone floating in front of me, I saw Cro'as standing at the entrance to the mine, and there were two more creepers standing with him.

"Cro'asss!" I said, smiling with my naturally-frowny mouth. "You've brought othersss!"

"Yesss," he replied. "Thessse creepersss are from nearby, and wanted to meet the *Mighty Cth'ka*…"

"Mighty Cth'ka??" I asked. "Who told you that?" If I could have turned red with embarrassment, I would have.

"It is what everyone calls you, my king," said a dull, low voice from behind me.

"Sssss..." I hissed slightly in surprise, then relaxed when I noticed that Zarek had approached quietly behind me. He stood tall and towered over us all, imposing in his golden armor. When that zombie swore to serve and protect me, man, he was serious! Was he coming up behind me now, just to stay close and protect me in case these creepers were unfriendly?? It seemed excessive...

I turned to Cro'as and the other two creepers.

"You guysss can jussst call me Cth'ka. Ssseriously. I'm no king..."

The two new creepers were staring at the block of stone that floated in the air between us. I put it down.

One approached.

"Great Cth'ka," it said in a gravelly, low voice. "My name isss C'Thor. I am from the plainsss to the sssouth." C'Thor nodded as if he was trying to show respect. "I have heard from Cro'asss that you can move objectsss with your mind. I now sssee that he wasss ssspeaking the truth. I will ssstay with you."

"Thank you, C'Thor," I replied. "Why do you want to ssstay?"

"I have a feeling that I should *be here*," the creeper responded. "At your ssside. Ssso I will ssstay…"

I smirked. "Okay…" I looked at the other creeper, who returned my gaze and stepped forward.

Cro'as spoke up.

"I do not know thisss creeper'sss name, my king," he said. "Thisss creeper doesss not ssspeak."

The mute creeper bowed, bending his stiff green body and crinkling as if he was made of dry leaves.

I tried to smile.

"Well, I welcome *both* of you to *my clearing*," I said. "You are of courssse welcome to ssstay." I looked around the meadow. "Although I can sssee that I will need to build another houssse."

"The name of thisss place is *the clearing?*" C'Thor asked.

"Well," I said. "That'sss what I've alwaysss called it. Maybe I should call it sssomething elssse now…"

"What did you call the foressst here?" Cro'as said.

"Darkwood," I responded.

"Darkwood," Cro'as repeated.

"Darkwood…" C'Thor pondered.

Over the rest of the day, I chatted with the three of them as Zarek kept a watchful eye. The new creepers followed me down into the mine a few times to look around, but there wasn't really anything they could do down there other than keeping me company.

Now, if only we could find more Crowns of Ender, I thought, and laughed to myself with a hiss.

Pausing the construction of my house's roof for a while, I started the foundation of a much larger building with a big common room—like a grand hall—next to my house and nestled up against the tree-line. If more creepers kept coming to join us, a large place like I had planned in my head would hold *quite* a few creepers indeed...

I've also decided, dear diary, to hold off on writing for a few days while I work hard on the mining and building. There's still a *lot of work* to be done before I leave with Skeleton Steve to see what Worla wants me to do for my *first task!*

Day 19

Okay, so it's been a few days, and I haven't touched this journal in a little while. Sorry. But I've been so busy!

Skeleton Steve finally came back yesterday, and was very happy to stay in his *own room* of my house. Oh—and my house has also been coming along quite nicely!

Also, the day before yesterday, *another* creeper showed up, and you'll never guess who it was!

It was *Cho'thos!* That's right—the creeper I met *very far* from here, back at the edge of the taiga forest where Skeleton Steve and I spent the day before heading down into the desert where we found that crazy village. The same place where I rescued Zarek from that hole in the ground!

What a small world.

When I first started my adventure with Skeleton Steve, it seemed like the world outside of

Darkwood Forest was so *huge*. But perhaps, the more I see and learn, the more the world seems *smaller* all the time.

But so *far!!*

I met Cho'thos *days* away from here. Why on Diamodia was he traveling so far? That village—the hole in the ground where I found Zarek—both of those places were *far to the north*, past other forests, on the other side of the extreme hills and that huge taiga mountain range...

"Cho'thosss!" I exclaimed. After Cro'as introduced him to me, I realized that I could still recognize him because of the long, slashing *scar* across his green body. That scar was from a fight he had with *the Steve*.

"Greetingsss, Cth'ka," Cho'thos said in a deep, hissing voice. "Ssso, a creeper *king* now? Interesssting..."

"Why doesss everyone keep sssaying that?" I responded. "I'm jussst a creeper, like you and the ressst of them."

"You have powersss, Cth'ka," he replied. "Look at what you build, creating housssesss and minesss, *just like* the Sssteve..."

"Well, I may as well, yesss?" I asked. "I have thessse powersss—I may asss well ussse them to help my people!"

"And that'sss why they will follow you, young one," Cho'thos said.

"How old are you, Cho'thosss?" I asked.

"Don't know," he responded, his voice sibilant and low. "Maybe older than you ... maybe not."

"I think you are," I said.

Day 20

Today it was time to travel to the *witch*.

Skeleton Steve, Zarek, and I traveled across Darkwood to the ridge where the forest changed into jungle down on the other side. My creeper friends all stayed back home. I tried to tell Zarek that he could wait there as well, but he wouldn't have it.

"You hold my life debt, Mighty Cth'ka," Zarek said in his low and rumbly zombie voice. "I am sworn to protect you, and will not leave your side."

"For how long?" I asked.

"Until one of us dies and I have failed," he responded, looking down at me, his eyes dark in the shadows of his golden helm.

As we walked along the ridge, looking down into the lush, green jungle below, heading north toward Lurkmire Swamp, I chatted with Skeleton Steve. I was reminded of the last time we talked on this ridge, before *and* after I was attacked by ocelots down there...

The difference was—it was *daytime* now. We didn't have to travel at night anymore.

Skeleton Steve rubbed his bony fingers along the metal of his shiny, iron helmet.

"I tell ya, Cth'ka, I don't know how I ever forgot," he said. "I mean—I've been around a *while* now, and I've had helmets and traveled during the day before, but it's like ... I just ... *forgot?*"

"That'sss weird, Ssskeleton Sssteve," I replied. "How do you forget sssomething like that?"

I gave him that helmet when we were in the stronghold's treasure room that held the Crown of Ender. Up until then, we only traveled at night, and hid in the shadows during the day, so that Skeleton Steve wouldn't catch on fire in the daylight.

He seemed surprised when Worla told him that the helmet would protect him from the sun.

He even almost *died* because of the sunlight back in that village when we were trying to keep away from the *Steve!*

"I don't know," Skeleton Steve said. "Now that I have the helmet, it's as if it's been *obvious* to me to wear it in the daylight all this time, but ... sometimes I ... *forget* stuff."

"Isss it becaussse you're *undead?*"

"Maybe," he responded. "I know *zombies* have memory problems—I've met quite a few with them, but—"

"I don't have any memory problems," Zarek interrupted, his voice slow and dull.

"Okay..." Skeleton Steve said. "Well, *most* zombies I've met have memory problems. Maybe *skeletons* do too, sometimes."

As we walked, I kept my old block of stronghold stone held up in front of me. Ever since I used that carved chunk of fortress stone to bash all of the bad guys in the stronghold to pieces during our getaway, I felt the need to keep it with me for self-defense.

Skeleton Steve had his bow.

I had my *stronghold block*.

Eventually, we made our way through the rest of Darkwood and emerged near the edge of the swamp.

Making our way through the muddy bog was easy this time. I wasn't afraid of water anymore, so crossing the deeper parts of the swamp didn't bother me, but I didn't *need* to. With my powers from the crown, all I had to do was put down my stronghold block, pick up lily pads and lay a path for myself across the water, then pick up my weapon again and keep going—all without slowing down.

While holding my stronghold block in the air, I could also … *almost* … feel the beginnings of *another invisible hand!* Even though I was holding my weapon in the air, I could *barely* feel the texture of the lily pads at the same time. I could *almost* touch more stuff around me…

I knew that it was just a matter of time before I could carry *two things* at once.

My powers were growing…

"Ssso what were you doing thessse last few daysss?" I asked Skeleton Steve.

He hopped onto a lily pad, crossed the water, then leapt back onto solid ground again. His bones *clunked*.

"Helping another friend," he said. "A *couple* of friends, actually. We had to go to the Steve's castle."

"Cassstle?" I asked. "The Sssteve hasss a cassstle?"

"Yeah," Skeleton Steve replied. "Just a little … *mini*-adventure—no big deal. But it *did* remind me of how close he lives! I've actually passed by it before, quite some time ago, but at that time I was heading to *Ahimsa village*, where I have another friend, and didn't really notice how close those places were to Darkwood Forest."

"Isss that the village we sssaw?"

"No," he replied. "It's another one. Closer, by far. You know the funny thing? Remember when we were attacked by the Steve in that village on the way to the stronghold?"

"Yesss, of courssse..."

"Well we figured that the Steve lived close to the village, because he kept going back there. But he doesn't. I wonder what he was doing by that village when we went through there before?"

"Ssssss ... who knowsss?" I responded.

When we approached Worla's witch hut, it was late in the afternoon, and the sun was still blazing, low in the sky.

Every time we've been to the witch's home in the past, it was nighttime. Now, in the light of the day, I could see that the swamp extended far to the east—it just kept going and going! I knew from experience that it only extended to the west a few hours' walk, then opened up to the grassy, horse-filled plains north of Darkwood.

But now, I saw something *new!*

To the north, not very far away, was a huge stone mountain that jutted up from the edge of the swamp and seemed very out of place. Not even an hour's walk from Worla's hut, the swamp rose up to a very skimpy forest, where there were only a few dozen sparse, brown trees before the grass and foliage disappeared altogether, and the mountain rose, naked and grey, full of sharp cliffs and topped a pointy peak!

"That'sss a *weird* mountain!" I said.

"Yeah, it really stands out, doesn't it?" Skeleton Steve replied.

Zarek followed behind me, saying nothing. His beady, black eyes peered around, combing the swamp for potential threats.

As we approached the modest wooden hut, propped up on stilts at the edge of a shallow and muddy lake, I saw the shadow of the witch appear on the deck.

"Well, well!" Worla cried from near her doorway. "Look at the three of you, walking around in the daytime like *proper* adventurers!"

"Greetings, witch!" Skeleton Steve exclaimed, as the strange woman gracefully slid down her ladder and approached.

Worla stalked over, heading straight toward me, her dark eyes lively amidst her severe and angular face, her hooked nose sitting like a great claw over her tight, grinning lips. Her hands were inside her robes, and she clutched her dark and mottled purple clothing close to her.

"Hello, Mighty Cth'ka," she said, her sharp voice cooing like she was talking to a child. She ignored the others, and stared straight into my eyes. "Are you *ready* for your first task?"

Her abruptness gave me pause, and I hesitated for a moment.

"Uh … yesss, Worla. What do you asssk of me?"

She cackled, and responded with high energy. "Easy! It's *easy*, my boy! Maybe a little hard work, but certainly a *simple* task for someone with your new … talents!"

As she spoke and smiled, I noticed that her teeth were sharp.

"Okay ... what isss it?"

"*Lava*, young creeper," she said. "I need you to get me some lava..."

"Lava?!" I asked. "Like..."

"Like the bright and red and hot and *burning* stuff, yes!" she replied. "I need some *lava* for a project I'm working on, but I have no way to get it, and no way to carry it. But *you do*..."

She smiled, and her eyes flicked to my crown.

"I *hate* lava," Zarek said suddenly.

Worla frowned at him, then looked back at me.

I looked at Skeleton Steve. He shrugged and smirked.

"There wasss lava in the cavesss by the ssstronghold," I said. "And on the beach, too..."

189

"Too far! Too far!" she said.

"Then where should I go to find sssome?" I asked.

"Don't know," she said. "But there will be lava *somewhere* nearby. Sometimes there are *pools* of it on the surface—especially in the desert! There's also *bald mountain* over there," she said, pointing with a long-clawed finger at the huge, jagged stone mountain behind her hut. "There might be some in the caves inside the mountain, or some caves in Darkwood forest. *All over!* If you can't find any lava pools on the surface, you have to go down into the caves until you're deep underground. There's *always* lava deep underground…"

Skeleton Steve spoke up. "What about your mine, Cth'ka? Have you found lava down *there* yet?"

"No," I said. "Not yet. But it isss very deep…"

Worla put her hands back together under her robe and nodded curtly. "Then there you go, creeper! Your *mine* is a good idea. You have a mine, huh? That's interesting. Well, if it's already deep, you won't have far to go to find lava."

"How much do you need?" I asked.

"I need to make … *eighteen* blocks of obsidian," she responded. "I need the same volume of lava as eighteen blocks like *that!*" She pointed at my stronghold stone block, which I had set on the ground next to me.

"How do I *get* the lava?"

"With the *crown*, dummy!" she snapped. "You know you can do more with that than just move *stone and dirt* around, eh?"

"Lava?" Skeleton Steve asked. "You think he can move *lava* with the crown?"

"I'm certain of it!" Worla said to him, then looked back at me. "If you can … reach out and touch dirt and stone with *the power*, you can *feel* water and lava just the same, right? Try it!"

She gestured with a sudden, rapid movement of a clawed hand toward the water next to her hut.

I looked at her, then the others, then took a few steps toward the water. Feeling out around me with my powers, I let the invisible fingers crawl along the ground toward the water's edge. I felt the dirt, the grass, the mud ... then dipped my invisible hand into the water.

I *could* feel it—the water. It was soft, and flowed all around my ghostly hand, but it was *physical*, and I could move through it, and around it. I passed my mind's hand through it like a paddle, and separated the water in front of me as if I did it with a *real* hand. The swamp water flowed around the shape of my power, then filled the void again as I moved through it.

But could I pick it up?

I tried to feel the water like a bowl, and scoop some of into the air, but it was slippery, and fell away from my ghostly manipulations. I couldn't even scoop up a little—how was I going to envelop a whole *block's* worth, like I did when I cut into stone?

How could I possibly do that? It was ridiculous...

"There, see?" Worla said. "You can touch it and move it. If you practice, you can get as much as I need."

I turned back toward her.

"But that'sss water. Not *lava*..."

Anger flashed in Worla's eyes for just a moment, then she softened again. Or was it just my imagination?

"What's the *difference*, Mighty Cth'ka?" she asked, her voice dripping over the *title* she gave me. "Lava is heavier than water, yes, but not heavier than that huge chunk of *carved stone* you have there. And it's hot—*very hot!* But will it burn your magic hands? I think not..."

"Okay," I said. "I'll try. Where do you want me to bring the lava?"

"Hmmmmm…" Worla pondered for a moment, looking sharply at the terrain around her swamp hut. Her eyes settled on an open field. "Come with me."

She led me to the field, then pointed at the brown, grassy ground in front of her.

Zarek followed close behind.

"Please pull a block of dirt out from *right there*," she said, pointing to the ground in front of us.

I did, and held the dirt block in the air.

"What would you like me to do with it?" I asked.

"Don't care!" she said, waving her hand. "Get rid of it!"

Casually tossing the dirt block through the air, I turned back toward the hole that was left in the ground. I saw Skeleton Steve and Zarek staring at the dirt block as it launched across the sky where we were all standing, and *flew* over field, past

Worla's hut, and cannonballed into the water of the swamp.

"*Holy cow...*" Skeleton Steve muttered.

"Now do it again ... seventeen times!" Worla said, "And leave some *space* in between, so when you come back with the lava, you can put it all into eighteen separate holes. Understand?"

"Yesss..." I said, nodding.

While Worla and my friends watched, I proceeded to use my power, strengthened by the last several days of mining, to effortlessly pluck blocks of dirt from the ground, one at a time, and toss them waaaay over to the swampy lake on the other side of the witch's hut.

Sploosh!

Ker-sploosh!

The blocks flew across the open air and landed in the water with enough force that they might have killed a mob if it was in the way.

Worla watched my work with a new kind of energy in her eyes. She might have been ... excited?

195

The witch's mouth slowly stretched into a wicked smile...

"Hold on, Cth'ka!" she said suddenly, and I halted a flying dirt block in mid-flight. Skeleton Steve gasped when he saw the block come to a sudden stop, hovering and twirling slightly in the air.

"Yesss? Isss thisss right?" I asked, tilting my head to the holes I was making in the field.

"Oh yes, yes!" Worla cooed. "Just fine. I was just thinking, instead of *wasting* all of that dirt, why don't you make a square dirt *pad* right over ... there...?" She extended a clawed finger and pointed at an open spot a little ways up from the water's edge behind the hut.

"Sure thing," I said, and rerouted the discarded dirt block to become the beginning of the dirt foundation she wanted nearby.

Focusing on my power, I completed the task, ending up with a nice grid of eighteen holes in the ground, meant to hold lava later, and a squarish dirt pad down the shore a bit from her home.

The sun was starting to go down, and I saw the square moon peeking up on the other side of the sky.

"Very good, creeper," Worla said, looking over my work. "That will work nicely. Over the next few days, as you bring the lava, just place each volume of it into these holes. When you're done, you can help me move it *all together*, so I can complete my project."

"Okay, Worla," I said. "Daysss??"

"Of course, Cth'ka," she said. "If you're going to your mine, it will take you ... well ... *eighteen* trips back and forth to bring it all here! Unless you can carry more than *one thing at a time*, that is..."

I sighed, and Skeleton Steve scoffed.

"Oh well," I said. "A deal'sss a deal..."

The witch smiled a curt smile.

"Indeed," she said. After a moment of silence, she spoke up again. "Well, you guys had better get moving then! I may or may not be here these next few days—away on other business. Just get *all of the lava* here, and either wait for me, or I'll come and find you."

"You know where I live?" I asked.

"I'll find you if I need to," she repeated. A chill ran down my spine at her words, and I didn't know why.

After Worla departed, disappearing back into her hut, we all decided to walk back home through the night.

Day 21

The next day, I was back in the mine, doing the same thing I had been doing for the last week, but *now*, I had a goal more than just gathering stone for the structures up on the surface!

Since I was trying to hurry and find lava quickly, so that I could get this time-consuming task *over with*, I didn't bother carefully placing each new stone block into its place on my home or the new creeper hall.

Instead, I stacked up all of the stone blocks along the side of the hill. Once this whole unpleasant task was done, I was sure I'd have a lot of fun building with a huge collection of blocks that would already be waiting up on the surface! Building things by mining and placing one block at a time was a *slow process*, of course!

And now, going deeper and deeper into the earth, I listened for the bubbling of the lava (I remembered that from when I saw all that lava down in the caves by the stronghold) ... but still, nothing.

All day I worked my way deeper and deeper. My stair-laden tunnel going down into the underworld was getting longer and longer—it was getting to the point where it took a long time to get back up to the surface, or to get down to the bottom!

But I had to remind myself that Skeleton Steve and I had to wander around in those caves for what—*maybe a day and a half?*—before we started coming across lava. And that was *without* digging.

Skeleton Steve hung out with me in the darkness at times, his eyes glowing red in the pitch black. It was a good thing we were *mobs* and could see in the dark. Then again, if we were Minecraftians, we'd just be using torches and stuff anyway...

"Do you know what you're going to do when we find lava?" he asked.

"Not yet," I responded. "I'll have to sssee when we get there."

"This is going to be a lot of work," Skeleton Steve said. "If this is just your *first* task, I'd hate to see what tasks *two and three* are going to be!"

"Yesss," I said, sighing with a hiss. "It'sss going to take *forever*. I've been thinking about that myssself. But what elssse isss there? I made a *deal* with the witch. Even if it'sss hard, it'sss ssstill worth it to have thisss crown..."

"Yeah, that's a good point," Skeleton Steve said. "I'd probably do the same thing for something that powerful, and I actually *have* arms!"

We laughed. Zarek laughed along with us from the shadows, and I jumped. Sometimes I forgot he was still there, but he was *always* there.

For the rest of the day, I dug and dug, deeper and deeper, but never heard the bubbling, and never found any lava.

At least I was amassing a *nice* stack of stone blocks up top!

When the sun went down, I went back to the surface, washed off in the stream, and hung

201

out with Skeleton Steve, Zarek, and the three creepers until the sun came up again.

Day 22

Today, I finally hit lava!

It was the middle of the day when it happened, and Cro'as was lingering near me, talking about finding more creepers when I heard the faintest bubbling through the stone.

"Why do you think we blow up, Cro'asss?" I asked, pulling a block out of the tunnel ahead of me.

"Beatsss me," he said. "Cho'thosss told me that he tried to blow up when he wasss fighting the Sssteve once!"

"Yeah," I said, carrying the block all the way back to the top, Cro'as and Zarek trailing behind me. "He told me that once. But the witch sssaid that that'sss how we make more creepersss."

"Really?" Cro'as asked. "That'sss weird…"

"Doesss it bother you that we know ssso little about oursssselvesss?"

"I've never been bothered by it," he responded. "But I'll alwaysss help you with whatever you ssseek to learn…"

"Thanksss," I said, and we walked up the stairs silently for a while. "Have *you* ever tried to blow up?"

"No sssir," he responded. "I don't even know how! I guesss it'll jussst come to me if I ever need to…"

Later, finally getting closer and closer to the bubbling sound, I pulled a stone block from the wall, and we were all surprised when the darkness was *flooded* with red and orange light, an intense heat hit me like a wall, and lava suddenly started oozing out of the wall … right toward us!

"Back!" I cried, backpedaling, trying to avoid tripping over Cro'as or Zarek. Little motes of fire and chunks of rock bursting into flame shot out toward us and around the tunnel, hissing and popping as the lava advanced.

Zarek made a small, uncomfortable moaning sound. Looking back, dazzled by the brilliance of the lava reflecting on his golden armor, I saw in his eyes that he was *terrified*.

We made our way backwards up a few steps and out of danger. The lava pouring out of the wall bled our way slowly, but eventually settled out and stopped moving.

After putting that stone block up on the surface, I returned to the lava, pulling more stone blocks out from around the flow into the tunnel, and eventually revealed a *massive* but short-ceilinged cavern with an impressive and equally-massive pool of lava cutting through the middle of it. The pool looked a lot like a wide *river* of lava, but it couldn't be an actual river, right? The lava had to end somewhere...

I had found the lava Worla wanted. There was plenty here—*more than enough* for her eighteen obsidian blocks' worth.

For the rest of the day, I sat on my crude stone stairs, and played with the lava with my powers.

I passed my invisible hand through it, parted it, and made it move. It was just like playing with the water, but the lava was a little more *solid*. And no, I didn't *burn* my magic hands...

However, try as I might, I still couldn't scoop any lava up into the air—I couldn't even pick up a glob of it! The molten stuff just kept running through my ghostly fingers. I could *move* it, but I couldn't pick it up. It was like trying to scoop up water in a cup full of holes.

I would have to figure out how to *close* those holes!

But it was *too hard*.

"You just need to keep trying," Skeleton Steve said at some point later, when he sat down with me in the dark, his bony features lit up red and orange from the lava light. "It's just something new. You'll figure it out. Keep trying!"

And I *did* try.

I tried and tried.

Trying to visualize my magic hand, I tried to shape it into a flat shape, then bend it around the lava like a box. I tried to scoop the lava again, even though that wasn't working—I even tried to scoop it up against the stone wall. But every time I tried to carry lava across the open air, I lost it all.

So hard.

Too hard.

This would *never* work.

There must be another way...

"Do you think Worla'sss back yet?" I asked Skeleton Steve.

"Who knows?" he responded. "What are you thinking?"

"It'sss too hard. It'sss going to take *too long!*"

"You can do it if you keep—"

"No I can't!" I cried. "Sssteve, thisss is imposssible!!"

"She's *right* you know, the witch. It's totally within your ability with that power to learn to do it! If you can pull a stone block out of a mountain, you can pull lava out of a pool. You've just got to—I dunno—make it more ... water-tight. *Plug the leaks*..."

"Sssssss," I sighed.

I tried again for another hour while Skeleton Steve patiently sat with me, then stopped.

"Maybe she can tell usss another way," I said, frowning at my bony friend. "Thisss isss ssstupid..."

"I dunno, Cth'ka. She'll probably be upset with you if you go back and tell her you can't do it. The best thing for you to do is to *keep trying*, even if it's hard, and eventually you'll figure it out. Really!"

I hissed, and glared at the lava pool.

"Maybe she'll have more ideasss on other wayss I can bring the lava *without* the crown..."

Skeleton Steve smirked, and looked at me with concern. "Yeah, maybe."

The lava bubbled and spat.

"It'sss ssso hard…"

"I tell ya what, buddy," Skeleton Steve said. "How about you keep trying the rest of the night, and if you *still* haven't figured it out, we'll go ask Worla for help in the morning, okay?"

"Ssssssss…"

"Just a little while longer. Besides, imagine what you can do if you can figure that thing out! You can freaking *throw lava* at your enemies! Terrifying!"

"Ssssss … okay, Sssteve," I said. I stood up. "Thanksss."

"No problem," he replied, standing. His bones *clunked*. "I'll go back up to the surface so you can concentrate, okay? See you in the morning?"

"Okay…"

I'd like to tell you that I tried hard for the rest of the night after Skeleton Steve left, but I'd be lying. The truth is that I tried for *maybe* another hour or so—good, honest trying—then I sat on the stairs and glared at the lava pool for the rest of the night.

Day 23

In the morning, Skeleton Steve, Zarek, Cro'as and I headed back to Worla's. The other creepers stayed behind to wait at what they were now all calling *Darkwood Fortress*.

It was funny. While I was working hard and struggling with harnessing my powers for moving the lava, the others were just playing up top, relaxing in the sun, and chatting about becoming a creeper army—creeper *soldiers*—under *Mighty Cht'ka, the Creeper King!*

If only they knew that Mighty Cth'ka was a *dummy* at using his new powers...

Mighty Cth'ka couldn't get the job done.

I sighed.

We traveled quickly and quietly for the most part, and arrived at Lurkmire much sooner than I expected. On the bright side, it looked like traveling here quickly and without dilly-dallying, chatting and looking around and such, would make

211

the trips back and forth with the lava pass faster than I initially anticipated.

When we reached the witch's hut, passing by the eighteen empty holes in the dirt, I whispered to Skeleton Steve.

"Do you think she'sss here??" I asked.

Skeleton Steve shrugged.

I noticed movement under the hut, and upon looking closer, I saw a *horse* of some kind move slightly, tied to one of the stilts of the house. In the shadows of the structure, I didn't notice it at first.

The horse was ... green?

It barely moved.

And as I peered at it more closely, I saw a *second* horse in the shadows behind it. But this horse wasn't green. It was white—bone white. And made of bones! A *skeleton* horse?!

"Worla!" Skeleton Steve called out.

I saw the shadows in the open window of the hut move, and in a quick moment, a head stuck out through the doorway.

"Who goes there?! Skeleton Steve? Cth'ka?! What are you doing back here?" It was Worla's voice alright. I heard a quiet "Be right back," and the witch emerged from her hut, shimmying down her ladder like an angry spider.

I took several steps forward away from the group and gulped.

Closer to the horses now, I could see that they were each burdened with heavy, leather saddlebags, and that the green one appeared to be a *zombie*. A zombie horse and a skeleton horse.

Worla must have had a visitor.

She approached me quickly, her face angry. Then, like flipping a switch, that predator's features shifted and softened, and then she was *smiling*.

Her eyes were still angry, and glittered blackly.

"Cth'ka," she crooned. "What can I do for you? I don't see any *lava*…"

"Yesss … um … Worla, I …" I stammered.

"Well out with it, young one! I'm busy!"

"I wasss wondering … if you might know of any other way to move the lava?"

She shook her head. "What are you talking about, creeper?! Just use the *crown!*"

"I've been … trying … but it'sss too hard! I can't figure it out. The lava keepsss sssssssslipping … it'sssssss … ssssssssss …"

I felt my heartbeat increasing, and my hearing suddenly felt funny. My vision was dimming around the edges…

"Calm down, creeper!" Worla cried. "You'll blow yourself up!"

I felt the bony hand of Skeleton Steve suddenly on my side. He was comforting me.

Good grief. I *was* working myself up!

Closing my eyes, I tried to calm down. I realized that I was hissing, so I stopped.

"Good job, Cth'ka. Now relax," Skeleton Steve said.

"Okay, creeper," Worla said, her voice a little toned down. "I don't want to get you all riled up, but you *knew* you'd have to learn this! Yeah, maybe it's hard, but I *need that lava*, and you're going to bring it to me! Figure it out! And hurry!"

"It'sss … hard. Really hard. I'm not jussst being a wusss here—I worked at it for a *long time* and couldn't do it! Do you have any other ideasss?"

"He *did* try, Worla," Skeleton Steve said. "The kid's been working on it literally all day yesterday."

She looked at Skeleton Steve and smiled, which shifted into a sneer. "Well laa dee da!" she said, then closed her eyes and rubbed one of her temples with a clawed finger. "Okay, well, I guess … you could always go to the Steve's castle and steal a *bucket* or something…"

A bucket! Of course!

215

The Steve probably had a bucket, if he had a whole *castle!*

"Ehhhh …" said Skeleton Steve. "That'd probably be *pretty* dangerous…"

"Yeah, well, it's either *that* or learn how to use the crown!" Worla snapped. "And Cth'ka, I really *encourage* you to learn to do it the *right* way, to learn to use the crown! *It can be done!* You just have to keep trying! Anything worth doing is worth learning how to do it right!"

I nodded and looked down, feeling stupid.

Everyone was so disappointed in me…

"Thanksss, Worla. I'll figure it out…"

"Please hurry, creeper. I need to make those obsidian blocks sooner than later, understand?!"

"Yesss. Okay…"

"Now if there isn't anything else, I've got to get back to my meeting…"

"Thanks, Worla," Skeleton Steve said.

216

The witch looked down at me again, cast a glance over to Zarek and Cro'as, then turned in a flash and zipped back to her ladder, up, and inside.

"Is it just me, or is she getting meaner?" Skeleton Steve said.

"It'sss my fault," I said. "I'm not getting the work done..."

"Eh, whatever. Let's do this! So you're ready to head back?"

"It'sss a good thing you jussst went to the Ssssteve'sss cassstle," I said. "You know the way from here?"

Skeleton Steve was surprised by that.

"Really??" he asked. "You want to go *steal a bucket* from the Steve??"

"I jussst want to get thisss over with," I said. "We can go ssstraight there from here, then go ssstraight home. If you guysss want to go with me...?"

Cro'as spoke up. "You can count on me, my king. I will asssissst you alwaysss."

217

"I'm with you, of course," Zarek said with his low, dull voice.

Skeleton Steve sighed.

"I'll try one more time to ask you to reconsider…?" he said. "I'll help you with this if you want, but did you forget how *dangerous* the *Steve* is? He's an armored *killing* machine! And *if* he has a bucket, it'll be inside his castle, and he'll probably be there too! You could just go *home*, now, and try to figure out the crown thing instead! I mean—you should know how to do everything you can with it eventually anyway!"

"Very sssmart, Ssskeleton Sssteve. Good pointsss. But I jussst want to get thisss finished. Thisss will be fassster."

"Alright," he said. "But don't say I didn't warn ya…"

With that, Skeleton Steve pulled out the compass he found in the stronghold library, and instead of leading us home to the south, he led us to *the Steve*, to the west…

The last time we traveled west from Lurkmire swamp at dusk was when we set out to find the *Crown of Ender*. When the sun went down, we had headed out to the west before, then turned north to follow the *Ender Eyes* through the horse valley and beyond. At the time, we didn't *know* it was north—we were just following the eyes.

But now, once we reached the familiar long, grassy plain, and saw horses standing in the silver light of the moon, we continued west to the far tree-line of a *new journey*.

It would be a short journey, though.

According to Skeleton Steve, to the east in the next plain over, on the other side of the upcoming forest, was another village called *Ahimsa Village*. Once we reached the village, we would turn north, and head up into the mountains where, eventually, we'd reach the Steve's castle.

I could almost imagine a *map* in my mind at this point. If we followed our old path to the stronghold, we would eventually run into the other village where we ran away from the Steve before—far to the north. And if this *Ahimsa Village* was to the west, or north-west, and the Steve's castle was to the north of *that*, then the other village to the north would be kinda-sorta east or north-east of the Steve's castle! The mob-killer could very well be positioned between *both* villages, which would let him visit and protect *both* of them…

Over the rest of the night, we traveled east until we found the village (I looked at it for a while, watching the torches flicker and the firelight inside the little houses go on and off), then skirted around Ahimsa to continue north.

Once we arrived at the foothills of the mountains to the north, we stopped and hid for a while, because we came across a great stone quarry—probably a place where the Steve gets stone of his own.

"I almost forgot about this place," Skeleton Steve said. "I didn't pass it a few days ago when I was here, but I've been here before. *That* was an interesting night…"

"Do you think the Sssteve isss here?" I whispered.

"I don't hear anything," Skeleton Steve said. "Last time I was here, he was using a pickaxe—a tool. Besides—it's night time! He's probably sleeping in the castle."

The stone quarry was a strangely shaped place where raw rock was cut out of the foothills of the mountains in great square voids. There was an artificially-created pool of water at the lowest point that we had to pass to go up and around the fake cliffs to continue to the north.

Up at the top of the quarry cliffs was a small hut with a torch over the door.

As we approached, I idly twirled my stronghold block, my mind itchy to throw it at *the Steve* if he showed up...

But he didn't appear.

We reached the top of the cliff, and Skeleton Steve eyed the hut.

"Let's check in here. He has a pool—there might be a bucket inside a chest in there..."

"Okay..." I said, preparing my weapon as Skeleton Steve opened the door.

"Aww—just a hut," he said. "No, wait—there's a ladder going down. There are also a couple of *chests*..."

Skeleton Steve disappeared inside, and I heard a wooden chest creak open. My bony friend spent some time looking over whatever was in there, then closed the chest and opened the next one. After a moment, he closed that one too, then stepped outside again.

"Well??" I asked.

"Nothing really," Skeleton Steve said. "Some metal, lots of cobblestone, some other rocks, a couple of stone pickaxes. I bet he hasn't been here in a while. No bucket. I took some *torches*." He patted his pack.

I deflated, and my stronghold stone sagged in the air.

We would have to steal the bucket from the castle...

Moving on to the north, we hiked up into the mountains, and continued to the lair of the Steve.

"Watch out for wolves..." Skeleton Steve said.

Day 24

By morning, we had arrived.

Creeping over the top of a mountain ridge, I saw a structure unlike anything I had ever seen. I mean—the *stronghold* where I found the crown was very impressive, of course, but it was underground and it was hard to appreciate its *size*.

The size of the castle below could be fully appreciated!

Down in the valley between two mountain ridges, surrounded by tall pine trees, was a green plateau, and on it was a single fortress structure about the size of a *whole village*. There was a huge, round tower—clearly the main part of the building—and other connecting structures areas around it that were more … square. More *normal*—like *my* house. The entire structure was made from carved stone bricks, it glittered with glass windows, and brimmed with artfully-placed torches.

In the morning sunlight, the torches weren't very impressive, but there were *many*, and I bet that at night, the whole plateau was brilliantly lit up to keep mobs from wandering in.

All around the castle were *other* features, too. There were multiple fenced-in areas containing various animals, and another large fenced-in area that looked a lot like the little farms from the villages—but *huge*.

Everything *the Steve* seemed to be doing here was huge…

As the plateau sloped down behind the castle to the lowest part of the gulch between the mountains, I saw the *blue* of a river or creek, and there was another smaller building on the edge of the water. *The Steve* must do something over there involving the river. Maybe it was a building for *drinking* water, or maybe getting some *food* out of it somehow. Maybe the Steve ate the squids…

"I've been here a few times now," Skeleton Steve said, "and I'm lucky this killer creature hasn't found me. My luck will run out one day…"

"Where would the Sssteve keep hisss bucketsss?" I asked, peering down at the massive structure.

"Beats me," Skeleton Steve said. "Inside, probably. Maybe a room with chests full of all of his *stuff*. Or not. If *I* could make things out of metal, I would probably keep all of the metal stuff in the same place next to where I made it. That's what *I'd* do."

"Down by the river house," Zarek said, surprising us. "Maybe he uses the bucket to get water there."

"Maybe he usssesss the bucketsss to get fish," Cro'as said.

"Eh … I don't know about *that*…" Skeleton Steve said. "The river house is a good idea, though. Maybe we should start there. If we find one and can get away without going into the main castle, all the better!"

"The farmsss," I said. "The farmsss have water, and he probably usssesss water *a lot* to make the plantsss. Maybe a chessst there with bucketsss..."

All good ideas. Plenty of places to start with. But which one? Once we started, we'd run out of time and be discovered *eventually*. Maybe we should start with the hardest of all—the castle.

"Okay, let'sss go," I said, walking over the ridge.

I felt Skeleton Steve's bony hand grab me.

"Hold on, Cth'ka," Skeleton Steve said. "It's broad daylight—we can't go down there right now! We've got to wait until tonight."

"Ssssss," I said. "We go in fassst and get out fassst. Probably not sssee the Sssteve at all!" I looked over at Zarek and Cro'as, and they looked uncomfortable between us.

"*No way*," Skeleton Steve said. "You wanted to do this, even though I advised against it, but it's *way* too dangerous to go during the day. That's when the Steve is active. Let's wait until he's sleeping tonight..."

"Come on!" I said with a hiss. "Let'sss do it fassst ssso we can go back home and get the lava!"

"No, Cth'ka," he said. "You want to take risks? I can understand that. But now you're not just playing with your *own* life—you're playing with mine." He jerked a bone thumb over his shoulder at Cro'as and Zarek. "And *theirs*. If we're doing this, we're doing it *right*."

"Sssssssss … fine," I said. "We'll wait."

So we sat in the shadows of the pine trees, watching the castle. I watched for the Steve, but we never saw him.

"I'm sssorry, guysss," I said later. "Sssorry for being impatient."

"It'sss okay, my king," Cro'as said. "I'm with you either way."

Zarek nodded.

"Taking the easy way out can be dangerous, Cth'ka," Skeleton Steve said. "That's how you get reckless. That's how bad things happen. It's important to do things the *right way*."

229

Over the rest of the day, there was no sign of *the Steve*.

"Maybe he'sss in a village??" I asked.

Skeleton Steve shrugged.

Once the sun went down and the moon was higher in the sky, we descended to the plateau.

"River hut first?" Skeleton Steve asked.

I nodded.

We quietly made our way through the tree-line around the edge of the castle grounds until we had to cross the river. My senses were on fire, and I listened for the *smallest sounds* to warn me that the Steve was coming.

But all was quiet...

I twirled my stronghold block nervously as we climbed up onto the wooden dock and approached the birch door.

Skeleton Steve opened the door with a quiet *creak*.

There were a variety of tables and cooking contraptions, and a single large chest.

Skeleton Steve opened it.

"Fish," he said. "Lots and lots of *fish* from the river, some boots, string, lily pads—a whole bunch of *junk*. No bucket..."

"Darn," I said, kicking the floor. "Let'sss check the farm..."

"Okay," Skeleton Steve said, and the others nodded.

We crept away from the fishing hut, and approached a large farm plot surrounded by a fence.

"How do we get in?" Zarek asked a little too loudly.

"Ssshh!!" Skeleton Steve said, holding his bony finger up to his skull face. "There's probably a *gate* around here somewhere, we just need to—"

I placed my stronghold block on the grass, then used my power, feeling the wooden rails of the fence with my mind...

231

Snap! Snap!

Pulling two rails out of the fence, the wood broke with a surprising *crack*, and we were left with an opening large enough for us to pass through. Skeleton Steve glared at me.

"Sssorry," I said, placing the two broken rails gently down on the ground. I picked up my stronghold block again.

We snuck into the farm, moving quietly among a variety of crops. I didn't really recognize *any* of them. At one point, Zarek reached down and pulled up what he would later tell me was a *potato*. Zarek likes potatoes. Rows of tall, golden grass of some kind waved in the mountain wind...

As we followed around the exterior wall of the castle, moving through all of the Steve's food plants, stepping around and over the trenches full of water, I looked for a chest. There had to be a chest *somewhere* full of his farming stuff— whatever *that* would be.

Eventually, I found it.

"Ssss ... There!" I whispered to Skeleton Steve.

He nodded, and approached the chest. Opened it and looked inside. My friend shook his head.

"No bucket," he said. "Just lots of dead plants, seeds, and a tool of some kind."

Looks like we'd have to do it the *hard* way...

Stealthily moving around to the front of the castle, we found the gate to the farm and let ourselves out, then approached the front door.

The Steve would be in there...

This is what you wanted, I thought. *Much easier to steal a bucket than to try again and again with that stupid lava...*

Was it?

How far did we have to go out of our way to get here and wait for nightfall? Would I have already figured it out by now if I just *tried harder* to learn the technique? We still had to get *back home*, and now we had to sneak into the Steve's castle and not get killed!

It seemed like a much easier idea when we were back at Worla's...

"Okay, let'sss go," I said.

Skeleton Steve opened the front door. Inside was a large hall, lit up by torches. The *whole place* would be full of torches, I bet.

I heard the faint ring of metal, and saw that Zarek had pulled his sword.

"What is that?" Skeleton Steve asked him, looking at the blade.

Come to think of it, Zarek's sword *was* different than Skeleton Steve's sword. Different than any other sword I've ever seen—shaped differently than the sword the Steve chased us with back at the village. It was longer, and thinner, with a longer handle and an edge only on one side.

"Katana," Zarek said.

"A *katana*, huh? Interesting. Never seen one before."

"I took it from an enemy long ago," the zombie warrior responded.

"Uh, guysss?" Cro'as asked. "The door isss open!"

Skeleton Steve and Zarek looked at him, then looked inside.

We went in.

The inside of the castle was quiet, save for the crackling of a large fireplace in the first room on the right. The room was lined with bookshelves (*I remembered the stronghold library*), and had a strange, obsidian table on the far end. An odd book sat idle on the middle of the platform. I started into the room, but Skeleton Steve stopped me.

"No bucket in there," he whispered.

We went on down a hall, past a staircase, and turned into a large stone room with multiple furnaces, an anvil, and various pieces of gear I didn't understand—probably for building *Minecraftian* things.

"Here we go," Skeleton Steve whispered, and led us into the forge room. He approached a series of wooden chests.

Creak. (Creak, creak, creak, creak...)

When he opened the first chest, the sound of it opening seemed to echo through the whole castle. Skeleton Steve froze silently for a moment, waited, then finished opening the chest.

"Lots of metal, coal, and ... ah!"

He smiled, and pulled out ... a *bucket!*

All four of us smiled in relief as Skeleton Steve took the bucket in one bony hand, closed the chest, and we turned to go.

And looked right at *the Steve*...

We all stood in shock for a moment.

I opened my mouth to say something, but nothing came out.

The Steve pulled an iron sword. It made a similar sound to Zarek's sword being pulled from its sheath earlier...

The Steve was wearing full iron armor. On his left arm was a brand new wood and iron shield. His eyes under the helmet were empty and without emotion. His face was bland and unreadable.

The Steve was *not like us*...

In a sudden flurry of activity, we all started yelling and running in different directions! The Steve charged, holding his sword high and his shield before him. He didn't make a sound, other than the *thump* of him pulling his shield into place. Zarek sidestepped, holding his katana with both hands, intending to put himself between myself and the Steve. Cro'as also charged against the Steve. I didn't know what he was doing, unless—

"Wait!" I cried. "Cro'asss, *no!!*"

Skeleton Steve, bucket in bony hand, darted around the coming melee, yelling "We just want a bucket! We just want a bucket!"

The Steve *clashed* into Zarek. They rapidly exchanged blows, faster than I could make out. At first, the Steve's sword came down, and there was a loud *clang* as Zarek met the blade with his own.

Then Zarek counter-attacked, but the Steve brought up his shield, and the katana cut a deep score into the wooden defense. The Steve's sword came down again, and glanced off of Zarek's gold shoulder armor. Zarek's sword flashed, and hit the shield again!

And all the while, I watched in horror as Cro'as approached the two swordsmen, flashing, hissing, sputtering, the gasses building up in his body *straining* at his green skin...

BOOM!!

My friend exploded. *The Steve* was blown back. Zarek was blown back. Skeleton Steve was thrown out into the hall. I was suddenly aware that I was tumbling across the floor.

"Cro'assss!" I cried. I hissed. I hardly heard my voice as I stumbled back to my feet. The room was partly destroyed. A wall was gone, and I saw through the hole into a room full of chests. A couple of chests had been blown to smithereens, and *countless* random items were strewn across the floor. Chunks and blocks of cobblestone were everywhere! I noticed that there was a hole in the floor where Cro'as had blown up, making a small ragged window into a basement level below.

The Steve was lying among all of the *stuff* in the chest room, but he was getting to his feet.

I was suddenly aware that Zarek was pulling me along.

"Come on!" Skeleton Steve yelled. "Let's get out of here!!"

The next few moments were a blur, as Zarek, Skeleton Steve and I stumbled back to the entrance of the castle, then ran out into the open air. I didn't look back, not until we were deep in the trees halfway up the ridge, heading south.

"*My block!*" I cried. I stopped, and Skeleton Steve and Zarek pulled on me some more to keep me moving. In the explosion, I somehow lost track of my *stronghold stone*. "The crown?! Do I still have the crown?!"

"You still have the crown!" Skeleton Steve yelled.

We kept moving, and didn't stop until we were well over the ridge.

"Are you okay, my king?" Zarek said finally.

I was dazed. My head was foggy. I felt like I had been hit with countless little pieces of flying rocks from an explosion. I *had* been!

"I'll be okay. Ssskeleton Sssteve? Do you have the bucket??"

I didn't see it in his hand.

"No, Cth'ka," he replied. "I dropped it in the explosion. But we had to get out of there! The Steve would have killed us if we stayed a moment longer..."

"No!!" I cried. I reached out with my power, and *smashed* a tree! Skeleton Steve and Zarek gasped as blocks of wood exploded from the tree trunk.

"We should have just gone home," Skeleton Steve said.

"Now there'sss no bucket, and Cro'asss is *dead!*"

240

I cried.

I didn't know that creepers could cry, but I did, and I bawled and hissed, and I pounded the ground with my powerful invisible hand. My friends kept their distance until I calmed down, then Skeleton Steve cautiously approached, putting his bony hand on my back.

"I'm sorry, Cth'ka. I'm sorry your friend is dead."

Zarek sheathed his sword, and sat on the ground.

"It'sss..." I stammered. "It'sss all my fault! I should have taken your adviccce and jussst did it right! I should have lissstened to you and Worla. Cro'asss would ssstill be alive. He'sss dead becaussse I tried to take a shortcut inssstead of doing it the *right way!*"

My friends said nothing. What *could* they say? I was right about all of it. And Skeleton Steve was too good to say *I told you so*. Not any more than he already did. Cro'as was gone, and it was all my fault.

241

Skeleton Steve's hand patted my back.

"We should get going," my bony friend said. "The Steve might still come after us."

"And I lossst my ssstone," I said.

"I know," Skeleton Steve said. "Maybe we can get another, huh? We still need to go back there for all of the treasure."

We walked.

Four, now three...

Over the night, we made our way back down the mountains, past the quarry, and around Ahimsa Village. Heading east, by the time we reached the plains outside Darkwood Forest again, it was morning.

Day 25

Today was terrible.

I'll never be able to forgive myself for getting Cro'as killed.

He was my friend, and he would have followed me to the ends of Diamodia. *My king*, he would say.

So he followed me to his death…

I made the wrong choice—the wrong choice as a leader, and I got one of my people killed. He was the first creeper to join my army, and the first life I lost, and for what?! To try to take the easy way out.

Well, not anymore.

From now on, I would do *right* by my people. I would take the hard path to do things *right*. I tried to take the lazy way out, and put my friends' lives in danger—killed one of them…

Not anymore.

243

We spent the first half of the day walking quickly back to Lurkmire Swamp, then turning south and making our way back home as fast as we could.

The others didn't talk much.

They followed.

And when we returned, I saw the happy faces of C'Thor, Cho'thos, and the mute creeper, and I stormed past them straight down into the mine. Before I disappeared into the darkness, I saw Skeleton Steve peel off of my path to talk to them, and heard the word *"Cro'as."*

For the rest of the day, I stared into the fiery glow of the lava, and reached out with my powers to wrap my ghostly hand around the oozing hot stuff in every way I could imagine.

I would win this.

I would conquer this technique.

I would do it for Cro'as, and to fill the gaping pit of guilt and regret in my heart.

All afternoon and evening I worked at that lava, and I failed over and over again. I continued to try and fail into the night, but did not give up. I would *never* give up again...

Day 26

I did it!!

I finally did it!

About halfway through the next day—it was hard to tell underground how much time had passed—I finally managed to get the *feel* right, and I lifted a glob of burning magma into the air, and was able to keep it from spilling out of my invisible hand. Not just for a second this time—as long as I wanted to!

"Yesss!!" I yelled to no one. Zarek startled behind me, sitting bored on the stone stairs for however many hours it had been. "I did it!! Zarek, I did it!"

"Very good, my king. At last!"

It was just as Skeleton Steve had said. It was a matter of *plugging the leaks*. I eventually came to understand that my invisible hand was kind of like a net. Easy to grab blocks of dirt. Harder with stone, because it seemed to *stretch out* with heavier things. But then, I strengthened it over time, and could now pick up heavy things without a problem. But there were still ... *pores* would be the best way to describe it. Today, I managed to, with my mind, clench shut those pores, and I plugged the leaks!

I felt it. I *knew*. I could do this *forever* now, now that I understood the *feel* of it.

Now that I could lift a small glob of lava, I increased my effort, trying to collect a large block's worth. Using the same concept I came to understand, I clenched around the mass of lava and plugged the leaks, and I heard Zarek gasp in fear and amazement as I lifted a large blob-block of magma from the lava pool, into the open air of the cavern at the bottom of the stairs.

"I've got it! I can do it!!" I exclaimed.

Zarek stirred, and I heard rapid footsteps coming down the stairs from the surface. I heard the *clunk* of bones.

"Cth'ka?" Skeleton Steve yelled from above. "Are you okay?"

"Ssskeleton Sssteve!" I yelled back. "I can do it! I did it! *Look!!*"

Skeleton Steve caught up and approached behind Zarek at the bottom of the stairs.

"Holy cow, Cth'ka! That's *amazing!* I mean—I knew you'd do it eventually, but I never imagined how *awesome* a floating block of lava would look!"

"Let'sss go up!" I exclaimed.

"Be careful!" Zarek cried, staying several steps ahead of me. "If you drop it up the stairs, you'll *burn yourself up!*"

I *was* careful. As fantastic as it was, carrying a brightly burning blob of lava in front of my face, I could feel the intense heat of it all over, and I was distinctly aware that if I slipped up, I'd get *fried.*

Eventually, I felt the sunshine on my face again, and stepped out into the day, holding the block of burning magma floating in the air in front of me.

The other creepers gaped in amazement, then all of my friends *cheered!*

"Doesss anyone need to *cook* anything??" I asked.

Everyone laughed.

Over the rest of the day, I walked the floating lava *all the way* to Worla's. It was a long time to hold my concentration, and at one point I felt the 'clenching of the pores' lapse, and thought I'd spill fiery lava all over the forest, but I caught it, and kept my hold. Everyone walked with me: Zarek, Skeleton Steve, Cho'thos, C'Thor, and the mute creeper.

Their support made me feel a lot better.

Halfway to Worla's, the sun went down, and our path was lit up brilliantly by the block of lava, casting red and orange light and a flurry of shadows all around us.

When we arrived at her witch hut, all was quiet. It seemed that she wasn't around. No horses under the hut either.

Walking the floating lava to the field of holes, I approached the first crude container, carefully moved the lava above it, then released my grip.

The blob of burning lava *splooshed* into the hole.

The swamp didn't catch on fire. The hole contained the lava just fine. Everything was fine.

Better then fine. *Great!*

I could finish the task!

Now, I just had to do that *seventeen more times*…

Day 27

Today was a very boring day.

Not much to talk about. But I learned from the last time I skipped writing in my diary that, even if you think nothing's going on, you should *still* write about it. Back when I thought I'd just spend a few boring days building, I ended up seeing Skeleton Steve return and be happy about his room, and I met up with Cho'thos again!

Always write...

But, even though I was ready to write about something unexpected and exciting, it was still a boring day.

My day consisted of picking up more lava, walking a *long* way with hot lava in my face, dumping it in a hole, then walking a long way back to do it again...

All in all, I tried to take the most direct route to Worla's possible, and I tried to work as

quickly as I could without being reckless.
Surprisingly, I was able to make the trip *six times!*

Before today, I never would have thought
that I could walk to Worla's and back *six times* in
one day—counting the night, of course.

Day 28

Today I did the same thing again.

Eighteen trips of transporting lava is *a lot!* Holy cow—this task is a doozy! Worla should have hired a *whole army* to do this! But then, who other than maybe *the Steve* would have been able to carry lava like this?

Just me.

I made the trip seven times today. Pushing even harder, I got an extra trip in there…

Only *four more* blocks of lava to go.

Today I did see something very interesting, though…

It should be pretty obvious that I could potentially use a flying block of lava as a really awesome *weapon*. Heck—Skeleton Steve mentioned that earlier, I think. It's just harder to control, being as I need to focus so much more on *plugging the leaks*. It would take a *lot* more concentration to use lava as a weapon than it would to throw around my *stronghold stone*, for instance.

But on my second-to-last trip, I *did* experiment with swinging the lava block around a little. It scared me some, the possibility of losing control and splashing burning lava around—maybe even on myself—but I was careful.

You would think that the obvious way to use the lava would be to swing it around like I already knew how to do with stone blocks. Zip it this way and that, and *smash* enemies along the way. Lava would do the same, of course, but it would *burn* them more than bash them, I think...

But while experimenting, I came up with *other* ways to use it as a weapon that's not as obvious!

I could use a lava block as a *defensive wall* to put between myself and an enemy. He'd have to get through the lava to get to me, and there aren't many mobs that could withstand *that*.

A lava block could also be used just to burn *through* stuff...

I tested this with a tree. No, not a tree in Darkwood Forest surrounded by *other* trees—that would be stupid! Once I was in the swamp, I found one of those weird, brown *scraggly* trees that stands all by itself, and I just *slowly* moved the lava block up to it, then *through* it. That block of lava set the tree *on fire*, and then cut its way through it pretty quickly!

And, of course, you could always just drop a block of lava on top of a bad guy's head! But that would be *very messy*...

Worla was still away from home. I hadn't seen her in ... what? Almost a week?

Well, what a long day. I'm looking forward to this being over tomorrow.

Day 29

Today, I had only *four trips* left to make! That field full of holes was starting to look very interesting—the dirt 'containers' were now almost all glowing with lava!

For the last few trips, Skeleton Steve came along with Zarek and I for support. The three creepers stayed back home.

The first and second trips went without event.

The third trip went without event as well, until we returned to Darkwood...

"Something's wrong," Skeleton Steve said as we approached my clearing. We had all been making jokes on the way back about ways to use lava blocks for pranks. They were all generally very bad ideas...

We broke into a run.

When I stepped out of the trees and into the clearing, I saw that my house...

Blocks, destruction … craters … the house…

The foundation of the creeper hall still stood, but my house was partially blown up! Sections of some walls were missing, ceiling rafters were broken and fallen, pieces of the floor were now craters.

What would make craters like that, other than—

"Cho'thosss!" I cried. "C'Thor! Where are you guysss?!"

The creepers were *gone!*

We approached the house, and I could see from the destruction, from the blast patterns, that two large explosions had taken place *inside* the house. Even the foundation was broken where … *two creepers* … had blown up…

"No!" I cried. "Who isss it? Who blew up?!"

In the commotion, I hardly noticed when C'Thor came up from around the back of the house.

"C'Thor!" I said. "You're alive! But that meansss..."

Cho'thos.

The mute creeper.

"Yesss, my king," C'Thor said. "Cho'thosss and the other perished..."

"What happened?!" Skeleton Steve asked.

C'Thor looked at him, then back at me.

"I wasss away in the foressst at the time, but it wasss the Sssteve! He came from the wessst and battled the other two. When I heard the explosionsss, I came back, but it wasss too late..."

"Did you *see* the Steve?" Skeleton Steve asked.

"I sssaw him running away, yesss," C'Thor said. "But he alssso left thisss..."

Walking over to the foundation of the creeper hall, the last creeper soldier pointed out a *single block* sitting in the middle of the stone pad...

It was my stronghold block.

I left it back at the Steve's castle.

And he brought it back to me.

What?!

"Why?!" I asked. "Why would he—?"

"Vengeance, my lord," Zarek said. "You blew up his house, so he has blown up yours."

"No, no, that *can't* be it," Skeleton Steve said. "There must be more of an explanation! The Steve is nothing to be trifled with, sure, but he's not *evil*."

"That'sss not all, my king," C'Thor said, looking back at the blown-up house. "He alssso ssstole all of your oresss."

"What?!"

I ran over to the house as fast as my four stubby creeper legs could carry me. Looking into the storage room, I saw that it was true. All of my stacks of various ores and coal were *gone*...

Skeleton Steve ran up to me, his bones clunking. "Now, Cth'ka, don't be too hasty here! This doesn't look like *just* the Steve. There's something *more* to this story, I'm sure of it! We have to figure out—"

"Where'sss the Sssteve?" I asked C'Thor. "Where'd he run to??"

"Uh … to the north, my king."

"To the witch," Zarek said.

"Let'sss go!" I said, and they all ran behind me to the north, but I stopped. "Wait," I said, turning to the mine. "There'sss one more block of lava to get. Let'sss finish thisss. Besssidesss—I may *need* it."

Gathering the last burning block of molten rock, I carried it as carefully as I could while moving quickly, and we made our way to Worla's home, grim and determined to fight—all of us except for Skeleton Steve, perhaps...

As we approached the glowing grid of lava holes near the witch's hut, the sun had already been down for a couple of hours, and the seventeen little, dirt pits burned brightly in the night in a *perfect pattern* on the ground of three rows and six columns.

Lovely.

Almost. There was one left to be filled...

As I approached the last empty hole, with my friends all around me, I listened and looked around for any signs of *the Steve*.

The swamp was quiet. It didn't look like the witch was around either.

With a final *gloop*, I dropped the last block of lava into the hole.

Finished.

At last!

We were all weary and stressed, so there were no cheers, although Skeleton Steve did give me a healthy clap on the back.

Just then, in the darkness off in the distance, I saw a flash of light.

"What wasss that?" I asked.

"What?" Skeleton Steve replied.

"A flash! Light, sssee, over there!"

Everyone turned and peered at the black horizon.

"I don't sssee anything," C'Thor said.

There was another flash of yellowish light. We all saw it.

"There!" I said.

"I saw it!" Skeleton Steve said. "What is—?"

Just barely, I could suddenly see two yellow, glowing forms buzzing around in the distance. Like ... fireflies.

Flash.

And then, we all gasped when a bolt of bright blue *lightning* sizzled through the air, and lit up *bald mountain* for just an instant.

Something was going on there!

Was it *the Steve?*

"Let's go check it out!" Skeleton Steve said, then broke into a run on the west side past Worla's hut. There was a ridge there just up the shore from the swamp lake, a path that would take us to the mountain.

"Wait!" I cried. "Should I bring sssome lava??"

"No!" Skeleton Steve called back. "There's no time!"

I ran after him, and Zarek and C'Thor followed.

As we bolted through the dark toward the mountain, we saw more flashes again and again. Some small and yellow. Once more, there was a bright crack of blue lightning! I could still see the yellow, glowing things circling around in the dark.

Whatever was going on over there was happening up on that huge cliff.

Could we get there in time?

Running after Skeleton Steve and his clunking bones, I watched my step through the mud while I also tried to pay attention the fireworks up ahead. Now, I could *hear* the explosions. Little fireballs streaked through the air, and lit up yellow whenever they impacted the rocky cliff.

We were almost there!

Skeleton Steve was ahead of me pretty far, but eventually, when I could see that he had a good vantage point, he stopped, and waved me over.

I struggled to catch up.

"What isss it??" I asked.

Skeleton Steve called back. "I think it's Worla! And *the Steve!*"

As if on cue, another bolt of bright lightning flashed through the sky, and *smashed* into the cliff, lighting up the whole area in a blueish-white light for an instant.

But an *instant* was all I needed to see!

267

Up on the large cliff of bald mountain, on the big outcropping I saw earlier from in front of Worla's hut, I saw the witch and the Steve locked in an epic battle!

The Steve was surrounded by patches of burning rocks, and stood holding up a burning shield as Worla twisted and flailed nimbly in the dark far away from him, presumably casting her *dark magic*. Above the battle, weaving in and out of the scene, were two creatures of *my size*, made of fire and strange rotating, glowing ... rods! The fire creatures dodged this way and that, occasionally stopping to launch a volley of fireballs at the Steve!

Foom foom foom!

Boom boom boom!

Three fireballs at a time, and the Steve would either dodge out of the way, catch them on his shield, or ... *amazingly* ... hit them with his sword and bat the flaming spheres away into the night.

The Steve looked wounded but ridiculously dangerous. Worla looked composed and determined. It seemed that he was trying to *get* to her—I was sure he could chop her up with his sword with little effort if he could reach her—but the fire creatures were keeping him busy!

I had to help...

"C'Thor!" I called out to my last creeper soldier.

"Yesss, my king?"

"Do *not* blow yourssself up, do you hear me?!"

"Asss you wish, my king!"

I charged toward the cliff battle and climbed the mountain as quickly as I could.

"Wait, Cth'ka!" Skeleton Steve called. "It's *too much!* Worla's got this! Stay out of it!"

"No, Ssskeleton Sssteve! The Sssteve killed my friendsss—I've got to help the witch!"

"You'll get yourself *killed!*" he cried after me.

I put one foot in front of the other. The edge of the cliff was coming—I just hoped I could clear the steepest part of the climb in time.

With the battle out of my vision for the moment, my heart leapt when I heard a weird sound. A strange combination of metal crunching, and an otherworldly cry ... of pain?

There was a crash, and the lights ahead over the stone cliff's edge above me were suddenly *dimmer*.

He just killed a fire creature, I thought.

Looking behind me, I saw Zarek, Skeleton Steve, and C'Thor struggling to catch up.

The flash of blue lightning lit up the sky again, and Worla cackled madly!

"*I've got you!*" she was screaming. "*I've got you! I've got you!*"

I reached the cliff, but couldn't get up!

No! I thought. Almost there, but I was *too short*. I couldn't jump. There was *nothing* to climb, I couldn't get up, I—

Reaching with my power into the stone under my feet, I enveloped the block I was standing on. I felt my invisible hand *all the way around it*, with me balanced on the top of it ... and I pulled ... *up*.

The ground under my feet jolted.

I heard Skeleton Steve gasp behind me. "*Cth'ka...!*"

"Mighty Creeper King!" said the awed voice of C'Thor.

I didn't think about the fact that I just made myself *fly* by carrying myself up onto the cliff with a stone block.

When I stepped off of the floating block, I allowed it to tumble down the slope below until it disappeared into darkness. I made it up just in time to see *the Steve* cornering the other flying creature. After dodging the creature's fireballs (*foom foom foom!*), he charged in, and his sword went snicker-snack. I vaguely saw the fireballs crash into a cave opening near the cliff's edge and smash apart something gelatinous and green...

With the crunch of metal on the creature's weird body, I heard the cries of its otherworldly pain again, and with a final strike, the Steve crashed his blade *through* its body, sending shards of the creature showering to the ground. The mob's internal fire went out, but areas of the cliff still set ablaze from the battle kept the Steve and the witch bathed in an orange glow...

"*You!!*" I cried. "*Sssteve*, you killed my friendsss!!"

The Steve and Worla both looked at me in surprise for a moment, the Steve with his blank eyes, and Worla looking like a monster. But the witch recovered from the shock more quickly, and as fast as a snake, pulled a vial of something from her robes and threw it at the Steve!

The armored mob killer didn't have time to react, and the potion shattered over his armored form. He immediately staggered from the effect, his knees buckling, those strange, alien eyes of his suddenly lolling from sickness...

Worla *shrieked* in joy. "*Yes!!* I've got you! You're *mine!*"

The Steve seemed to pull himself together for an instant, stood strong, and charged at Worla, sword high and ready.

"No!" I shouted, and reached out with my power to bash him, just like I did to the tree. I felt my invisible hand connect powerfully with the Steve's armored body, and the mob killer suddenly *snapped* through the air, flying away in the opposite direction.

I swatted him away like a bug...

The Steve's shield went flying one way, his sword went the other, and the Steve himself flew backwards out into the night ... over the edge of the cliff!

The malicious glee in Worla's face suddenly transformed to instant fury!

"What?! *No!!*" she shrieked. "*Idiot creeper*, what have you done?!"

My belly suddenly felt like it turned to ice...

What happened?!

What did I do wrong??

Worla sprinted over to the edge of the cliff like a dangerous animal, her limbs long and lean and her whole body made of spikes and claws. She was *terrifying* in battle!

"No!" she howled. "*Gone! No!*"

With a quick glare back at me, she focused her attention back to where the Steve was last seen, flying over the edge of the cliff, then she reached both hands up into the air, arms spread apart. Her claws glistened in the firelight.

"I ... I'm sssorry, Worla! I—"

"*Silence*, fool! I must concentrate!"

With her hands reaching high and her arms spread, I saw a strange magical effect start emanating from her body into the air, like dark oily bubbles appearing, rising, and popping, for several seconds until the bubbles all popped, and *three creatures* appeared in the air around her!

In the dim light of the dying fires, I could see that they were small—half my size. They were of a light blue color, like ice, had wispy white wings that kept them hovering around the witch, and each of the creatures held a small, metal sword.

"After him!" Worla shrieked at the newcomers. "Bring me the Steve! *Bring him to me!*"

The three flying demon-creatures departed without a word or a nod, making a beeline with their rapid, little wings over the edge of the cliff, and disappeared into darkness.

I heard the footsteps of my friends approaching. It sounded like they found a way up. Turning back for a moment, I saw Skeleton Steve and Zarek running up, weapons drawn, followed by C'Thor struggling to keep up.

The fires calmed down, and so did I. So did Worla, it seemed.

"Worla," I said. "I'm sssorry. I wasss trying … trying to help!"

The witch stayed facing away from me, peering into the darkness over the cliff where the Steve had disappeared—where she sent her strange, magical little imps…

She turned, changed back to the mostly-friendly and sometimes scary Worla that I was use to.

"Ah, Mighty Cth'ka," she said, laughing to herself. "*That* was impressive. You just *swatted* him right off the cliff, didn't you? It's okay. Thanks for trying to help."

"He did?" Skeleton Steve asked.

"Why did you want to catch him ssso badly?" I asked. "He'sss defeated. He ran away! He won't messs with you anymore."

The witch shook her head. "Doesn't matter now," she said. "You know that *the Steve* is immortal, right?"

"What'sss *that* mean?"

"That means, young creeper, that he never dies. He just comes back."

"Oh yeah," I said. "Ssskeleton Sssteve told me about that once…"

"He'll be back," she said.

"He killed my friendsss," I said, biting back the tears. "All we did was try to sssteal a bucket, and he blew up my houssse, killed my friendsss, and ssstole all of my ssstuff!"

The witch made a face of concern. I had no idea if it was real or not.

"Poor thing," she cooed. "That's terrible. And then he must have come here to kill me next, I suppose. But you *took care* of that Steve, didn't you?"

"I guesss I did," I said, shaking the sorrow out of my head. "But now what? He knowsss where we live! He'll surely come *back* for me after that!"

Skeleton Steve put his hand on my side.

"We'll be with you, buddy," he said.

277

"And I," said Zarek.

"And I, king," said C'Thor.

"Do not worry, Cth'ka," Worla said. "I plan to investigate this, and come up with a course of action." She paused, and peered out over the swamp, back to her hut. I looked at what she was staring at, and saw the glow of my lava. "I see you have gathered some *lava*, creeper. I knew you had it in you!" She smiled. "Did you … perchance … get *all eighteen?*"

I felt myself standing a little taller.

"Yesss," I said. "I did. I learned to ussse the crown."

"Very good, young one. Very good!" The witch smiled genuinely, at least for once. "Let us tend to it in the morning. Will you all wait down there for me? I have more business to tend to up here until the dawn…"

"Of course," Skeleton Steve said, and we all turned to go.

Day 30

"It's called a *portal*," Worla said.

We were standing in the field outside her hut. The lava glowed in all eighteen holes, but the fiery light was diminished in the brightness of the day. I could still feel the heat, though.

"Where's it go?" Skeleton Steve asked.

"Tisk tisk, Skeleton Steve. Haven't you seen a *nether portal* before? I think you *have*."

"No," he replied. "Why would you say that??"

"*Eh* ... no matter," she replied, then turned back to me. "What I need you to do is to move dirt blocks into the places I tell you, and we'll make a *cast*. That's something designed to hold something else. Then, you'll move one of those volumes of lava *into the cast*. That puts the lava where we want it! Then, I'll have you pick up some *water* from the swamp, and dump it over the lava in the cast..."

"What'sss all that *do?*" I asked.

"That's how we make *obsidian*, creeper!"

"Ssssoundsss complicated," I replied.

"All you have to do is do what I say," she said.

"Okay," I said. "Let'sss do it."

Worla cackled. "*That's* the spirit! Obsidian is a *wonderful* building material. It's one of the strongest stones on Diamodia, it's used for *magic*, and can even withstand the explosion of creepers!"

With that, as my friends watched from the field, I helped Worla create obsidian blocks, one by one, using dirt casts, lava, and water, all in the pattern she designed. She had me build it on top of the dirt pad I created near the water a week ago. I would move dirt until there was an empty space where she wanted to obsidian to set, dump some lava inside, then cool if off with water. Once the lava was cooled, I'd remove the dirt around it, and in its place was a brilliantly *black* block of dense, super-solid material that glittered in the sun yet also absorbed the light around it at the same time...

Amazing.

Ultimately, I helped Worla make eighteen of these blocks, all attached together to form a large doorway—a *portal*—four blocks wide on the top and bottom, and five blocks tall, including the four corners.

Something about the dark stone, the obsidian, was *beautiful*. And something about it configured like a giant doorway ... was *foreboding*.

Worla looked the happiest I'd ever seen her.

When all of the dirt was cleared away, the witch pulled out a small, shiny stone and a piece of metal from her robes, *struck* the two objects against each other inside the doorway, which made a bright, falling *spark*, and the portal *came alive* in all its terrible glory...

A *film* of purple magic-stuff spread across the open space inside the doorway, warbling and wobbling, and a *moan* emanated from the gateway—a sound low and deep that reached inside my body and made my bones shiver…

Purple motes of light jumped off of the dizzying magical sheen in the doorway, hopping off every which way, just like how lava spits pieces of sizzling rock and fire…

Whatever was on the other side of that evil, purple doorway—I didn't want to know!

Worla looked at it with glee. It was as if she totally forgot we were standing there.

"At last…" she whispered to herself.

A little while later, she thanked me for completing my first task.

"Now, you should take a *break*, Mighty Cth'ka—a short one anyway—before your *second* task."

"When'sss a good time for me to *return?*" I asked.

"You don't have to come back this time," the witch said. "I will be leaving on some business soon." I looked over at the portal, and heard it moan and yawn its evil music. "Take some time to *rebuild* your *Darkwood*. When I'm ready for you to perform your second task, I will come to you…"

"Okay, Worla," I said.

After a few goodbyes, Skeleton Steve, Zarek, C'Thor, and I turned to go. Worla had also asked me if I was beginning to understand how much I'd eventually be able to accomplish with the *Crown of Ender*. I told her that I did. She didn't see me make myself fly—at least I didn't think so…

"You flew," Skeleton Steve told me while we were walking. "At least, not *technically*—you were actually riding a block that you were moving through the air, but that's pretty much *flying*…"

"I know," I said.

Day 31

I decided to start Darkwood again from scratch. After moving a lot of stone blocks, my clearing was a normal clearing again.

The house—or what was *left* of it—was now gone.

The beginning of the 'creeper hall' I was making was also gone.

I pulled all of the stone blocks apart, one by one, with my powerful, invisible magic hand.

Or ... *hands*. I was starting to feel more of a ... *second* hand take shape. I was sure that it would be a while before I could carry *two* things at once, but I knew I'd get there.

I was giddy at the idea of it. What if I could carry my stronghold block and a lava block at the *same time?* Or ... what if I could ride *one* block around in the sky—flying—and use the other magic hand to wield *another* block as a weapon?! Amazing...

For the nineteenth time, I carried a hot, sizzling blob of burning lava up from the bottom of my mine. My friends stood by in the grass, surrounded by yellow and red flowers, and watched as I dropped the volume of lava into a dirt cast where my house used to be.

Sploosh. Sizzle...

Returning with some water from the stream on the other side of the clearing, I *cooled* the block of lava, and removed the dirt cast when it was safe.

And I smiled as I looked upon the *first obsidian block*—the first block to the foundation of the *new* Darkwood Fortress...

A house and a hall might work for *villagers*. But *this* was going to be for my creeper army. My *creeper soldiers*. And I would not allow our home to be destroyed in battle again! I didn't want a beautiful home like *the Steve's*, still so vulnerable to being damaged by an explosion!

I also wouldn't build separate houses.

Darkwood Fortress would one day be a massive, imposing structure of *invincible black stone*, large enough to house *hundreds* of creepers, strong enough to withstand any attack, durable enough to withstand creeper explosions—there would surely be *more* explosions, for how *else* would a creeper army fight?

Zarek and C'Thor cheered for me, for Darkwood Fortress, while Skeleton Steve looked on in concern.

After spending a moment feeling good about creating my own obsidian, I turned and went back down into the mine.

I would need a *lot* more lava...

Box Set Book 3 - Diary of a Creeper King

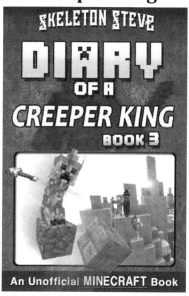

Mighty Cth'ka the Creeper King is ready for his second task!

While working on his obsidian Darkwood Fortress, Cth'ka is approached by Worla the Witch and asked to perform his second task--to kill a fellow witch!! Sure, the witch of the icy mountains is probably evil and is planning on spreading her ice magic into Darkwood Forest, but is Cth'ka okay with being Worla's assassin?

As more and more creepers join his creeper army, Cth'ka sets off on his dangerous mission with Skeleton Steve and Zarek the zombie, but have his powers grown strong enough to help him kill a witch? And is there something more sinister going on with Worla and her three tasks??

Day 32

Today I laid my *twentieth* block of obsidian.

I'm just taking a break, though. I expect I can do *another* twenty—no, *forty!* … before I stop for the day.

The sky right now is clear and blue, and the cool breeze of Darkwood Forest is calming my hot and blistered skin. *Hot and blistered* is a good way to put it—I've been working *all day* at carrying lava up from the bottom of my mine!

Every trip I took from the huge magma pool deep in the earth under *my clearing* meant that I had to carefully balance a brightly burning blob of molten rock in front of my face as I climbed dozens of stairs back to the surface! Then I'd dump the blazing hot stuff into a dirt cast attached to the fortress foundation I was working on.

Rinse, repeat!

I felt confident in my ability to avoid spilling the lava, and it was a good thing I did! If I did trip up, even a little, I would probably set myself on fire as a spilled blob of lava made its way back down the stairs ... *through me.*

But I'm careful. I do it *right*. I learned that lesson well enough the last time I tried to rush something and got my friend, Cro'as, killed...

Twenty blocks now of beautiful, black obsidian—it's like a slab of *night sky* amidst the green grass and yellow and red flowers.

And it's *just the beginning*...

Now that I've taken down what remained of my house and the beginning of the great hall, after *the Steve* blew it up, I've got a much different and *better* design in mind for Darkwood Fortress!

Twenty blocks of obsidian isn't much, but man, it's going to be worth it!

Four hundred blocks will be a good foundation for a castle! Twenty by twenty—it should be a good size for a first level. Then I can start on the walls, then a ceiling, and start building *up*. Up into the sky, until from the top level of the fortress, I can look out over *all* of the dark oak trees in all directions...

Darkwood Fortress will be amazing ... and it will be *all* obsidian!

Sure, it would take a long time. And I'll probably need to find more lava at some point. But if I was to be the leader of a creeper people, if an army of my brethren would be living with me ... I'll do this *right*.

Eventually, I'll be done with Worla's three tasks, and would be able to work on this fortress *all the time* until it was complete.

And *the Steve* wouldn't be able to blow up my place, my friends, and my stuff again...

"Cth'ka!" C'Thor called as I dictated my story to Skeleton Steve, staring at the deep and glittering black fortress foundation. My skeleton friend paused, lifting his writing quill.

"Yesss, C'Thor?" I asked.

I heard the clanking of metal shifting as Zarek the zombie moved near me. My bodyguard

293

was sitting in the grass near me, always close by, and perked up when he sensed outsiders approaching.

Walking along with C'Thor, there were *three* new creepers I hadn't met before...

"What isss that??" one of the newcomers said suddenly, looking at the four by five slab of obsidian sitting on the grass clearing.

"Sssilence!" C'Thor snapped back at him. "You are addresssing *Mighty Cth'ka!* Wait for me to introduce you!"

I chuckled. This was ridiculous.

"It'sss okay, C'Thor. What am I, a king of *two creepersss* right now?"

"Sssorry, sssire," he responded, then looked back at the three creepers.

"Welcome, creepersss, to Darkwood," I said, and nodded.

They nodded back.

"Thisss," C'Thor said, motioning to the creeper who asked about the obsidian, "isss Cad'mus." He motioned to the others. "Thisss isss C'den, and thisss isss Ca'desss."

"It'sss nice to meet you all," I said, nodding again. "Thisss isss Ssskeleton Sssteve here with me, and Zarek there." I pointed at my friends with a small creeper foot.

"Hey there," Skeleton Steve said. "Nice to meet you guys. Where'd you come from?"

The three creepers looked at Skeleton Steve with blank expressions, then turned back to me.

Cad'mus spoke up again. "Mighty Cth'ka," he said. "Ssso it'sss true? You can move thingsss when other creepersss cannot?"

"It'sss true," I said. "And to anssswer your quesssstion from before, that'sss *obsssidian*. I am usssing it to build a fortresss for usss. *It* will not be harmed by explosionsss."

The creepers collectively made a sound of awe.

295

Skeleton Steve watched the conversation for a moment, shrugged, and looked back down at the journal he was writing.

After some conversation where I learned that Cad'mus came from the other side of Darkwood forest, C'den came from the southern plains (just like C'Thor), and Ca'des came from the snowy mountains to the west, C'Thor led the creepers away to allow me some space to get back to work.

For the rest of the day and well into the night, I went on, collecting lava from the lava pool at the bottom of my mine, dumping it in a cast on the surface, cooling the lava with water from the stream, then breaking the cast and rebuilding it for the *next* blob of lava.

At times, especially when I was doing something easy with my powers, like moving around the dirt blocks from the obsidian casts, I found that I could still feel things around me—even when I had a dirt block floating in the air in front of me!

This was new.

Usually, whenever I held a block with my invisible *magic hand*, the concentration needed to keep a hold of it made me lose track of the rest of the world around me—with my *powers* at least...

But now, more and more, it was like another magic hand was growing, and I felt that soon I'd be able to move more than one thing at a time!

I'd been thinking about it these last few days—especially after the battle on bald mountain, when I instinctually made myself *fly* by riding a block I carried with my powers to bring me up onto the cliff.

I had surprised myself there! Desperate to help Worla in her battle with *the Steve*, unable to climb the rest of the way onto the cliff with my stubby, little creeper legs, I found a solution without even thinking about it.

The power of the *Crown of Ender* was definitely becoming second nature to me. But what was the *extent* of this power? Would I eventually have a *hundred* invisible, magic hands, and be able to control the world around me in a constant tornado of rearranging?

I smiled, but I was also a little afraid...

Who would I become if I could do anything and squash anything in my way? Would I go crazy with power and lose my desire to help creeperkind?

I'd have to be careful!

Sometimes, today, I played around a little with the new, growing power of the *second* hand. Especially when I was working with the dirt casts. I'd lift one of the dirt blocks, and, while I still had one in the air, I tried to feel, then envelop, then lift *another*...

But I wasn't quite there yet.

Not yet.

Soon...

Day 33

"You've got it!" Skeleton Steve cried from below me. "Be *careful* now, Cth'ka! If you fall, you'll really get hurt!"

The block was very wobbly under my feet, and seemed a lot smaller than it really was—I had to squeeze my legs together to keep them all directly under me!

I was flying...

Or ... *hovering* at least.

In the mid-morning, I took a break from building the obsidian foundation to sit in the sunshine with Skeleton Steve and Zarek, and one of us started talking about flying. Before I knew it, I was trying to balance on a block of raw stone, *high* above the ground!

It took *a lot* of concentration. Not only did I have to focus on carrying the block (*carefully! I was on it!*), but I also had to concentrate on my *own* balance!

Talk about a mind-body connection!

Well, I wasn't flying up as high as the tops of the trees—this was still new to me, and I didn't want to kill myself falling! But I was at least half-way to the treetops! Higher than where I had started building the roof on my *last* home.

It was amazing!

Looking down, I could see Skeleton Steve and Zarek staring back up at me, a serious look of worry on my skeleton friend's bony face. Zarek hovered around in the grass sort of ... below me ... as if he was thinking of trying to *catch me* if I fell.

The four creepers stood off at the edge of the trees, looking up at me in undisguised *wonder*.

Keeping a tight hold on the mental invisible net around the stone block, I moved the platform sideways a little—toward the center of the clearing. The stone moved a little faster than I meant for it to, and my knees buckled briefly as I caught my balance.

"*Whoa!*" Zarek cried on my behalf, his dark eyes widening under the brow of his golden helm.

Inching the block along, I moved from one side of the clearing to the other.

Descending to be a little closer to the ground, I moved through the air, little by little, toward the stream at the far end of the clearing until...

I released my hold of the block, and it disappeared from under my feet.

Gone.

Sploosh!

"Cth'ka!!" Skeleton Steve cried when I emerged from the water, and I heard them hurrying over. Bones clunked, and Zarek's armor jangled with each heavy step.

I laughed—long and hard! Floating in the water of the stream, I looked up at the sky, and looked over to where my stone block had plummeted to the ground when I released it, now stuck in the dirt at the edge of the water.

"It'sss okay!" I exclaimed. "I wanted to dive in the water!"

301

My friends approached. I could see C'Thor and the creepers hurrying along behind them too, but creepers, like me, were slow.

Skeleton Steve smirked, then laughed.

"Cth'ka, just a few weeks ago, you couldn't even put your *foot* into water," he said. "Now you're flying around with magical powers, diving into it!"

"Sssshh!" I replied. "Don't tell the othersss!"

As the other creepers arrived to see if I was okay, we were all laughing.

Later, I was back to work on the fortress foundation.

Four hundred blocks was *a lot!*

I had already laid down ... I don't know ... a hundred or so maybe? Probably a bit less. And I still had a *long* way to go. When you think about how big you want a floor to be, so many blocks by so many blocks, you don't really think about how many blocks it *really* takes to fill in the space in between!

The lava pool underground was huge, and went on farther than I could tell at the moment, but I could see that I had already taken a *good chunk* out of it.

Surely there would be more lava pools like that down there.

But where else can I find lots of lava? I thought.

I'd have to figure something else out eventually, but things were okay for now.

C'Thor brought back *even more* creepers today. Right now, I don't remember their names, but I'd make sure to learn them. If my army grew by a few creepers every day, it wouldn't be long before I wouldn't be able to remember everyone! C'Thor would have to be my ... *second in command* I guess. And he would need his *own* commanders under him, to keep track of ... squads?

I don't know—this might get complicated...

Once the sun went down, I stopped working on the obsidian floor for the day. It was also getting hard to work with all of those creepers crowding around me every time I brought up a blazing blob of lava.

After some more practice with my *second hand*, and plenty of conversation with Skeleton Steve and Zarek, I decided to go for a *night flight...*

The sky was dark and full of stars, and the rising square moon cast a silver light across the valleys. The leaves of the dark oak trees all around and below me were *black*.

I felt a little more comfortable now, like I was getting the hang of riding the block, but I still had to be *super careful!* Even though my body wasn't jolting around as much, and I wasn't losing my balance every time I moved the block in a sideways direction, I still had to remind myself that *creepers weren't designed for riding things through the sky!*

One mistake, and *foop!* I would plummet down to the ground and maybe break my neck!

Even though I was more balanced, I still moved the block pretty slowly.

But, after flying across the tops of dozens of trees, heading randomly to the *west*, crossing another clearing, then *zipping* across the tops of another cluster of dark oaks ... I realized that I was going *faster!*

Careful, I thought...

Eventually, I slowed myself down, and realized that I had travelled a decent distance away from home! Back behind me, I could see the rise in the forest where the hill rose up on the one side of my clearing, though it was mostly a sea of black.

Up ahead, the trees of Darkwood went on for a while, then broke apart as the landscape transitioned from forest to the cold, western mountains. Far in the distance, I could see the ground as a choppy, silver vista of snow and ice.

I continued toward the mountains, gliding silently through the night sky. *Not too fast*—but faster than I could walk!

If I *really* got the hang of this, I'd be able to fly fast! As fast as I could throw the blocks, really. But I bet there's definitely a limit as to how fast I could fly and still keep my balance on the block.

Unless I built some sort of safe thing with walls that I could sit in...

I stopped.

There was movement up ahead.

Just outside the forest, walking through the snow, was a strange shape I didn't recognize—not a random passing zombie, skeleton, or creeper...

Lowering my block to skim just above the treetops, to help keep me hidden, I flew closer...

Nice and slow ...

As a creeper, I could see through the darkness just fine, and when I was close enough, I saw a strange, plodding green horse ... with a *witch* on top.

Worla?

No. Not Worla. This must have been *another* witch...

She looked a lot like Worla—long and lean, swaddled up in robes, her face cruel and her nose long and hooked over her face—but her robes were of a bluish-grey color, and a single ice-blue *gem* sat in the band of her hat.

The horse was a zombie horse.

I had *seen* that horse before, tethered under Worla's hut along with a skeleton horse the day we traveled to Lurkmire to ask the witch for help with the lava task...

This was *another* witch.

A friend of Worla's?

She had apparently visited a couple of weeks ago when I saw the zombie horse under the hut, but ... passing by again?

I lowered my flying block, and watched the witch from inside the treetops. Only my head poked out into the night, but I wasn't worried. A *creeper head* probably looked like all of the leaves around me.

Except for the crown, I thought.

The strange blue-robed witch continued on, her zombie horse plodding through the snow, until she veered right, and started heading west up into the mountains.

Interesting.

I didn't stay long, though. Once the witch was faced away from me, I raised my block higher into the night sky again, and flew home.

Tomorrow would be another big day of building...

Day 34

"Mighty Cth'ka," a hard-edged voice exclaimed, almost startling me into dropping a blob of lava onto the grass.

Zarek's hand darted to the hilt of his sword, then immediately relaxed, as we all turned toward the sound … and saw that it was Worla.

The witch had come…

Probably to give me my second task, I thought. Just like she said she would.

She stood at the edge of the trees, not far from the entrance to my mine. Her body was wrapped in her normal dark, mottled purple robes, and she almost blended into the late afternoon shadows of the trees. Her cowl was black and hid some of her face, but I could see the pale, hooked nose, the wolfish grin, and the glittering of her black eyes.

"Ssssss … Worla," I said, catching the lava and making sure that my magical grip on it didn't slip. "Jussst a sssecond. Let me put thisss down..." A tiny drip of molten stone fell and set some grass on fire. I stepped on it.

The witch nodded, and I placed the lava into its intended cast.

"I see you're making use of the *obsidian technique* I showed you," she said, then cackled madly. "*What* on Diamodia are you *building??*"

Skeleton Steve and Zarek exchanged glances.

"Darkwood Fortresss," I responded, turning back to her. "You told me that obsssidian can withsssstand *creeper* explosionsss. After the Sssteve blew up my friendsss and my houssse, I decided to make a houssse he couldn't hurt again."

"Clever creeper," she responded. "Clever, clever." She looked over the obsidian pad. By now, I had lined out the twenty by twenty border, and was starting to fill it in, one block of obsidian at a time. "And a *big place*, too! Why so big?"

Some of my creepers had emerged from the woods, and were standing around us. Not all of them—it was morning, and C'Thor and a few others were gone. They were probably out scouting around the area looking for even *more* recruits.

"Lotsss of creepersss are coming," I responded. "I'm building a fortresss where we *all* can live."

Worla laughed again.

"Ah yes," she said. "The legacy of the *Mighty Cth'ka*. As I have foreseen, it's all happening for you right now, isn't it?"

"I guesss…"

"Well are you ready for your *second task*, creeper king?" she asked, stepping forward from the trees casually into the clearing. Her pitch-black eyes darted to Skeleton Steve, then to Zarek, then she took in the several frowning faces of the creepers around us.

Behind her, where she was standing in the shadows, I could see the gleam of bone. There was the skeleton horse. That horse must have been *hers*. Its sides bulged with full leather saddlebags.

"Yesss, Worla," I said. "I'm ready. What do you asssk of me?"

She smiled, and approached close enough for polite conversation.

"Mighty Cth'ka," she said, "there is another witch nearby, with … wicked intent. She's an *ice witch*, and seeks to … expand her domain."

"*Another* witch?" Skeleton Steve asked, his tone annoyed.

What did he mean by *that?*

Worla frowned at him. I felt in his tone that he was alluding to something else between him and Worla from another time…

"What'sss that mean … *expand* her domain??"

Worla looked back at me with a snap.

"It *means* that she wants to *take over* your Darkwood forest, Cth'ka!" she said. I felt a chill go down my spine. "She is an *ice witch*, like I said, from the ice spires to the west, and yearns for *more power*, and will be using her ice magic to

312

expand into Darkwood forest." She paused. "That means, Cth'ka, that she'll be bringing snow and ice into Darkwood and *freezing* the forest to add to her domain..."

"What?!" I asked. "Why??"

"Ah, who knows?" Worla responded casually. "Some witches are focused on nothing but power and becoming the *strongest* witch. I don't care for such things." She made a dismissive gesture with her clawed hands. "But she wants more *power*, Cth'ka, and she seeks to come here to this place where you live. To *your clearing*."

"But ... ssss ... what can I do about that?" I asked.

"You must *stop her*, Mighty Cth'ka!"

"Ssstop her?" I asked. "Kill her??"

"Yes, young creeper. Use the power of the crown, and put an end to her conquest! Defend your home!"

"You want me to *kill a witch?*" I asked. "Yesss, I can do a lot more with thisss crown, my powersss, but I can't kill a witch! Why me??"

In that moment, I suddenly remembered seeing the blue-robed witch last night, riding her zombie horse into the snowy mountains. Fear clenched my stomach when I realized that if she had seen me, she might have blasted me out of the sky with a lightning bolt, or *worse*...

Worla lifted a thin, clawed finger in air and opened her mouth to speak, but Skeleton Steve interrupted her.

"A witch can't kill another witch," Skeleton Steve said. "Isn't that right, Worla?" He smirked. "They're all too resistant to each other's attacks."

Worla frowned at him.

"Yes, Skeleton Steve, that's true," she said, her voice full of venom. "But that is only *part* of the reason I'm not doing it myself. I am still investigating *the Steve's* attack on your home, Cth'ka." She looked back at me and smiled. "And while Witherynn is a fellow witch, I certainly don't condone her attacking the home of my *friends*. But she's coming, Cth'ka, with her snow and ice magic, and will *freeze your home* if you don't *stop her*. I cannot do it, *Mighty Cth'ka*. For this, I need your help—you and your magnificent powers..."

Something didn't feel right, but a deal was a deal...

Witherynn.

The ice witch on the zombie horse.

"What'sss the plan?" I asked.

Skeleton Steve cocked a bony eyebrow at me, but he and Zarek came closer as Worla went into the details.

She pointed out that Witherynn the ice witch lived in what she called the 'ice spires' to the west. West of Darkwood was a large range of snowy mountains—I'd never been very far into them because I *hated* the cold, but apparently the evil witch lived beyond the snow-covered mountains that I could see from the edge of my forest.

Not too far, though, Worla pointed out. It should be a pretty quick task. The witch's icy home was apparently not even a day's journey from the edge of the snow.

At one point, Worla pulled out a rolled up piece of paper and unfurled it on top of my obsidian foundation.

A map...

I had seen one of these only once before, and that was when Skeleton Steve found the map in the library of the stronghold where we found the Crown of Ender.

Her map was huge and complex, and I had a hard time understanding what I was looking at. But when she pointed a slender claw at a big, dark green blob, I knew right away that it was Darkwood.

"Here we are," she said.

In that instant, I scanned around the map, around her finger. I saw the jungle to the northeast, as well as a few crude drawings of small square buildings within. To the north was Lurkmire swamp, and I saw a drawing of her hut, and a depiction of bald mountain to the north of *that*. Lurkmire extended *far* to the east! *Way* farther than I thought it did!

I saw the plains and the forest to the west, and a little drawing to the north of that of what must have been *Ahimsa village*. Once the trees started again to the north of the picture of the village, the taiga went on for quite a ways, until there was a large, menacing drawing of a *skull*. I knew from experience that *that skull* must have been *the Steve's* castle.

And there were *other villages!* To the east of the skull, to the north of the skull—plenty to the west, and to the north—even more still. Villages all over!

One of those little towns, presumably the one to the east of the skull, in the middle of a *desert* it looked like, was the village where Skeleton Steve and I had been attacked by *the Steve* on our first adventure.

I even saw the *ocean*, near the top edge of her map, where we had used up the last *Ender Eye*,

317

and found the stronghold down below in the cave system there! I could see a dark rift in the trees southeast of the shore—that must be the ravine where we climbed out from the depths of the underworld. But the *stronghold itself* was not marked...

Maps are amazing!!

"And here," she went on, trailing her clawed finger across the forest to the west, over a large white area and pictures of mountains, "is the witch's home. She has a *small* home—small on the *outside*—made of ice and snow, in the middle of a valley surrounded by ice spires. Once you climb into the mountains, you'll start to see the ice spikes. Just keep an eye out for the spikes—you can't miss them! Witherynn lives near the tallest one; like another mountain, made entirely of *ice!*"

I suddenly noticed that Skeleton Steve's bony hand was inside his pack, like he was going to pull something out, but he changed his mind, and said, "So we just go directly *west?* And look for the tallest ice spire once we see the area full of spikes?"

"You got it, Skeleton Steve," she replied. Before I could make out any more details, she rolled up the map and pulled it back into her robes. "This should hardly take any time at all, Cth'ka," she said. "Not like the *last* task."

"Okay, Worla," I said. "I'll ssstop ... Witherynn."

"Mighty Cth'ka," Worla purred. "Your home, your *people*," she said, waving a hand at the other creepers, "depend on it! Complete your second task, then return to me. Understood?"

"Yesss," I said, nodding.

"*Stop* Witherynn, then return to me!" the witch repeated, then walked back to her skeletal horse, mounted it effortlessly, and rode off into the shadows of the trees.

We all watched her go for a while, then stood, silent and thinking.

"So I guess we're going to kill a witch," Skeleton Steve said. "Again."

"Again??" I asked.

319

"Never mind," my skeleton friend replied. "I'm just starting to feel a little *weird* about Worla's motives..."

"Sssss," I said, hissing while thinking. "Well at any rate, she'sss evil, right? Thisss ice witch..."

"If you don't mind doing Worla's *dirty work*," Skeleton Steve said.

"What elssse isss there?" I asked. "I *have* to, right?"

"Yeah, I guess," Skeleton Steve said.

"At leassst it'sss for good," I said. "To protect the foressst!"

"Yeah, sure."

"What'sss that you were grabbing, Ssskeleton Sssteve? What'sss in your pack?" I asked.

"Oh," he replied, putting his bony hand back in there. He pulled out a rolled up sheaf of paper of his own. "I have my own map too—you remember the map I found in the stronghold's library?"

320

"Yesss…"

"I was going to pull it out to compare it to Worla's, but I'm feeling a little … *odd* about her lately, and didn't want her knowing I had it. Is that paranoid?"

Skeleton Steve unrolled his own map out onto the obsidian blocks, and I could see that it was *far* less detailed than Worla's. But it did have many detailed narrow paths through areas where my friend had traveled after our adventure—places where I'd never been. Multiple paths led to *the Steve's* castle, and it looked like he'd done a lot of traveling in deserts…

The snow and ice lands to the west were uncharted.

"At leassst we'll be filling out that ssspace on your map," I said.

Skeleton Steve rolled up his map and stuffed it back into his pack.

"Yeah," he replied. "It'll take a long time to fill it up like the witch's map."

"Let'sss leave in the morning."

"Okay," Skeleton Steve said. "And she just said 'stop her'. Hopefully we can get this figured out without bloodshed."

"I guesss we'll sssee..."

Day 35

When the sun came up and all of the undead mobs (except for Zarek and Skeleton Steve) caught on fire, we were already standing at the edge of the forest. I had my *stronghold stone* with me, and my friends looked ready for another adventure—even if it was a short one.

As Darkwood forest continued to the west from *my clearing*, the ground became more hilly, and by the time the forest ended, where we now stood, the terrain had grown steep and the trees grew right up to the edge of the snow.

A long, rising plain of blinding white snow extended west before us, climbing higher and higher until tall, imposing mountains sprung up out of the ground.

One of the creepers I met the other day, Ca'des, stood with us.

He was *from* the snowy area ahead.

"Do you sssee the three mountainsss in the dissstance?" he asked in a scratchy voice.

Several mountains sprawled out on the horizon, but *yes*—there were *three mountains* clustered together...

I nodded.

"You will climb up the plainsss until you get to thossse three peaksss. Once you go over thossse, you'll sssee the ice ssspikes on the other ssside."

"Have you ssseen Witherynn the witch before?" I asked him.

"No sssir," he replied. "Are you *sure* you don't want me to go with you guysss?"

"Yesss, Ca'desss," I said. "Ssstay here with the othersss. The witch will be easssy to get to if you ssspeak true, and we'll be back sssoon."

"Yesss, my king," Ca'des said with a nod, and turned back to the forest. With quiet creeper steps, he disappeared into the trees.

The cold wind blowing down from the icy plains made me shiver.

Once the sun made me feel a little warmer, we set off, crunching through the snow to the west.

It seemed like it took *hours*, crossing that steadily rising snowy plain, but it was only early afternoon when we finally reached the foothills of the three snow-capped mountains. Looking back down the vast, frozen expanse we just crossed, I could see the mottled colors of Darkwood Forest far in the distance, hazy through the cold air.

Climbing the mountains was more difficult.

This land was cold, my feet were numb, and my body was stiff!

Sure, I could have just floated on my stronghold block, but that wouldn't have been fair to my friends, who had to trudge through the snow.

Or ... *friend*. Only Zarek seemed to be bothered. The zombie warrior looked rather displeased as his armored feet crunched through

325

the snow and ice. All of that metal must have been very cold. Then again, he was undead. Did he even *feel* the cold? He was acting like he did.

Skeleton Steve didn't seem to mind the cold. His thin, bone legs and bony skeleton feet punched through the snow with ease, and he moved with just as much grace as normal, his body *clanking* and *clunking* as we went on.

As we neared the top of the mountain we were climbing, watching the other two mountains on either side loom over us and block out the sun, I heard a low *woomph* from around a bend.

An animal sound? A *wolf* maybe?

"What wasss that?" I asked, my lips frozen and hard to move.

Zarek and Skeleton Steve looked up ahead, both shielding their eyes from the glare of the white snow.

A low, rumbling *roar*…

We all stood up straight.

"That'sss not a *wolf*, isss it?" I asked.

"Bigger than a wolf," Skeleton Steve said.

"I know what it is," Zarek said with a low, dull voice. His zombie lips cracked in the cold as he spoke. "I've been in places like this before..."

Suddenly up ahead, from around a corner, came a *huge* white animal, tromping slowly through the snow. Some sort of *predator* animal, judging by its thick head, long teeth and claws...

"What?!" Skeleton Steve asked, pulling his bow.

"It's a bear," Zarek said. "A *polar* bear. Don't worry. It'll mind its own business as long as—"

His words were interrupted by a small cry—a miniature version of the polar bear's grunting sounds a moment ago...

Looking down, I saw a small, white animal approaching—a miniature version of the adult up ahead. How did it get so close to us ... so quickly? How did we not *notice* it?

It was a *little* polar bear. It looked up at me with bright, black eyes. Was it … smiling?

"Uh oh…" Zarek said, pulling his sword in alarm.

ROOOAAARRR!!!

The huge polar bear up the pass sprang into action, sprinting through the snow, a bellowing bundle of deep rumbling sounds of anger, claws and muscles, and a large mouth of thick, gleaming *teeth*…

"Run!!" Skeleton Steve cried.

We broke to the left, sprinting across the icy incline, spraying snow all around! The polar bear pounded the frozen ground behind us, roaring and running after us for a while, but as we increased our distance away from the young one, the great white beast eventually broke off pursuit.

With one last roar and a grunt, the bear turned around, and walked back to its cub.

I realized that I could have just used my *stronghold stone* to kill the beast, but in that moment, all I could imagine was just getting away!

"Calm down, Cth'ka," Skeleton Steve said suddenly.

Was I *hissing??*

"Ssssss … I could have … sssss … killed it," I said.

"Why didn't you?" Zarek asked, sheathing his katana.

"It ssseemed … well … I've ssseen baby animalsss before. I think that wasss itsss *baby*, and the polar bear wasss just trying to protect the little one I think…"

Skeleton Steve put a bony hand on my back and smiled.

"Very wise observation, Mighty Cth'ka," he said. "You sure have a good heart, my creeper friend."

As the sun set and the air chilled (*so cold!!*), we crossed the peak of the middle mountain. In the silver light of the square moon, I could see ice glittering in the distance like tall, strange spikes of glass in the night.

Heading down the other side of the mountain, we reached the ice spikes when the moon was high in the sky. However, even though we could see well enough in the darkness, all of the ice spires looked the same, and I didn't see one taller than the rest—I sure didn't see a whole ice *mountain* like Worla described...

"I'll get up higher to sssee," I said, climbing up onto my stronghold block.

"Be careful," Skeleton Steve said. "It's very cold, and your block could get slippery!"

Nodding at my friends, I raised the block and flew straight up into the night sky to see if I could make out any other landmarks.

There it is, I thought.

In the dark distance, past the ice spikes and a small clearing in the snow, was another mountain. Not very tall, since we were already very high up in the mountains, but it shone and reflected the light of the moon. Maybe … it was less like a mountain, and more like a really *big and fat* ice spike!

A mountain of ice...

But there were hundreds of ice spires between us and the ice mountain! It would be very confusing to cross the weird forest of spires in the night.

We'd have to wait until morning...

As the three of us settled under an overhang at the edge of the ice spike landscape, I sat in the cold, thinking about being at home, feeling *nice and warm.*

And I played with growing my *second magic hand*...

Not yet.

But soon...

SKELETON STEVE

Psssssst!!
Liking the story? Don't forget
to join my Mailing List!
I'll send you *free books* and stuff!
(www.SkeletonSteve.com)

332

Day 36

The ice spikes were *brilliant* in the daylight!

Brilliant, and *weird*. What a strange, exotic land this was!

I was grateful for the sunshine. There was a reason I never tried heading out here to the west before—creepers hate the cold! And for good reason. I was freezing and miserable. But the rising sun helped me to warm up a *little*.

Still, it wasn't really *that* warm. These ice spikes all around us, reaching up into the sky like odd, crystal *swords*, wouldn't be melting any time soon...

We never ran into that polar bear again, but after having its baby sneak up on us, almost *invisible* in the bright, white snow, I kept my eyes peeled and paid a lot more attention to what was around me!

As we walked through the ice spikes, continuing west toward where I saw the 'ice mountain' landmark from up above last night, we stared in wonder at the sharp, crystalline structures all around us, frozen and towering over our heads. Light shined through the spires, and cast rays and rainbows all around...

By the time the sun was high in the sky, we had passed a *hundred* ice spikes it seemed, and the terrain opened up in front of us ... just a little ... to reveal a small, snowy clearing.

It was like an oasis in a desert—a modest open area of snow, a few trees, and a small creek, and behind it was the largest ice spike of them all!

But that wasn't the most *interesting* thing.

In the middle of the small, snowy clearing was a little white home.

It was made of ice and snow.

Some sort of ... *igloo*. Skeleton Steve would tell me the *name* for that sort of structuré later.

Behind the witch's igloo was the largest ice spike of them all—practically a *mountain* of ice! Blue and translucent, the ice mountain reflected the light of the morning, and the sun pierced the crystalline structure, making it bright, somewhat see-through, and *dangerous-looking*. With all of its edges and cracks, I could also see what looked like a *path*, cut out of the ice and winding up the sides of the mountain, leading to an *ice cave* at the top...

So ... Witherynn the witch lived in the igloo, and also did her business—whatever *that* was—up at the top of the spire behind her home.

"That's it," Skeleton Steve said, pointing at the small home with a bony and frosted-over finger.

We stood at the edge of the snowy clearing, surrounded by towering ice spikes. The igloo sat at the *opposite* edge of the clearing, up against the huge spike mountain.

Everything was quiet.

"Where'sss the witch?" I asked, trying not to let my voice shiver in the cold.

"Maybe inside," Zarek said, his green face crackling with ice.

"Let's approach quietly, from the side," Skeleton Steve said. "If she's inside, we should be as close as possible before she hears us, so we can get to her before she uses her magic!"

We did.

Crunching softly through the snow, we snuck up to Witherynn's house along the edge of the clearing. As we approached closer, I could see that there was a single wooden door in the front, facing the open, snowy field.

I didn't hear any sounds coming from inside.

The igloo was a small place. Whatever space it held wouldn't be very big, and if the witch was inside, we'd be in for a quick and close battle once we were through the door!

Skeleton Steve pulled his bow.

Zarek pulled his sword.

"Let me go first, my king," the zombie warrior said, the blade of his katana shining in the light from all of the ice spikes casting sunlight around us.

I nodded. "Go in quickly and move to the sssside, ssso I can get in with my block..."

We stood all around the door, getting ready.

"One," Skeleton Steve said, grasping the door handle. "Two ... *three!*"

Throwing open the door, Skeleton Steve stepped aside and nocked an arrow on his bow. Zarek rushed through the doorway, sword low and ready, then stepped out of sight to the right side. With my powers, I pushed my stronghold stone through the entrance, ready to smash whatever was on the other side, then I stepped inside, too—

And there was no one home.

The inside of the igloo was indeed small!

Covering the entire floor was a white carpet. A single bed with red blankets lay on one side of the room, and a crafting table and furnace were on the other side. Between the two

Minecraftian tools was a single, bright red torch, stuck in the ground.

"Jussst like the Sssteve..." I said.

"What?" Skeleton Steve asked, stepping inside.

"Thisss ssstuff," I replied, "isss jussst like the Sssteve'sss ssstuff we sssaw in hisss cassstle."

Stepping into the igloo and out of the wind, I already felt loads better! It wasn't cold in here. A little *cool* maybe...

"But where is the witch?" asked Zarek.

Skeleton Steve shrugged. "Maybe she's out doing something."

I looked toward the ice mountain behind the igloo, even though it was on the other side of the wall. The igloo had no windows. A couple of blocks of solid ice let in a small amount of light from outside.

"Maybe she'sss up on the mountain," I said.

Zarek paced around the open area in the middle of the room. His feet plodded around on the carpet.

Plop plop plop plop…

He was clearly itching for a fight.

"So what now?" the zombie asked.

"I guesss we should head up there," I replied. "I sssaw a path of ice going up the sssides."

Zarek paced around, gripping his sword.

Plop plop *thunk* plop…

"Okay, my king," he said.

Skeleton Steve was watching Zarek closely.

"Hang on, Zarek," my bony friend said, putting up a hand. "What was that?!"

"What?" Zarek responded.

"Uh …" Skeleton Steve waved a bone finger around at the floor in the middle of the room. "Walk around there again!"

339

Zarek looked at me, confused. I nodded. Whatever Skeleton Steve was getting at, he's never steered me wrong in the past...

The zombie warrior shrugged, and clomped around on the carpet some more, pacing randomly like he was.

Plop plop plop plop plop *thunk* plop plop...

"There!" Skeleton Steve exclaimed. "What was that??"

I heard it too.

Zarek moved back.

Plop plop *thunk*...

He stomped his foot a few times.

Thunk thunk thunk...

"There'sss sssomething in the floor!" I said.

Zarek stared up at us, his dark black eyes surprised.

340

"Zarek, pull back the carpet!" Skeleton Steve said.

"Hold on," I said. "Zarek, ssstep back…"

My zombie bodyguard moved away from the center of the room as I set my stronghold block down near the entrance of the igloo. Reaching out with my invisible hands—one strong and powerful, the other still small and weak—I felt the carpet, wrapped my power around it, felt the packed snow underneath…

Rrrrrrripppp!!

With almost no effort, I pulled the white carpet off of the ground, tearing a large chunk of it out of the entire carpeted floor. My friends gasped. I tossed the torn-up carpet onto the bed.

In the center of the igloo, previously hidden under the carpet, was a wooden trap door!

"Hurr? Hungh!! Hurrrr!!"

From far away, under the trapdoor, I heard the faint voice of a villager calling out to us.

"*Hurrrr!!*"

SKELETON STEVE

We all looked at each other.

Skeleton Steve seemed puzzled.

"It's a villager!" he said. "I can understand him. He says ... he's held *captive??* He's crying out for help."

"That'sss weird," I said.

"You speak *villager?*" Zarek asked, cocking a green eyebrow.

"I understand it, at least," Skeleton Steve replied. "Come on—let's go see!"

Reaching down, Skeleton Steve undid the latch of the trap door, and pulled it open. He stashed his bow, then started down the ladder.

"Long ladder," he said, looking up at us. "Your block won't fit, Cth'ka. Be careful..."

I looked up at Zarek.

"You go next, my king," he said. His face wasn't frozen anymore, I noticed. We were warming up in the igloo. I felt pretty normal now, myself! "That way, you will be between him and I…"

"Sss … okay," I said, carefully crawling into the shaft after Skeleton Steve. By leaning against the far wall, I was able to lower myself down with my small, creeper legs. I hoped we wouldn't have to get out in a hurry, though!

When I finally reached the bottom of the ladder, occasionally looking up to see Zarek climbing down above me, I followed Skeleton Steve into a strange room.

I was immediately reminded of the stronghold. We were now deep underground, and the walls were made out of the same stronghold stone—some cracked, some carved with designs, some covered in moss—some just like my block weapon I left upstairs.

On my left was a large, wooden chest. Ahead on the left was some sort of *bedroll*—maybe somewhere for Witherynn to take a nap in between experiments? On the right was a large wooden shelf with an odd glass and metal apparatus … some sort of *witch stuff*, I guess. And there was a large, metal bucket full of water. Skeleton Steve would later tell me it was called a *cauldron*.

But the strangest thing about the room was the far wall! There, under a single torch in the middle of the wall, were two … prison cells. Behind the iron bars, held captive, were two villagers in purple robes, one in each hold.

Or, rather, *one* was a villager.

The other was a *zombie*—a villager once upon a time…

Upon seeing a skeleton, a creeper, and a zombie warrior climb down the ladder, the living villager, who was crying out for us to *help him* in his villager language, holding the bars of the cage, suddenly *freaked out!* Screaming and pushing his body up against the back wall of his cell, the odd fellow covered his head with his hands.

"Hmmm! Hurrrr!!!"

"What'sss he sssaying?" I asked.

344

"Oh, about what you'd expect," Skeleton Steve said, leaning in close to me so that I could hear him over the panicked cries. "Get away from me, *oh no*, stay away, don't hurt me—stuff like that."

I looked at Zarek, and noticed that he was staring at the villager, his eyes squinted. Was that ... *drool?*

"What isss thisss place?" I asked.

"I've never *seen* a place like this before," Skeleton Steve responded. "This must be some sort of *laboratory* of Witherynn's. My guess is that she's doing experiments on villagers? Turning them into zombies, maybe?"

The villager zombie in the other cell was just standing still, watching us with lifeless zombie eyes. Its skin was green just like Zarek's, but the purple robes it wore were still fresh and mostly-clean.

It spoke.

"What are ... *you three* ... doing here?" the zombie asked, slowly.

345

"We're looking for the witch," Skeleton Steve replied. "How long have you two been *down* here?"

The zombie villager pondered, staring at the stone wall.

"Don't … know," it said.

"What'sss your name?" I asked.

"My name … *don't know*."

"Okaaaay…" Skeleton Steve said, turning back to me. "Let's get out of here," he said.

"We've got to free thessse guysss, don't we?" I said.

"Yeah, sure," Skeleton Steve said. "But *first* we should deal with Witherynn. If she gets back while we're down here, we'll be trapped."

"Good point, my king," Zarek said, finally snapping his eyes off of the living villager. "Let's go back up. I will go *first*."

We climbed the ladder back to the surface. It *sure* was a long way!

Back up in the small igloo, I was relieved to see that there wasn't an evil witch waiting for us.

Skeleton Steve closed the trapdoor after we were all out. I could still hear the cries of the villager from down below, along with the less urgent moans of the villager zombie...

"Who goes there?!"

A wicked and hard-edged voice suddenly rang out from outside. A voice a lot like Worla's, but a little ... smoother ... softer...

My stomach turned cold, and we all jolted in surprise.

The witch!!

She's back—just outside!

Looking back to where I left it, I grabbed my stronghold block from the icy floor and lifted it into the air with my power.

"Who's in my home?!" Witherynn shrieked. "Step outside, or *be destroyed!*"

Clunk. Clank.

347

Skeletons?

Were there *skeletons* outside?

I looked at Skeleton Steve. He shrugged.

"Let'sss charge out together?" I asked.

Zarek nodded.

"I'll go first," Skeleton Steve said, "and send an arrow at her to give you two time to get outside—"

"*Get out here, Steve!!*" Witherynn shouted.

"Sssteve?" I whispered.

She must have thought it was *the Steve* poking around in her house.

Zarek readied his sword. "I'll go out after Skeleton Steve, my king, then you come out and use your block!"

Without another word, Skeleton Steve readied his bow and ran out through the door. As soon as he was out, I heard the *twang* of his bow, and a cry of pain from the witch.

Zarek rushed through the doorway next, his heavy feet thumping, and his sword splitting the cold air as soon as he was in the sunlight. The zombie warrior darted to the right.

Holding my block in front of me, I stepped out, and tried to take everything in at once...

Up ahead, in the snowy field, Skeleton Steve was nocking another arrow and stepping to the left. In the middle of the field was the witch I had seen the other night—much like Worla, but dressed in bluish-grey robes, with a bright blue gem (like ice) in her hat. She was clutching at an arrow that stuck in her shoulder, her hooked and angular face grimacing in pain, her other hand pulling something from her robes. A glass vial of something *red*...

Around her and positioned to shoot at the doorway were four skeletons I had never seen before! They were blue and white, their bones frozen, and their eyes glowing with a pale globs of light—much different than the sharp pin-pricks of red light in Skeleton Steve's black eye sockets—and they were dressed in pale blue rags, piecemeal armor, and aiming their bows right at—

Several arrows flew through the air! I swung my block up in front of me to act like a shield, and heard the *tink* sounds of the stronghold stone defending me. Another arrow flew wild, and the fourth landed in Zarek's golden armor as he charged through the snow at one of the archers.

The zombie warrior's katana came down, and he smashed the blue skeleton to pieces! Skeleton Steve shot a second arrow, which flew through the air at the witch and hit her in the stomach. Witherynn grunted, then threw the glass vial down at her feet. Just as quickly, she pulled *another* vial from her robe...

With as much strength as I could muster, I threw my stronghold block out at the first blue skeleton that shot at me. My weapon crashed through the skeleton like a wrecking ball, showering the snowy field with bones and scraps of blue cloth. Pulling the stronghold stone back to me just as fast, I arced its flight path through the next enemy skeleton, who was taking aim at me again.

My stronghold block smashed through its back, sending the archer's arrow flying wild into the sky, and my opponent sprawled into the snow!

As the last blue skeleton took aim at Zarek, Skeleton Steve spun away from attacking the witch, and shot his own arrow at the archer, hitting it square in the middle of its bone forehead. The archer's head snapped back, but it focused on its attack again, firing at Zarek.

The zombie warrior turned and took the arrow on his armor, then charged.

The witch threw the second vial at Skeleton Steve. My skeleton friend spun to her again, nocking another arrow, as the potion shattered on him, splashing him with a turquoise fluid.

"Get her, Cth'ka!" he cried, then his voice slowed down. "*Uuusssee yyyoouurrr ssstttoooonnee!!*" I watched for a moment, astounded, as Skeleton Steve … slowed … down. His turning to the witch slowed, his arrow, nocked, his bony fingers … pulling on the bowstring … back … slowly … in *slow motion*…

"To me, my Strays!!" Witherynn cried. "Kill the intruders!"

She pulled some sort of wand from her robes, aiming at Zarek, who closed with the skeleton archer with the arrow sticking in its skull. My zombie bodyguard swung his katana, and the archer's skull, arrow and all, flew up into the air, then tumbled to the ground.

I had to do something before she used whatever that weapon was on Zarek...

Focusing on my power, I made my stone fly through the air, arcing toward the witch from above...

With crunching sounds of snow and ice all around us, I saw *more* of the blue skeletons ... the *strays* ... pulling themselves out of the frozen ground...

Witherynn aimed her wand at Zarek as Skeleton Steve *slowly* took aim at her ... then looked up in surprise at the huge stronghold stone block flying toward her head!

Thump.

I squashed her.

She fell to the snow, holding one hand up to protect herself, still trying to aim the wand. Bringing the stone block up again, I threw it down on her another time.

Thump.

Squashed her again.

The witch cried out in pain. "*Stop!!*" she cried, her voice breaking and gurgling. "No more, I beg you, *stop!!*"

I raised the block high over her again. Zarek turned to face some of the strays approaching from the ice spikes.

"Ssstop your sssskeletonsss!" I exclaimed.

The witch made a sound of fear and pain.

Skeleton Steve remained aiming at her, almost stuck in time. His skeletal body seemed to shine with a turquoise magical glow, under the slowness effect of her spell.

"Bless you!!" she cried. "Okay, I give up! *Strays!! Leave us! Stand down!*"

My stronghold block twirled slowly in the air above the witch, and she held her hands up in fear, staring at my weapon, cringing and making small whimpering sounds.

The *strays* at the edge of the snowy clearing backed up and disappeared into the ice spikes.

Skeleton Steve *slowly* lowered his bow…

"You'd better not *try anything*, Witherynn!!" I cried, keeping my block high and ready, as I walked up to the fight. Zarek lowered his sword and stood waiting, seemingly ready to spring back into action. Skeleton Steve was reacting slowly, still under the effect of the magic!

As I approached closer, I could see that the witch was very wounded, crushed under my block—*twice*—but her body was pulsating with a red energy and visibly mending itself.

Pop.

One of Skeleton Steve's arrows popped out of her shoulder, falling into the snow.

Pop.

There went the other one.

Witherynn was *regenerating* very quickly, but she still lay in the snow submissively, still acted like she was near death...

"Who are you?" she asked, her voice still quivering with fear, but much more composed. "You know *me*, but *who are you??*"

"It doesssn't matter who we are, witch!" I responded, and she cringed as I made my block waver in the air. "You are planning on attacking my foressst, and I won't let you!"

"Your fore—what are you *talking* about?" she asked, her pretense of being mortally wounded dropped for the moment. "You..." Her eyes suddenly lit up, just as black and beady as Worla's, her mouth opening into a slight smile. "You're that *lava* creeper, aren't you?"

"Darkwood Foressst isss under *my protectio*n, Witherynn!" I responded, speaking as forcefully as I could. "You'd better ssstay away!"

"Who sent you?" Witherynn asked. "Why are you here??"

"The gig isss up, witch!" I said. "Worla told usss that you were planning to expand your domain down from the mountainsss, and you won't be doing it in *my* landsss!"

"*Worla?*" Witherynn said. I could see the wheels turning in her head, and she stared *through me* for a moment. "Worla ... sent you *because* ... I'm attacking your dark oak forest?"

"Let's just kill her and get out of here, my king," Zarek said.

She looked up at him, then back at me, alarmed.

"My king!" she said. "You ... don't need to *kill* me! I'll leave you and your forest alone! You can ask ... Worla..." she sneered. "I am a *witch of my word*. I'll stay away—I promise! You can tell ...

Worla ... that I won't be bothering you *or her* anymore..."

"Sss ... how do I know you're telling me the truth?" I asked, twirling my block over her head. "How do I know you'll ssstay away?"

"Oh, powerful creeper king, it's because I need to stay in the cold to live!" she said. "I'll ... find somewhere else to expand into. There's ... an empty valley to the other side of the mountains. I'll go there!"

"What about your prisssonersss under your houssse?"

She scowled for a moment, then her face transformed into a submissive grin again. "What *about* them, my king?"

"You have to releassse them!"

"Oh, of course!" she said. "You clearly care *so much* about other mobs!"

"What are you *doing* with them?" Skeleton Steve asked suddenly. He was speaking normally again.

The witch looked up at him.

"Such strange eyes, skeleton..." she said, marveling for a moment. "Why, I'm trying to heal the villagers, of course! I'm taking those that are zombies, and turning them into *villagers* again!"

"Really?" Skeleton Steve asked.

The witch looked back at me.

"Please leave me, creeper king. I will not harm you or your lands. You can tell Worla that I've ... seen the *error* of my ways. The *council* will be visiting her soon..."

"Very well," I said. "But you'd better not be lying..."

Day 37

"Hopefully that'sss enough for Worla," I said.

We were on our way back to Lurkmire swamp, making our way down the long, sloping snowy fields again. I couldn't *wait* to be out of this miserable, cold biome! Soon, I'd be done with my *second task*, and I'd be back home, working on the obsidian fortress!

"I don't know," Skeleton Steve said. "There was something *mighty fishy* about that conversation..."

"But Worla *did* sssay to *ssstop* her—not kill her..."

"That's technically true, Cth'ka," he replied. "I just hope this was enough. All of this *witch business* is starting to feel pretty foul to me. I don't know what to believe anymore. Really, I'm not looking forward to your *third task*."

"It'sss true," I said. "There'sss sssomething *bad* going on with Worla I think." My little creeper feet were numb, crunching through the snow. I *hate* the cold! "But Witherynn felt weird too. Maybe all witchesss are jussst bad newsss..."

"I'm starting to think so," Skeleton Steve replied.

"Thisss will all be over eventually," I said.

"Yes. And do you still think the crown was worth the price?"

"Oh, of courssse!" I replied.

We walked quietly for a while, our feet crunching through the ice and snow.

"Ssskeleton Sssteve?"

"Yes, Cth'ka?"

"You'll ssstill help me ... with my third tasssk, right? I mean—if you're not busy on another adventure sssomewhere??"

"Sure, Cth'ka," he said. "Of course. You're my friend. Friends help each other."

We finally reached Worla's witch hut at night. Instead of passing through Darkwood, we saved time by following the edge of my forest to the north until we reached the western edge of Lurkmire swamp, and then it was just a few hours' walk from there.

The witch watched as we approached, then leapt down from her hut's upper deck as we neared, running toward like a lean predator. She grinned ear to ear, her teeth sharp and menacing in the moonlight.

"Mighty Cth'ka!" she exclaimed. "You return!"

"Yesss, Worla," I replied, setting my stronghold stone down onto the swampy grass. Her eyes followed the block greedily, as if she loved my weapon for some reason...

"So ... *success??* Witherynn is *no more?* You've saved the forest?"

"We ssstopped her, yesss," I said, a chill going down my spine.

Skeleton Steve shifted his weight next to me.

Clunk, clank.

Zarek watched me, and Worla, without expression.

"Fantastic!" she exclaimed, letting out a gleeful cackle. "Now we can move on to—wait..." The happiness melted away from her face. "*Stopped* her? What do you mean you *stopped* her??"

"Well, I..."

I swallowed.

Skeleton Steve was right. She wanted Witherynn killed. I was supposed to be Worla's *assassin...*

"Out with it, creeper!" she snapped. "What do you mean, you *stopped her?!* Is Witherynn *dead* or isn't she?!"

"Well, she promisssed to—"

Worla threw her hands up into the air with a shriek. "Are you *kidding* me?!"

"She sssaid that she'd … expand to a valley inssstead and…"

"Worla," Skeleton Steve said suddenly. "Cth'ka showed her mercy as she begged for her life. She vowed not to come down into the fore—"

"*Oh, shut up*, Skeleton Steve!" she snapped at him, then turned back to me, her eyes like obsidian daggers. "Does she know who *sent* you??"

"She sssaid that she won't be bothering me … or you … anymore. That she'sss ssseen the errorsss of her waysss. Oh, and that the *council* will be ssseing you sssoon! Pleassse, Worla, I—"

Worla gasped a long, exasperated sound, her eyes wide, her face almost screaming at the sky. Her hands—her long fingers tipped with thin, wicked claws—curled up, and I thought she was going to *claw her own face off* for a moment…

The witch composed herself again, and looked down at me, her black eyes burning through my head.

"Cth'ka!!" she shrieked. "Witherynn is evil! And she *lies!* And now she's going to *kill us all* with her ice magic!!"

We all gasped.

"But … but she—"

"You've got to get *back out there*, creeper!" she cried. "Get back out there and kill her while you still have the chance! It was *she* that destroyed your home!"

"What?!" Skeleton Steve replied.

Worla ignored him. "Witherynn *blew up your house*, Cth'ka, and killed your friends!! Are you going to stand for that? Now *hurry!* And get back up there and kill her dead before she goes into hiding and kills you in your sleep or takes an army of strays to your home!"

"But, Worla," I cried, my head spinning, "the *Sssteve* blew up my houssse!"

"Yes, dummy!" she snapped. "They were working *together!* I know it! I figured it out while you were gone. That's why I was trying to capture

364

the Steve the other night! They're both working against you! *Now go!!* You must hurry! You must trust me! *Kill Witherynn* and save your forest and avenge your friends!!"

"Okay," I said, unsure of where I stood now.

"And don't just 'stop' her again, creeper! Your task is to *kill the witch!* Bring back the gem from her hat to prove to me you did it *right* this time!"

"Sss … her *hat??*"

"Yes! *Her hat!* The *ice gem* in her hat!! Is there something wrong with your creeper ears? If you talked to her already, surely you *saw* it!!"

In a jumble of confusion, the witch sent us away, and before I knew it, we were following the edge of Darkwood Forest again, heading *right back into* Witherynn's cold and snowy domain…

Day 38

The way back to the igloo at the top of the icy mountains was slow going.

We didn't speak much.

I was embarrassed for thinking that Worla would be satisfied with us making Witherynn promise to leave us alone. After all, my *instinct* knew better. After all this time working with the witch, I should have known that she would sugarcoat the task, but really intended for us to do the *bad* thing...

Dirty work.

Skeleton Steve was right.

And my bony friend didn't speak much either, because he probably knew better too, and allowed us to return to the swamp on our merry way without listening to his *own* instincts.

He probably wasn't too keen to be an assassin either.

And Zarek … well, he was just *Zarek*.

My zombie warrior buddy just followed wherever I went, not judging, not trying to sway my thoughts, except maybe in battle.

And now, the battle was constant!

Ever since we set foot in the snowy biome, we had been beset by those *strays*. It's as if Witherynn was sure we'd be back, and sent an *entire army* to slow us down.

At first, it didn't seem like they were too much of a danger to the three of us. After all—we were *hardcore adventurers* now! Between Zarek's flashing katana and golden-armored defense, Skeleton Steve's deadly bow, and my stronghold stone that could *obliterate* anything in my path, we usually made short work of them.

But as we got closer to the three mountain peaks, the strays started attacking in larger groups. I even took at arrow at one point myself, it piercing my side and chilling me to the bone with some sort of *cold magic*, something that made it hard to move and made me … *slow* … *down* … for a while…

By the time we reached the ice spikes, it was night time again, and we were all wounded. Skeleton Steve had taken a few hits, Zarek was like a *pin cushion* in his golden armor, and fairly wounded himself, and my arrow wound gave me serious second thoughts about being able to defeat Witherynn a *second time*—especially if she knew we were coming!

Up until now, I also kept trying to use that growing *second* invisible hand. We really needed a second block flying around through the air! I might have avoided being shot if I was able to use a second block as a shield, and my friends would have been better off—less hurt at least—if I was able to smash through the army of strays with *two* blocks instead of one.

But, try as I did, it was impossible!

That second magical hand just wasn't ready.

Not yet.

I really hoped I'd figure it out by the time I really needed it...

Heading through the ice spikes in the dark, I had a pretty good idea of where Witherynn's igloo was, but the strays kept attacking us from all over, and my friends were starting to have a lot of trouble defeating them.

For now, we'd have to wait.

Surrounding my little group with a wall of ice blocks, pulled from the landscape around us, I set up a good defensive position for the night, and we settled in to rest.

We would attack Witherynn in the morning...

Day 39

As the sun came up over the icy horizon, I watched as the daylight crept through the ice spikes around us, towering over us, casting rays of cold light everywhere like we were in an alien world of glass and diamonds...

I looked at my friends.

They were grim.

Skeleton Steve looked weary, wounded in three different places by the arrows of the strays. He had pulled the arrows out over the night, but his cracked bones still showed, and I was reminded of the time we were wounded and trapped at the bottom of the stronghold.

Back when he thought he was at the end, Skeleton Steve, missing an arm and wounded from the zombies, the skeletons, the silverfish—all the bad mobs that attacked us in that dark place—just ... sat down.

When all hope was lost, he wanted to just *sit and think* for a while.

Until I found the crown...

Zarek still showed *multiple* arrows sticking out of his body! One even stuck out of his golden helmet. I was sure that several of those arrows were just stuck in the armor, but I was also certain that a few had gotten through...

The zombie warrior was determined, and his face was firm and unmovable—just like it always was.

He would stick by me until the end.

I had my arrow wound, in my side, and had used my powers to pull the arrow out. There was a wound still, a *hole* in my side, but it was so cold outside that I could hardly feel it!

As the terrain around us lit up with daylight, I could see that on the other side of my defensive ice wall ... were strays.

Lots of them!

They stood quietly, sometimes pacing, their bones clunking here and there, staring at us through the ice with their weird, glowing white eyes, their frozen bones gripping their bows, ready to attack once we tried to escape our resting place.

"There are at least … *thirty* of them?" Skeleton Steve said, breaking the silence. "Forty?? It's hard to tell through the ice. It's as if they keep coming out from behind the spires…"

"What do we do, my king?" Zarek asked, pulling his sword. "I can kill *many*, but we are all wounded and there are *too* many…"

"Oh, my friendsss," I said, smiling with my frowny face. "I wasss jussst waiting for the light."

They looked at me.

"Ssskeleton Sssteve, do you remember the ssstronghold?"

"Of course, Cth'ka. What are you getting at?"

"Remember what I did through the door'sss barsss?"

373

He smirked.

"It'sss the sssame," I went on. "I can feel *everything* out there…"

And it was *true*.

The strays couldn't get through my ice wall, which surrounded us on all sides … *except* above. Until this ice wall melted—*if* it melted—we were safe. And I could do *whatever I wanted* to the bad guys outside…

Reaching out with my powers, my *invisible magic hands* felt the world around me—the slick ice blocks of the wall, up, *over* the wall and down the other side, the packed snow and ice of the ground out there, the slick exteriors of the ice spires all around, the cold bones of the strays pacing, the frozen wood of their bows, even the frosty clothing they wore and the frigid feathers of their arrows…

Concentrating, remembering back to the first time I used the powers of the crown to save our lives back in the stronghold, I launched my stone block weapon over the wall, and proceeded

374

to smash up *each and every one* of the strays that waited for us on the other side!

Zarek and Skeleton Steve stood and watched, smiling, laughing whenever we saw a particularly entertaining explosion of frozen bones.

With my warped vision through the ice wall, I watched my dark grey stronghold stone fly back and forth, shattering the strange, blue skeletons into bone dust! I killed the ones near the wall, then watched for others approaching, and killed them too. When the action started to die down and I ran out of targets, I put my block down into the snow and bone dust, and felt out with my powers to see if there were any skeletons left moving out there...

Eventually, I opened up the ice wall enough to let us step outside into the destruction.

Skeleton Steve immediately began collecting as many of the magical *slow* arrows as he could find. Zarek stayed close to me as I looked around at the many piles of bones I created.

I picked up my stronghold block and we moved on.

Once we approached Witherynn's clearing, we had dealt with a few more skirmishes, a few more battles with small groups of strays here and there, but I was getting the feeling that the witch was running out of soldiers...

"*Strays! To me!!*" the witch was calling, standing in front of her home.

It was as if she was *summoning* the blue, frozen creatures from icy mountain itself, and the strays always appeared, pulling themselves out of the snowy ground.

But there were only a few left.

As we approached, shooting and slashing and smashing through all of the strays in our path, Witherynn glared at me from in front of her igloo, and pulled that wand from her robes again.

"How can this be?!" she shrieked, and make a menacing cry as she stabbed the wand through the air at us.

A sound exploded through the air like a blinding snowstorm, and a torrent of ice and snow hurtled toward us—mostly toward Zarek. I was reminded of Worla's lightning strikes when she was fighting *the Steve*, but instead of lightning, it was some sort of cold magic! And instead of zapping down from the sky, it was coming straight at us from her *wand*...

I had just long enough to block myself from her attack with my stronghold stone, but Zarek was hit full-force! As the zombie charged through the snow, his sword held level with his body, ready to slash into the witch across the clearing, he was blasted with the cold magic! When the white flurry died down, my undead bodyguard was coated from head to toe with ice—*frozen solid!*

"Zarek!" I cried, and launched my stronghold stone at the witch.

Skeleton Steve fired off another arrow at another stray.

My block weapon *zipped* across the clearing toward the witch, and crashed into her igloo as she barely jumped out of the way, punching a huge hole through the wall and sending chunks of snow and ice blocks flying all over!

Missed!

I scowled, and pulled my stronghold stone back toward me at great speed.

Witherynn jumped back to her feet, her black eyes wide with terror, and she clutched the wand and her robes and ran away!

"*Curses!*" she cried. "What to do, *what to do?!*"

No way, I thought. She was *not* going to get away from me this time, not by deceit, not by running!

I plopped my stronghold stone down into the snow in front of me, and climbed on, immediately using my power to grab the block— with me on it—and flew up into the sky!

"*Cth'ka!*" Skeleton Steve cried from below. "Wait for me!!"

"She'sss getting away!" I shouted back down at him. "Ssstay with Zarek!!"

Out of the corner of my eye, I could see Skeleton Steve suddenly turn his attention to another stray, and focus on his bow again...

Moving more quickly on the block than I ever had before, desperately trying to stay balanced, I flew, riding the stronghold block through the sky, low enough to (*hopefully!*) not kill me if I slipped up. Up ahead, past the igloo, I could see the witch scrambling toward the huge ice spire—the ice mountain, toward the bottom of the chiseled path winding up the side that led to the top.

Toward whatever secret *witch* place she had up there...

Witherynn looked over her shoulder, saw me in the sky, and shrieked.

"Strays!" she screamed, frantically. "*To me!!* To me, strays! Oh *darn darn darn!!*" The witch reached the bottom of the path up the spire, and started her ascent, running up as quickly as she could on solid ice.

A handful of strays appeared, emerging from the ice of the spire as if they had been waiting inside...

I suddenly realized what a *dicey situation* I was in!

Even if I caught up to the witch, what would I be able to do from a floating block? It took *all of my concentration* just to keep flying and not fall off! Not to mention, she'd eventually start *blasting* at me with that cold wand of hers, and the strays would be firing arrows...

Speaking of arrows...

I gripped the edges of the stone block with my little creeper claws as I pulled it to the left, dodging out of the way of an arrow whistling toward me from below.

"Kill the creeper!" Witherynn cried from the ice path up the spire. "*Strays!* To me!! Kill it! *Kill it!!*"

I'd have to figure out how to use that second magic hand, *and fast!!*

Dodging another arrow, I tried to split my concentration, tried to feel around on the ground down below for something I could use...

Snow!

Snow should be easy!

With that elusive second hand, I reached out and felt for the surface of the snow near a stray. I could feel it, the cold, wet, gritty surface, I could feel where I'd need to reach in ... pull out a block of snow...

Whoa!!

The block I was riding suddenly *dropped several feet* and my heart raced up into my throat as I caught my balance!

Okay ... still flying...

Not dead yet.

Darn!

I couldn't quite pick up a second block!

An arrow whistled through the air past me.

381

"To meeeee!!" Witherynn was shrieking from higher up the spire.

This wouldn't work. I'd have to land up there somewhere so that I could use the block as a weapon.

I flew after her.

As I rose up higher and higher, getting closer to Witherynn on the spire, I saw a handful of strays here and there, waiting on the winding, rising ice path. They took aim and fired, even though I was far away. I dodged their shots, and watched the arrows sink through the air to the ground.

I wondered how Skeleton Steve was doing...

"Get away, creeper!" Witherynn suddenly shouted at me, and I looked up in time to see her aiming the wand. I cut hard to the left, just as a blast of cold magic unfurled through the air, dissipating as it passed me!

That was too close, I thought.

If I fell from the block now, as high as I was, I would probably be killed by the fall...

What was I going to do??

She was almost at the top...

Flying in suddenly behind her, I decided to land on the path *behind* the witch, out of sight, where the path wrapped around and around the spire going up. I'd catch up on foot and kill her with my block...

When I was close and about to step off onto the slick, blue path, Witherynn appeared again from around the corner!

"Die, creeper!! *Die!*"

Good thing I was still on my block...

I flew back out into the open again, crouching down and clutching on as best I could, desperate to stay balanced as a blast of cold magic flooded the place where I was just trying to step down. Scores of stinging ice crystals and numbing cold snow and wind brushed the right side of my body. I *took the pain*, wishing with all my might that I had the strength to keep it together—stay on the block. Keep flying...

Just the edge of the blast hit me.

But I was still in the air.

My right legs were numb, but I was still alive and holding on.

I saw another stray heading up the path, and dodged aside as it launched an arrow through the air at me. Witherynn continued her ascent.

We were almost at the top of the spire. What crazy weapon or defensive thing did she have up there that she was trying so hard to get to?? I had to stop her before...

I peered into the ice cave as she reached the top and stepped into what looked like some sort of ... *library?* Bookshelves, all surrounding a central obsidian table with a single thick tome just like ... well, just like the one I saw at *the Steve's* castle!

And I was *seeing* this because I followed her right up in there, through the air, swooping in close and exposed, because I *knew* that I had to stop her before—

Witherynn turned toward me, backing up through her books, past her obsidian table, putting the library between her and me, standing at the other edge of her platform, her back to the open world of ice and snow on the other side of the spire...

Her face was twisted and terrified.

I was *also* terrified! My block and I were in her sights, vulnerable, hovering a hundred feet in the air...

But I knew what I had to do!

"No, creeper!!" she screamed, panicked. "It's *Worla!* She's—"

She aimed the wand, gritted her teeth, and...

Gripping onto the block with my feet, I let go of my concentration and focused everything on the witch. My powers snapped out at her like a *battering ram*, through the open space of her ice

385

library, over the books, through the blast of ice and snow flying toward me, and *smashed* into her body! The witch flew off of the other side of the spire, blue-grey robes fluttering in the wind, arms flailing, and plummeted off into the open sky...

The stronghold stone block I was riding *also* plummeted for a moment, enough to allow me to duck below her magic cold attack, and I fell for several feet before my concentration snapped back to flying ... and then I was stable again, hovering in the air.

I heard the witch's cry as she fell down, down to the icy ground below!

My heart was racing, and I felt the stinging cold of her magic dissipating down over my head, but *I was alive*. And the witch—

Focusing on flying again, I zipped around to the other side of the ice spire and looked down. The blue form of the witch was sprawled on the ground far below. I didn't see any strays anywhere—had they *disappeared* when she died??

I saw Skeleton Steve hurrying over to Witherynn's fallen body, far below.

Descending, I hurried to catch up.

"Cth'ka!" my friend cried up to me as I approached the ground. "You made it! Holy cow, that was *insane!*"

Jumping off of my stronghold block, I was thrilled to be back on the ground again, even if it was freezing cold and wet!

"Sssssss Ssskeleton Sssteve, I—"

It was hard to speak. My heart was hammering in my chest! Looking over, I saw Witherynn's body as a dark blue spot in the snow nearby.

"Are you okay?" my friend asked.

"Yesss, I think ssso," I said. "Zarek??"

"Still frozen," Skeleton Steve said. "On the bright side, all of the strays *wandered off*, so he's perfectly safe, I think!"

We both looked at Witherynn and stood silently for a moment.

She coughed.

Looking at each other quickly, we ran to approach her. I carried my stronghold stone in the air next to me.

Next to the witch, looking down, I could see that she was … *not* going to make it. That was quite a fall! She was dying, but not dead yet. When I approached near her, she no longer looked at me in fear, but in … sadness.

"Creeper," she whispered, and coughed again.

"Yesss, Witherynn?"

"I know …" she coughed. "I know you think … you are doing the *right thing*." She coughed and winced in pain. "There is … *more*."

"What are you talking about?" Skeleton Steve asked.

"Listen!" she snapped, her voice barely there. "Worla … the *vindicators* … she's …"

Witherynn faded into another coughing fit. "Wele ... gu ... wele'gumali..."

"She'sss not making any sssenssse," I said.

"She's dying," Skeleton Steve said, looking down at her sadly.

"You fools!" the witch cried with a little more volume, then coughed again. "*Poor* creeper ... I see you ... *bound* ... *Geas!*" She gasped, coughed, and sputtered. "*Beware* ... Worla ... the witches..."

Witherynn raised her wand at us again, and we jumped back, ready to finish her off, but she only blinked weakly.

"Take..." she said, and handed the wand to Skeleton Steve. "It's ... Worla..."

With that, Witherynn went into another coughing fit, gasped, then died.

Skeleton Steve reached down and took the wand from her long, clawed fingers.

"I feel kinda *bad*," my friend said.

"Yesss," I responded, looking down at the dead witch. "Me too."

"What do you think that stuff was about Worla and ... vindicators??"

"It'sss Worla," I said. "I wonder what she meant by that..."

"More sneaky witch stuff," Skeleton Steve said. "I swear, my friend, once we're done with your three tasks, we're going to have to stay away from all of those evil witches..."

We turned.

"Oh," I said, turning back. "Don't forget ... Witherynn'sss *hat*."

"Oh yeah," Skeleton Steve said.

My bony friend stashed the magical cold wand into his pack. I wondered if he'd even be able to *use it* someday. Or maybe it was part of some big conspiracy involving Worla and *vindicating* or some other witch babble...

"What'sss a ... *Geasss?*"

"No idea…"

Eventually, we made our way back to Zarek and the igloo. My poor zombie warrior friend was *frozen solid* in a thick sheen of ice.

Skeleton Steve had a brilliant idea of me using the crown to move frozen Zarek into the igloo so that he could thaw out and break free from the ice! So I did. And while the ice around the zombie warrior melted, Skeleton Steve and I went back down into the dungeon to release the prisoners and grab whatever loot we could find.

The zombie villager promised that he wouldn't try to eat the living villager if I released both of them at the same time, but I played it safe and made them take turns. The living villager was still mostly out of his mind when I pulled the iron bars off of his cell with my powers, so it took him some time to scream and flee his way over to the ladder. He eventually made his way out of there, howling in fear the whole way.

When I released the zombie villager, it wasn't in any hurry to leave.

Inside the chest, we found an apple made of gold, some Minecraftian food (which we left behind), and a green gem. Skeleton Steve called it an *emerald*. I insisted that he kept both the golden apple and the emerald, since I couldn't think of a single use for them, myself.

Sure enough, and fortunately long after the living villager was gone, Zarek thawed out and was still alive. Or ... *unalive*. Undead. Still moving and thinking and speaking, anyway! He wasn't destroyed, and I was glad.

"I have failed you, my king," he said.

I scoffed. "Sss ... you're fine, Zarek. I'm fine. We're *all* fine. You were frozen sssolid by the witch'sss magic! It'sss okay. I guesss thessse thingsss happen."

"Yes, my king."

"Now let'sss go home," I said.

"That's a *great* idea," Skeleton Steve said.

Day 40

Through the night and most of the day, we walked home.

When we stepped out of the snow and onto the crunchy and grassy forest floor again, I breathed a sigh of relief!

"Let'sss hope we don't ever have to go back *there!*" I said.

As we dried out and warmed up back in the comfort of Darkwood, on two different occasions I caught a glimpse of a few creepers here and there walking in the same direction we were.

By the time we returned home, I was amazed at how *busy* my little clearing had become...

"My king!!"

It was the voice of C'Thor. He approached me from a bustling and wandering group of—*I don't know how many*—creepers! There were creepers congregating in little clustered groups all

393

over the clearing, amidst the green grass, the yellow and red flowers. They stood around and chatted with each other by the mine, by the creek, even standing around on the obsidian foundation of Darkwood Fortress.

"C'Thor!" I exclaimed. "It'sss good to sssee you—good to be back!"

Zarek's dark eyes were lively and darted around the clearing as he stayed close to me and scanned for possible danger.

"Holy cow, Cth'ka!" Skeleton Steve said. "Look at all the creepers!!"

"Welcome back, my king!" C'Thor said, hurrying up with a creeper I didn't recognize on each side. "Sssee how your army hasss *grown*, Mighty Cth'ka!"

Upon hearing those words, all of the creepers around us gradually stopped whatever they were doing, halted their conversations, and turned to look. I heard the faint footfalls of dozens of creepers as they made their way over, staring with sad-slanting eyes and frowning faces, all looking for the one called *Mighty Cth'ka*.

"What'sss going on??" I asked C'Thor. "Where did all thessse creepersss *come from?*"

"My lord, there is a buzz in the foressst! Word hasss ssspread *far* about creepersss gathering in your army!

"But it'sss jussst been a few daysss!" I said.

"Yesss," C'Thor responded. "But when *one creeper* goesss out and bringsss back three, and then each of thossse go out and bring back three, and each of *thossse* go out and bring back three—"

"That's a lot of creepers..." Zarek said.

"Sssay sssomething to them, my king!" C'Thor said.

My eyes widened and I looked over to Skeleton Steve.

He shrugged.

"Hey," he said. "You *wanted* to bring your people together, remember?"

I gulped.

Stepping onto my stronghold stone, I gripped the edges with my claws ... and lifted myself a little into the air with my powers.

"Sssssssssssssssssss!!" Voices hissed and gasped all around me.

"Sssss ... he fliesss!!" a random creeper said.

A sibilant murmur swept over the crowd of creepers. There was ... I couldn't even *count* them all! A *hundred* maybe??

"*Sssilence!!*" C'Thor shouted.

The hissing died down.

"Welcome, creepersss, to my Darkwood Foressst!" I said.

All of the eyes stayed on me. I heard a small hiss here and there. Looking down at Skeleton Steve, I pleaded with him for help with my eyes. He gestured with his bony hand.

Go on, he seemed to say.

"We creepersss have never been together asss a *people*. But we are a great race! And I am *proud* to welcome you to ssstay with me here, in my *clearing*, the future sssite of *Darkwood Fortresss!* This foressst isss my home, and if you want, it will now be *your* home too! *Together*, we will learn more about oursssselvesss and the creeper people. Asss your leader, I will do my bessst to lisssten to you and to keep you sssafe. I believe that in time, creepersss all over Diamodia will learn of thisss place, and will travel here to join usss, and we will finally know what it meansss to be a *creeper!*"

I opened my mouth to say more, but I was suddenly tongue-tied, and couldn't think of anything else to say!

"Thanksss to *all of you*, and welcome again to Darkwood Foressst!"

As I lowered my stone block back to my closest friends, I felt embarrassed, and like I wasn't *ready* to be a leader. But Skeleton Steve, C'Thor, even Zarek, all smiled up at me! The crowd of creepers erupted into cheers and shouting, and the clearing was filled with a collective hiss. Just when I thought the noise was about to die down, at least one creeper out there started chanting, and before long, the entire green congregation had joined in...

"Mighty ... Cth'ka! Mighty ... Cth'ka! Mighty ... Cth'ka! Mighty ... Cth'ka!"

"Oh goodnesss," I said quietly to Skeleton Steve. "Thisss isss nutsss!"

My bony friend clapped me on the back and smiled, even chanting along in jest for a moment...

For the rest of the day, once I was able to get the mass of creepers to clear some space for me, I worked on the obsidian fortress. Dozens of creepers watched me work while the rest of them milled around the clearing. All evening, I heard words of amazement as newcomers watched me move blobs of lava, glowing brightly in the early night, as I created *obsidian* with dirt casts and water.

Would my twenty-by-twenty fortress even be *enough?*

Day 41

In the morning, Skeleton Steve, Zarek, and I returned to the witch.

It was a somber walk, as Skeleton Steve and I contemplated the dying words of Witherynn. There was something dark and sneaky going on with Worla, and the dead witch had us concerned. I couldn't even remember some of the words she was babbling—something about ... gumali? Wele'Gumali? Whatever *that* was...

"Probably nothing," Skeleton Steve said. "Sometimes, I guess, when you're dying, you say all *kinds* of crazy things..."

"Have you ssseen a lot of mobsss die?"

"Yeah, I suppose," Skeleton Steve said. "Not slowly though. Mostly in battle. So, really, I guess I don't know all that much about babbling while dying. Just *speculating*, I guess."

"She *did* sssay *'beware Worla'*..."

"Yeah," my friend replied. "She definitely said that..."

By the time we reached Lurkmire swamp and Worla's home, all three of us were surprised by the bustle of activity going on there.

Worla's hut stood at the edge of the swampy lake as always, and the obsidian portal with the evil, purple magic field warbling inside it stood nearby. However, all around the portal and beyond it to the east was now a large construction site!

The dirt pad I built under the portal was gone, replaced by a *floor!* And not just *any* floor—it was a small part of what looked like the beginning of a *huge building!* On a cobblestone foundation, there was an extensive birch wood floor being built that looked like it would be the first floor of a massive structure that seemed *very out of place* in Worla's swamp! So far, all I could see was the cobblestone foundation, the birch floor, and the early framing of some outer walls in places.

Working on the building were a dozen or so ... villagers??

No—not villagers.

They *looked* a lot like villagers—their clothing was similar, their faces the same, the same big, bulbous noses and thick brows over serious eyes. But they were *different*. For one thing, they were dressed mostly in grey and black, with dark bluish-grey pants (that reminded me of Witherynn's robe), and wore severe-looking overcoats with two rows of buttons down the front. Their skin was grey and colorless, and their brows were scowling and of the deepest black.

The other thing was that they *felt* weird. As we approached Worla's home, they all stopped as a group and stared at us, their eyes black and piercing and full of bad intentions. Something about them I couldn't explain. Like they *didn't belong*...

As the three of us stared at the massive construction project, and the strange workers stared back at us, I almost didn't notice when Worla turned away from the building and greeted us.

"Cth'ka!" she cried, as she turned away from the construction and approached with a dangerous grace. "You're back!" She stopped and narrowed her eyes. "You *have* completed your task, haven't you??"

I sighed.

"Yesss, Worla," I replied. "Witherynn isss *dead*."

The witch smiled like a wolf and walked up closer, her hands together under her robe.

"So, you have the gem??" she asked.

Skeleton Steve reached into his pack and pulled out Witherynn's hat. The ice gem glimmered in the afternoon sun.

"Excellent!" Worla exclaimed. "You have done *well*, Cth'ka! I was right to—"

"Now, lisssten here, Worla!" I hissed, feeling a coil of anger building inside of me. "I am *not* your asssasssin! I just have one more tasssk to—"

"Yes, yes!" she interrupted, waving her clawed hand to dismiss my words. "I *understand*, Mighty Cth'ka! It's fine. It's time for your—"

"What's going on here?" Skeleton Steve asked. "What's all the construction? Who *are* those guys??"

The witch frowned at him. "Them?? They're nothing. Just a new project. They're *vindicators*. Don't worry about it." She turned back to me. "Now, Cth'ka, I'm ready to give you your *third and final task!* Complete this task for me, and you'll be free to go play army in your forest and whatever. Are you ready?"

"It dependsss," I said.

"Are you *ready* or *not ready*, little creeper??" she asked, adding a knife's edge to her words. "These tasks are *mine to assign*. You have agreed! Now cut the attitude and tell me—are you ready?!"

I felt myself burning hot, and tried to calm the hiss building inside me.

"Yesss, witch. What do you asssk of me?"

403

"Cth'ka, for your third task, I need you to *kill the Steve...*"

Box Set Book 4 - Diary of a Creeper King

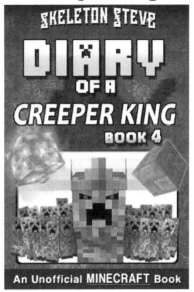

"Cth'ka, for your third task, I need you to kill the Steve..."

The good-hearted Mighty Cth'ka and his friends are back for the conclusion of the Creeper King series. Cth'ka only has one task left to perform for Worla the witch--but it's something he really doesn't want to do! After all, he's not an assassin!! But stuck under the power of the witch's binding spell, does he really have any choice?

With Skeleton Steve, his bodyguard Zarek the Zombie, and an ARMY OF CREEPERS, Cth'ka sets off to assault the Steve's castle in the mountains. With his powers growing, fighting bad mobs is one thing, but can Cth'ka really defeat the Steve? And what sinister plans lie behind the scenes with Worla the witch and her vindicators?

Day 41 - continued

I felt myself burning hot, and tried to calm the hiss building inside me.

"Yesss, witch. What do you asssk of me?"

"Cth'ka, for your third task, I need you to *kill the Steve*..."

What?!

I heard Skeleton Steve gasp next to me.

As I stood, surprised, I watched Worla's face. Her twisted and sharp features came together in a wolfish grin, and she stared at me with those beady black eyes, waiting for me to respond.

I shook my head.

There was *no way* I could do that. Heck, I even just told her that I wasn't her assassin, and she completely *ignored* me!

"Calm down, little creeper," Worla said suddenly, and I realized that I was hissing. She waved a clawed hand in a dismissive gesture. "Yes, *the Steve*. He has been our enemy for a long time, and has caused lots of grief to *both* of our homes, has he not?"

I thought back to when I returned home to find my house blown to bits and all of my collected ores stolen. Three of my creeper friends were dead, forced to explode and destroy my property...

"Yesss," I said, finding my voice again, "but Worla, like I sssaid, I'm *not* an asssasssin! I—"

She loomed over me with a terrible quickness, thrusting a claw into my chest.

"*You*, Mighty Cth'ka, are *whatever I deem you to be*, as long as you are still bound to me!"

I felt Zarek move behind me; heard his armor shift as he reacted to Worla getting in my face. The witch's eyes darted up to my bodyguard.

"*Back off*, zombie! Or I'll sic the vindicators on you!!"

My own eyes darted to the group of dark villagers, all clustered together and standing nearby. They watched, still as statues, the early afternoon sun showing their skin to be colorless and grey—so out of place, even in the muted colors of the swamp! Their black brows furrowed, and their dark eyes watched us intently.

Some of them were leaning on iron axes.

A chill ran down my spine.

Something about those ... vindicators ... was ... *unnatural*.

"It'sss okay, Zarek," I said. "Let'sss not fight."

Worla snapped her attention back to me and smiled. "Okay, Cth'ka, so here's what you need to do—"

"I didn't agree to thisss, Worla," I said. She frowned viciously when I interrupted. "I'm not your persssonal hired killer! After Witherynn, that'sss *enough killing* for me..."

Skeleton Steve spoke up. "Worla, surely there must be something *else* Cth'ka can do for you? There must be someone else working for you who can take care of *the Steve?* Cth'ka would be better for other tasks. What about Zebulon? He's *already* killed—"

"Stay out of this, Skeleton Steve!" she snapped. "This is between the creeper and I, and I have my reasons! It's none of your business." She turned back to me. "Now, Cth'ka, we had a deal!" Her clawed hands gestured to the *Crown of Ender* on my head. "You agreed, you are *bound*, to perform three favors for me when I require them in the future. Those were *your words*, when you agreed and *promised* to do these three tasks in return for my help in finding *that crown*."

"But I never sssaid that I would *kill* anyone!" I shouted.

"Three favors! Three tasks *of my choosing*. It doesn't matter what they are! The tasks are *mine alone* to choose, and you *must!* I could ask you to bring me magma cream from the Nether. I could ask for you to destroy a village! I could ask you to bring me an *end rod!*"

"Then sssend me to get an ... *end rod?!* I don't know what that isss, but I'm *not* a murderer, witch!!"

I realized that I was *hissing* again, and tried to calm down.

"I don't want you to get me an *end rod*, creeper," she replied, her voice like a knife's edge. "I want you to *kill the Steve*. That's it! *That's* your third task, and then you'll be free. It's not like I'm asking you to kill an innocent here—*the Steve* is *your* enemy as well as mine!"

"And what if I don't?!" I asked, squinting and staring into her fearsome eyes.

She sneered, showing her sharp teeth.

"Creeper," she said, her voice dripping with venom. "There is *magic* at work in our deal. You cannot refuse my task. Bad things will happen to you if you try." She broke her attention away, looking at my companions for a moment, then easing up on her tone. "Now—you'd best head home and get started! I'd like you to return here tomorrow with several creepers. At least *ten* of

411

them, if you have that many. I'll enchant them to help with the assault..."

The more she talked, the more I felt like I was hopelessly stuck performing this task I didn't want to have anything to do with.

Yes, *the Steve* did all of that nasty stuff to me.

He even attacked Skeleton Steve and I back on our first adventure, back in that village, and we almost died! Both of us!

But I am not a killer.

I'm a *leader*. And a visionary for my people.

Not an assassin...

I sighed with a big hiss. *May as well get this over with*, I thought.

"Are you listening, Cth'ka?" the witch asked suddenly, her voice sharp and annoyed. "The charged creepers will—"

"Yesss, Worla, fine. I'll be back with ten creepersss."

She smiled. There was no longer any sugar coating. The witch knew that I hated doing this task, and also knew that I had no choice.

Worla wasn't my friend anymore.

"Good then," she replied. "Get back here with those creepers, and you can be on your way to *the Steve's* castle."

Without a word, I turned away and started heading back to Darkwood. My friends snapped to and followed, Skeleton Steve's bones *clunking* as he moved.

When we were a distance away, Skeleton Steve spoke up.

"Cth'ka, this isn't the first time I've seen the witch send someone out to kill one of her enemies," he said. "I'm thinking, when you're done with … all of this, and free from whatever *magical spell* she has over you, we shouldn't deal with Worla anymore…"

"Why didn't you sssay anything when we had to kill Witherynn?" I asked.

"Up until now, I didn't suspect that Worla was in the wrong," he replied. "I bet Witherynn was evil, *sure*, but I think Worla's getting into some pretty *dark* stuff. I'm starting to think that *she's* the bad guy here..."

"I feel ssso ... ssstuck..."

"I know," Skeleton Steve said, putting a bony hand on my back. "We'll get through this, buddy. Hopefully without anyone else getting hurt."

Day 42

I changed my mind.

No way, I thought, sitting in my clearing surrounded by over a hundred creepers.

There was no way Worla could force me to kill *the Steve* for her. My people were looking up to me to lead them, to be a good example of a new *creeperkind*. I would *not* take my army and just go *squash the Steve*, like I was the witch's own personal weapon that she could toss around!

She'd have to find someone *else* to do that...

I didn't know what I was going to do, or what I could do about getting a *different* third favor from her, but I did have a huge fortress to build, and that lava wasn't going to become obsidian all by itself!

So ... I'd deal with it tomorrow.

For most of the day, I resumed construction on Darkwood Fortress. My creeper army watched me move the lava for the most part, crowding around an open path I used to pass between the mine and the twenty-by-twenty obsidian foundation.

As I walked from the mine to the worksite, carrying bright and burning blobs of magma, the multitude of creepers lined up on both sides and gasped in awe, whispering among themselves in hissing voices, like two *walls of green* with lots of frowning faces.

"Give the king sssome ssspace!!" C'Thor had to yell at them from time to time.

Every time I took a break from working, C'Thor led me around, introducing me to various soldiers in my army, telling me about how he divided them all into squads with team leaders, who reported to him.

C'Thor was shaping up to be a pretty great *general!* At least, when it came to organizing the army and keeping them in line.

There were so many creepers—and more coming all the time—that after meeting one new soldier *here*, another *there*, I promptly forgot their names as I met new faces.

One creeper however, among the throng, definitely stood out…

"Thisss," C'Thor said, indicating another soldier, "isss C'Ssscorp."

C'Scorp was different.

He was a lot like the other creepers— maybe a little *larger*—but what made him stand out was that his entire body was completely enveloped in some sort of … *energy field!* C'Scorp's eyes were lively and intense, his mouth pressed together tightly as if he was always trying to keep control of himself.

The energy field was *lightning!* Electricity, blue and sparking, arced around his body, his face, his eyes, in a constant state of flux! Even when the creeper opened his mouth, I saw streaks of blue fire zapping across the open space.

C'Scorp's energy was intense!! And when he spoke, I immediately got the feeling like this creeper wanted to move, wanted to attack—that standing still was torture and he was probably doing everything he could to just avoid *blowing up!*

"HELLO, MY KING!!" C'Scorp exclaimed, barely holding in his extreme enthusiasm. "I MUSSST SSSAY, YOU'RE AMAZING!! EVERYTHING YOU'RE DOING … SSSO GREAT!!"

"Thank you, C'Ssscorp," I replied. "I appreciate you joining usss here."

"YESSS SSSIR!!" he responded, beaming, lighting streaking across his smile. "I AM *THRILLED* TO SSSERVE YOU SSSIR!! I CAN'T WAIT TO *BLOW UP* IN THE FACE OF YOUR ENEMIESSS, MY KING!! I WILL BE A GOOD SSSOLDIER!!" He hopped on the ground in excitement, and several creepers around him winced.

"C'Ssscorp," I said, "what happened to you? Why are you ssso … full of … *lightning??*"

"OH, MY KING!!" he replied. "I WASSS OUT ON THE PLAINSSS ONE NIGHT IN THE RAIN AND WASSS SSSTRUCK BY LIGHTNING!! BUT DON'T WORRY—I FEEL SSSUPER!! I JUSSST … WANNA *BLOW* … WANNA BE A GREAT SSSOLDIER SSSIR!!"

"I sssee," I said. "Well, thank you for your dedication, C'Ssscorp. Hopefully you don't … *blow* … too sssoon!"

C'Ssscorp looked confused for a brief moment, then smiled again and gave me a dramatic nod. "YESSS SSSIR!! I WILL BE HERE FOR YOU, SSSIR!!"

Returning the nod, I continued with C'Thor, meeting other creepers, but my thoughts kept returning back to the lightning-struck C'Scorp.

When I acquired the *Crown of Ender*, it was because I did not want to die. I did *not* want to blow myself up, and I was desperate to figure out a way to live a fulfilling life of bringing my people together without blowing myself up one day!

But meeting C'Scorp reminded me that, even though I felt that way, there were probably many creepers that were *more than happy* to blow themselves up for whatever reason was important to them.

And what did Worla say so long ago?

"*Because*," the witch had said, her words returning in my mind, "*creepers are quite happy to blow themselves up. It's their destiny. It's how they make more creepers.*"

Just because I wanted to live didn't mean that I had the right to deny my soldiers' desire to blow *themselves* up, if that was what they wanted. We were an *army* after all. How else would an army of creepers fight?

I was the leader of a massive army of dedicated, walking bombs...

When the time came, C'Scorp would be happy to blow himself up in the face of my peoples' enemies, and I had a feeling that my intense new friend was hoping that such an occasion would happen *sooner* rather than *later*...

Eventually, I became tired, and decided to rest for the night.

There would be no working through the darkness *tonight*.

420

It had been a long several days fighting the ice witch, and I was just starting to feel the exhaustion of it.

Or so I thought…

Day 43

Today I decided that I would work on the fortress some more.

Something nagged in the back of my mind that I would need to take care of this *third task* thing one way or another, but I just didn't want to deal with it.

Not yet.

Not today.

I would *not* be Worla's assassin. I was one of the good guys—I wouldn't be a killer, even if the victim was *the Steve!*

Down at the bottom of my mine, I was starting to get a little worried about my lava lake. Soon, the fortress foundation would be finished. Four hundred blocks of obsidian! But my seemingly infinite lava lake deep down in the earth didn't look so *infinite* anymore...

Now, I wasn't just scooping up blobs of molten rock from the bottom of the stairs anymore.

I had taken so much lava out of the pool, that now I was walking through a large, empty stone tunnel for quite a ways—previously full of magma—to reach the glowing red lava that remained. From what I could see, looking at the magma as closely as I could without burning my face off, there would be enough to finish the foundation, maybe get a little ways into building the first level's walls, but *then* … I might run out. And after *then*, I'd have to dig around some more to find another lava pool, if there *was* one.

Something was wrong, though.

As I made the trip, back and forth, back and forth, again and again, from the lava pool back up to my fortress on the surface, and vice a versa, I was slowing down…

Once, climbing the long mine staircase, heading back up with a burning blob of lava in front of me, I actually slipped on the stone floor and almost killed Zarek and I with the magma I was carrying!

I stumbled, my legs suddenly weak, and lost my hold on the invisible *net* of my powers holding the lava in the air. As the dangerous, burning stuff splashed down onto the stairs above us, Zarek reached out, grabbed me around the waist, and rushed me down the staircase out of the way of the deadly, burning flood oozing down toward us...

When my zombie friend saw an opening, he pulled us to the side, and let the lava flow past, down, down to the bottom of the mine!

"Are you okay, my king?" he asked in a dull but intent voice.

"Yesss," I said. "Thanksss. I don't ... don't know what *happened* there..."

"Maybe you should take a *break*, sire."

"Yesss, okay, I will..."

Over the rest of the day, it seemed that I was becoming more and more susceptible to accidents, so I eventually stopped working.

Skeleton Steve, Zarek, and C'Thor sat with me, all watching me, as I wheezed and breathed hard.

Was I getting *sick* somehow?? That never happens! I've never been one to just *get sick*...

I was a very healthy creeper!

"What's the matter, Cth'ka?" Skeleton Steve asked.

"I don't know," I said. "Jussst a little *sssick* I guesss."

Once I felt better in the evening, I worked a little longer, pressing myself hard to finish the foundation. There weren't many open spaces left to fill in the obsidian floor anymore! I was *almost done*, and would soon be able to start on the walls!

When I took another break before nightfall, I watched my general, C'Thor, put the army through exercises. What an *amazing* thing to watch! C'Thor had such potential as a military commander!

To think that just ... *a month and a half ago?* ... I was sitting in this clearing by myself

426

without the crown, enjoying the sunshine and waiting for night so my friend, Skeleton Steve, could come out of hiding...

Now, I looked over the large obsidian foundation of my future fortress (*and could see Darkwood Fortress in my mind!*), and all across the clearing was well over a hundred creeper soldiers, split into squads, doing drills, directed by *my* general—and they all followed *me!*

Little old me.

As C'Thor yelled orders at one squad at a time, I watched as the organized clusters of creepers moved as *units*; taking several steps forward all together, then stopping, and backing up.

It was beautiful!

C'Thor also put them through ... *hissing* drills. I could only imagine that he was actually encouraging them to *almost blow themselves up*, then, he would have them stop and calm down.

Amazing.

I watched as a particular squad, on demand, all started hissing, shaking, sputtering, their bodies convulsing and stretching...

Then C'Thor would call out another command, and they'd gradually get back to normal.

Among the throngs of creepers in the dimming light, I could easily make out C'Scorp, his entire body glowing with blue lightning energy, swirling around him like a storm of deadly intent.

I coughed, and spat up some weird green stuff.

Strange, I thought. I couldn't remember the last time I got sick like this. Hopefully, I'd be better tomorrow...

Day 44

I won't be writing much today.

Last night, I was hoping that a good rest would make me feel better, but it didn't. Things are worse!

I tried to build, and even managed to finish the foundation! But as exciting as that was, I wasn't in any mood to celebrate. Going up the stairs was getting very difficult, and each trip back and forth from the fortress to the lava, and back again, felt like walking for *days*...

Eventually, I started getting *woozy*. My head started spinning, and it was everything I could do to avoid just laying down for the rest of the day.

"You don't look too good, Cth'ka," Skeleton Steve said. "You're pale ... and your eyes are all ... sunken..."

"Like a creeper *zombie*," Zarek said.

After resting for what might have been *hours*, I tried to resume work on the fortress, and

429

was only able to make the *first block* of a new wall before giving up on building for the day...

Every time my friends looked at me, I saw concern in their eyes.

Even Zarek.

My creeper army, always milling around, was very curious, and they were starting to whisper among themselves (*sssick ... he'sss sssick*), but C'Thor did what he could to keep them drilling and practicing away from me.

If this gets worse, I don't know what I'm going to do...

Day 45

I am not an assassin...

I am not an assassin...

Was this sickness because of *Worla?*

Bad things will happen if you try...

Today was even worse!

My head was spinning, I was having a hard time breathing, and I was frequently coughing up more green stuff.

What *was* that green stuff? *My insides??* My stomach tied up in knots.

Was I going to die??

"Cth'ka," Skeleton Steve said. "Cth'ka, can you hear me?"

"Wha?? Yessssss..."

I drifted away for a moment, then heard his voice again.

"He's coming back around. Cth'ka, can you hear me??"

Opening my eyes, I saw Skeleton Steve standing above me, along with Zarek. I could hear C'Thor's voice like waves of water in a dream. He was addressing the army.

"And he'sss turning sssick becaussse of the *witch*, but we'll fix it! We will ssserve our *king*, *Mighty Cth'ka*, and when he'sss better, we will be sssuccessssful asss a *gloriousss creeper army!* I need ten volunteersss for the asssault!"

"I VOLUNTEER, SSSIR!!" a familiar voice cried, intense and excited. "I WILL SSSERVE MIGHTY CTH'KA AND SSSAVE OUR KING!!"

"Thank you, C'Ssscorp," C'Thor said, his voice muddy in my head. "I need *nine more* creepersss for the sssspecial attack team..."

"Cth'ka!" Skeleton Steve said, cutting through the fog in my brain. There he was, still standing over me. "Cth'ka! You're back!" he smiled.

"What'sss going on??"

432

"This is the work of the *witch*," Zarek said in his low voice.

"Hey, buddy," Skeleton Steve said. "You're dying because you're refusing to kill *the Steve!* You must be. It's Worla's binding magic! We have to go ahead with the task, or you'll *die!*"

"Sssss ... okay," I said, struggling to my feet. "I don't feel ssso good..."

"Yeah, you don't *look* so good either," my bony friend replied, helping me up. "Look, I've talked to C'Thor about the ten creepers—I hope you don't mind. We've got to get you and them *back* to the witch, so she can *enchant* them or whatever she was going to do..."

"Okay," I said weakly. "Let'sss go. What time isss it?"

I looked up, and the sun made me close my eyes. The light hurt my head so bad...

"It's the afternoon," Skeleton Steve said. "It'll be a long walk with you like this, but we should get there tonight or tomorrow morning, maybe. Hang on, we're still getting the creepers..."

433

"Where'sss my … ssstone…?"

"I will protect you, my king," Zarek said. "Don't worry about your powers for now…"

In a haze of getting a group of ten creepers together, including C'Scorp, we started the fevered journey to Lurkmire Swamp.

It was going to be a long, slow walk…

Day 46

We walked through the night and into the morning, stopping frequently so that I could rest and cough up more green yuck. In the slow, quiet moments under the moonlight, in between the dizzy spells, I tried to move dirt blocks around with the *crown*, but my control was ... unpredictable. Eventually, I stopped trying to use my powers, because I was afraid of accidentally hurting my friends.

By noon, we reached Worla's domain.

I could barely see, and the forest and swampland was swimming around me. With the help of Skeleton Steve and Zarek, guiding me along and encouraging me to keep moving, we made it down to the witch's hut.

In my woozy vision, I saw the dark, creepy eyes of the vindicators looking at me. While everything around me was moving and twirling, making me dizzy, I could see their stony, grey faces frowning at me, black brows furrowed over intense glares.

The huge structure built around the Nether Portal seemed to be larger…

Were there … walls?

"Well, well … what do we have here?" Worla's voice emerged like a poisonous snake from the tumbling, sick world around me. "Mighty Cth'ka, you're not *looking* so good!"

"Give him a break, Worla," Skeleton Steve said from somewhere on my left. "He's come around. We're here to do the third task."

I felt Zarek's strong hands steady my body.

"She approaches, my king," he said.

"Worla," I said, trying to concentrate. "What'sss … what'sss wrong with me??"

"It's the *Geas magic*, I'm afraid, young creeper," she responded.

Geas.

That word stood out, and I remembered … Witherynn said that word when she lay dying after falling from her ice spire. I just thought it was nonsense at the time...

"Geasss...?"

"I *told* you that if you refused the task, bad things would happen, did I not?"

I heard her voice keenly, even though I had a hard time focusing. Squinting, I could *see* her now, a looming dark shape in front of me. I gasped in terror. She went on.

"It's a good thing your friends got you here when they did. Another day, and you might be a pile of green mush!" She cackled, and my stomach felt cold. "I sssee you brought the creepersss for *enchanting*. Are you ready to proceed??"

"I ..." My head swam, but I still knew how I felt. This was wrong. All wrong. "Worla, I jussst ... I can't do it! It'sss *wrong!*"

She seemed to darken in front of me.

"Cth'ka, don't!" Skeleton Steve pleaded.

"You won't?!" Worla shrieked. "Still?!" I sensed her taking a step back, then felt a change, a crackling in the air. Crackling? Like lightning? No ... more like ... *bubbles popping?*

Suddenly, I felt the bulk of Zarek moving behind me.

"Get down, my king!!" he bellowed.

"Fine!" Worla shouted. "If you're going to break the deal, then I'll take this back!"

I heard the sound of Zarek pulling his katana...

"Worla, don't!" Skeleton Steve cried.

Listening to my bodyguard and dropping a little lower, I felt him move again, and heard the flapping of small wings—multiple sets of small wings.

The katana sliced through the air above me with a wicked sound, and I heard the breaking of metal, and a strange gasp of a creature being wounded.

In the next moment, I felt something tugging at my head...

438

The crown!

"NO!" I cried, as I felt the Crown of Ender being pulled off of me!

It was gone.

Even though I wasn't using my powers at the moment, while I was so *out of it*, I could still feel around me, and now ... there was nothing!

Nothing! It was gone!

My powers—the crown—gone!!

I saw the body of one of the little flying creatures hit the ground, cut to pieces by Zarek. Shaking my head and squinting my eyes, I focused on my surroundings. I saw two of the little imps flying back to Worla, who stood in front of me scowling. They were carrying the crown.

Vexes, I remembered. *She called them Vexes.*

Skeleton Steve was shocked, and didn't seem to know what to do.

The vindicators were approaching quietly behind Worla, like a wave of darkness and steely axe blades...

I could hear my chosen creepers hissing behind me.

"Ssstop!!" I cried. "Creepersss, ssstand down! Zarek ... Ssskeleton Sssteve..."

Zarek moved to stand in front of me, shielding my body, holding his katana low and ready.

"We had a *deal*, Cth'ka!" Worla said, her voice cutting above the din, slicing through fog in my head.

"Keep it!" I said. Skeleton Steve gasped. "Thisss isssn't worth getting my friendsss hurt over, and I will not be your asssasssin anymore! I found the crown to ussse to *defend myssself*—not to ussse to kill!!"

Worla's face became deadpan.

"Keep it?" she asked. "Really?! Your *friends* are worth more than your powers??"

"I won't be your ssslave and your killer, witch!"

"So be it," she said, her voice quiet and low. Then, in a flash, she pulled a vial from her robes, and threw it at Zarek! Before any of us could react, the potion shattered on his armor, and he was enveloped in a sickening, green cloud.

My zombie friend staggered to the ground.

"Take him," Worla said.

The vindicators rushed Zarek, moving fast and efficiently, axes high. Zarek raised his sword in defiance, but they beat him down as he choked in the green cloud of Worla's potion.

"*No!*" Skeleton Steve and I both cried.

"Don't kill him! Not yet!" Worla shouted, and her vindicators beat him almost to death, but stopped. "Take him to the mansion," she said. "Put him in a cell…"

"Worla!" I cried. "Leave him alone—your fight isss with me!!"

"Wrong," she said.

"Let him go!" Skeleton Steve cried.

"Or what?!" she replied. "You think I'm scared of one skeleton archer and a bunch of creepers? Now, let's get back to business!"

"Ssss ... what?!"

"Cth'ka, you're going to complete my task for me, or you'll die, *and* your zombie friend will die. Get it?!"

My mind was a blank...

What could I do?!

"Sss ... okay..." If I could have cried, I would have. Coughing several times again, I spit more green stuff onto the grass. "What am I sssupposssed to do?"

"You are to kill the Steve, then destroy his entire compound. Do you understand? *All* of the castle, the other buildings, the crops—everything! I'm going to enchant these creepers ... *are you paying attention?!*"

I shook my head, trying to clear the fog of the sickness.

442

"I'm ssso … woozy…"

Worla scoffed, and I was barely aware of her waving her hands through the air.

And it was like she pulled a blanket off of my mind…

My head *cleared*. I could see—hear—everything again! I wasn't dizzy anymore, and my feet found themselves *solid* under me. I could stand up straight! Worla stood in front of me, scowling, and holding her clawed fingers splayed out in the air like she just finished casting some sort of magic. Skeleton Steve stood at my left, my ten creeper soldiers, including the electrified C'Scorp, stood behind me, and I saw a handful of vindicators carrying a beaten-up Zarek into the huge building, the structure more progressed now with its construction.

The other vindicators, maybe a dozen (*were there more now?*) stood around and behind Worla, ready to get into action. They stared at me like hateful statues, all holding wicked iron axes. Two of the little Vexes hovered over each of Worla's shoulders. One of them held a tiny sword. The other held my crown…

"What?!" I stammered. "What'sss … how am I?!"

"Can you understand me now?" she asked impatiently.

"Yesss … *Zarek!* You won't hurt him??"

"Oh yes," she said. "I'll *definitely* hurt him if you don't do as you're *told*. I'll *kill* him, creeper, if you don't hold up your end of the bargain! And *you'll* die too, sick and weak just like you just were. The only way for you to be free of the magic, is to *truly believe* that you have completed your task!"

"The crown," I said. "Will you let—" I was interrupted by a nasty coughing fit, and spit out more green stuff. I looked at the witch in confusion. "I'm not … all the way better?"

Worla sneered. "That's to remind you to stay *focused*, Cth'ka. Now, if you play *nice*, I'll give back the crown, enchant these creepers, and—do I have to repeat what I already said? Tell me, young one. What did I just instruct you to do, before I lifted the curse?"

Curse?

I thought back.

"Sss ... to ... kill the Sssteve, dessstroy the cassstle and all other buildingsss, dessstroy the cropsss?"

"Good," she replied. "After you do, return to me, and I'll release your friend back to you. Take your time making sure everything is destroyed! Leave *nothing* undone! But if you *do nothing* like these last few days..."

I looked down at the *mansion*, as Worla called it.

The vindicators and Zarek were already inside, behind the half-built walls. I couldn't see my friend.

"Undersssstood," I said. I wanted to threaten her, to make sure Zarek isn't harmed, to make sure she wouldn't *betray* me somehow, but what could I say that would mean anything?? *She* was in the position of power here…

After all of that, Worla proceeded to enchant each of the creepers to make them like C'Scorp.

"I see you already have *one* creeper hit by lightning, eh?" she asked, as if everything was normal and we weren't *just* fighting, as if she didn't just kidnap my friend. "That's a rare sight!"

She directed each of the creepers to stand on their own, and one by one, the witch called down a bolt of lightning, just like I watched her do in the battle with *the Steve* up on Bald Mountain several days ago! Skeleton Steve and I flinched with each lightning bolt, as they *cracked* through the air and set the grass on fire. But each creeper hit by Worla's magic seemed better off for it—swirling with electrical energy just like C'Scorp, suddenly extremely energized and aggressive, and riled up about the coming battle!

When the process was finished, after Worla returned the crown and I could feel my powers *sweeping* back into me, we led the charged creepers back to Darkwood to join up with the rest of the army.

One man down...

Day 47

"I'm so sorry, Cth'ka" Skeleton Steve said again.

"It'sss okay, Ssskeleton Sssteve," I replied. I no longer felt like my cheerful self. "We'll get thisss over with, and get Zarek back! And if that witch hurtsss him again..."

Using my powers, I lashed out at a random tree, and made its trunk *explode*, sending chunks of dark oak and leaves showering all over!

"I didn't know what to do," my skeleton friend said. "I couldn't think of any way to make a difference..."

"Thisss will all be over sssoon," I replied.

"Hey—through all this craziness, I've been thinking about *the Steve*. Our encounters with him and what he's done to you."

"Ssso?"

Skeleton Steve shrugged. "Well, when he attacked us in the village by the stronghold, he was—"

"He wasss protecting the villagersss, yesss. We were jussst more mobsss to him."

"Yeah, exactly! And, I've encountered him before, too, by myself and with other friends like you. I helped fight him when he was about to kill *a friend of a friend* once, but ... he was really just killing chickens, and ... he *chased* me once in the rain, by the quarry, but then let me go! And he attacked us in his castle the other day about the bucket, but *we* were the invaders, you know??"

"Ssso what?! Are you trying to sssay that he'sss not ssso bad? Right when we're sssupposssed to go kill him, or me and Zarek will die?"

Skeleton Steve shot me a worried glance, then tried to play it off with a shrug. "I'm sorry, Cth'ka. I guess—I don't really know where I was going with that..."

We walked quietly for a while, then I spoke up again.

"I don't know if *the Sssteve* was really the one who dessstroyed my houssse," I replied. And it was true. I was doubting it more and more.

"Why do you say that?"

"Well," I responded. "Firssst, Worla sssaid that *he* did it. Then, when we didn't kill Witherynn, sssuddenly it was the Sssteve *and Witherynn* that did it!"

"What are you getting at? Are you … suggesting that … *Worla* did it somehow??"

"It ssseemed pretty convenient asss a way to make me do what she wanted," I said. "I dunno…"

I coughed and spat some green stuff onto the ground.

Later, when we arrived back at my clearing, C'Thor gathered the army before me. Many of the creeper soldiers marveled at the 'special attack team', all *ten* of them now glowing and shrouded with the arcing, sweeping *lightning energy.*

I gave my army a speech about the villain, *the Steve*. About how he hates creepers and how he came here and killed some of their fellow soldiers, blew up my house, and stole our resources. I told them that our mission was to destroy him and his castle grounds, for the good of creeperkind.

I hated it. I hated myself for lying, but my soldiers needed to be sure and confident in what we were doing.

Skeleton Steve put a bony hand on me for reassurance.

He understood.

When I looked over at him, he returned a look of compassion.

To completely destroy the farm, and to make it easier to destroy the wooden structures, I figured that I should bring some lava.

But how?

After contemplating how to travel with lava *and* my stronghold block for a while, I decided to build a small platform … a small *flying* platform. My army watched in admiration as I built the vehicle— a small 'flying boat' of *just enough* blocks to carry me and a blob of lava, much like an obsidian cast (except made of *stone* instead of dirt), with a seat in front! As an added bonus, I added blocks to the side to keep me more secure while I flew—no more clinging on and maybe falling off.

I don't know why I didn't think about it before!

It was like a flying … *seat*, with a stone container of lava behind it.

Taking my *stronghold stone* in one of my invisible magic hands, I placed it over the lava, sealing the burning magma safely inside, and stashing my weapon for later use.

"Brilliant!" Skeleton Steve said. "And when you get more powerful, you can make a bigger, *heavier* one that can also carry me and Zarek!" He laughed, but the merriment quickly petered out.

Once my flying platform was loaded with lava, and the troops were ready, we set off!

Up until now, there was never in the *history of Diamodia* a march of creepers like this, one hundred and sixty green soldiers crawling on as an organized unit over the landscape. I'm sure it was a sight to see for any of the random mobs we encountered out there.

I, Cth'ka the creeper king, led my army out of Darkwood toward Lurkmire swamp, then, turned west to cross the plains, the shallow mountain range, then again into the plains where Ahimsa village waited on the horizon...

Flying low in the air, I used the powers of the crown to glide slow and low above the terrain, followed by dozens of squads of grim and determined creepers. At the front of the army, in the middle of the great formation of soldiers, was the unique unit of glowing-blue, charged creepers—the *special attack team*.

C'Thor and his two assistants walked at the head of the army—my *general* and most trusted soldier frequently looking up to me in case I needed him. Skeleton Steve also walked along near the front line, out of the main formation.

Once we reached the village, we didn't avoid it.

Why should we?

There was no reason to be stealthy with such a large force of mobs like this!

As we approached Ahimsa village, I could see, from up high, that the villagers in town were freaking out! They screamed and squawked at each other in their strange, villager language, gathering together and hiding indoors.

For a moment, I was tempted to ask Skeleton Steve what they were saying, but I had a pretty good idea.

"Creepersss, do *not* harm the village!" I shouted from my flying platform.

"*Sssir, yesss sssir!!*" my soldiers answered in unison from below.

I was suddenly giddy with excitement...

We passed through the village like green water, all of my creepers flowing through the streets, around the buildings, and out of the north side as we headed up the valley toward the mountains. Flying above, I couldn't see what my creeper soldiers could see down in the streets, but I bet they were getting a good view of the villagers cowering inside their homes, watching with terrified eyes from the windows!

There were no explosions—no damage.

We moved on to the north.

By the time we reached the forest's edge, flowing around the Steve's stone quarry and climbing up into the mountains, the sun had gone down, casting silver light over all of the creepers moving quietly along the grassy ground.

We marched through the night, ever northward through the woods.

If *the Steve* happened to be out on a nightly stroll, he would be in for *quite* a surprise...

I watched from above as all of the random mobs that came out at night looked around in confusion, stepping out of the way of our march. Many of the zombies and skeletons down there demanded to know *'what's happening?'*, but my soldiers were well-trained, and stayed focused on the assault.

More than a handful of random creepers we came across decided to follow and slip into the ranks...

At this rate, we were bound to reach *the Steve's* castle by dawn...

Day 48

The day of the big battle.

I raised my flying platform higher into the air between the trees—just high enough to see *the Steve's* castle from the mountain ridge.

The last time I was here, on the ground at least, Skeleton Steve, Zarek, and I were *running away* back toward Ahimsa village. Cro'as was dead. My first creeper follower had blown himself up to save me from *the Steve*, blowing a hole in the castle's wall and floor!

We were going to do a lot more damage than that this time...

I coughed and spit.

Felt sick to my stomach.

Not because of the *Geas* magic—but because my army and I were about to level this *whole place* before me, and kill a Minecraftian that I had no interest in killing.

Looking down onto *the Steve's* plateau, I took it *all* in one last time—the massive castle with a central, round tower and glistening glass windows; fields full of Minecraftian food-crops, pale in the morning light and blowing in the breeze; multiple fenced-in areas full of animals; a small dock and fishing hut near the river.

Soon, it would all be no more, and it would all be my fault.

"My fault," I said aloud, wishing that someone could make me feel better, but I was too high in the air. None of my friends down below heard me.

Worla's fault, I thought.

But I still squirmed inside with guilt. Yes, it was me doing the deed, but her magic would kill me if I didn't, and worse—she'd kill Zarek, too. The witch left me with *no choice*. I could sacrifice *myself* to do what's right, sure, but I won't kill my friend...

Lowering myself down, I approached C'Thor and Skeleton Steve.

"Sssire?" my general asked.

"So what's the plan?" my bony friend said.

"We approach in sssquadsss," I responded. "Until we're on the groundsss. Then, I'll park my platform and join in when the Sssteve appearsss. C'Thor, direct the *ssspecial attack team* to make the biggessst breaksss in the cassstle. Then the otherss attack until the cassstle and the river building isss no more…"

I shook my head to clear away the guilt that was gnawing at me.

"What about *the Steve?*" Skeleton Steve asked.

"When he comesss," I said, swallowing back the disgust of what I had to do, "I'll take care of him. We'll improvissse."

"Yesss, my king," C'Thor said, turning to the army.

"C'Thor??" I said. He turned around. "Don't put yoursssself in danger. And make sure the

461

sssoldiersss know ... well ... let'sss try to lossse as *few* creepersss asss posssible, okay?"

"No unneeded explosionsss, *got it!*" C'Thor said, then got to work.

"You ready for this?" Skeleton Steve asked.

"Yesss," I responded. "It'll be easssy. What can the Sssteve do, really? There are ssso many of usss. I feel bad. He'sss *doomed*."

"Cth'ka," Skeleton Steve said, looking me in the eyes, "I'll do my *best* to figure out a way to make this better for everyone."

"Sss ... I don't know what you mean, but okay, Ssskeleton Sssteve..."

C'Thor yelled out at the group. "Okay, let'sss do thisss by sssquadsss! Sssspecial attack team in the center! Sssspread out when we get clossse. Don't wassste your livesss! Let'sss go!!"

With that, my army approached the nicely manicured land of *the Steve*. When we all reached the field full of torches, the Minecraftian still hadn't revealed himself. I landed my flying platform in the open grass area, then, pulled my stronghold block off of the lava container.

I was tempted to try to take the lava along too, but I wanted to focus on *the Steve* first. Just one magical hand for now. Things might change in battle...

"Ssspecial attack team, front and center!!" C'Thor yelled.

The ten glowing, charged creepers approached and fanned out into a spread formation. As I watched, I saw C'Scorp notice me. The large, original charged creeper smiled brightly, then focused his attention on the castle, seemingly set and determined to make me proud.

It felt so amazing to have all of these creepers devoted to me. My heart swelled in appreciation for their dedication. I felt a little sadness at the thought that several of them would not return home, but reminded myself that they wanted to do this...

I loved them. I loved these creeper people. And they loved me for it.

"Firssst three, attack!!" C'Thor yelled.

Just then, I saw a flash of movement up on the balcony.

It was *the Steve*.

He must have stepped out to see what all of the commotion was.

I bet he was surprised...

In the instant that *the Steve* looked out from what must have been his bedroom, I noticed that he was unarmored—just wearing a blue shirt, and darker blue pants.

The Minecraftian ducked back inside.

The first three charged creepers approached, each spreading farther and farther apart from each other as they neared the castle. *The Steve* was still inside when the charged creepers started hissing, convulsing; one closing to the main tower by the front door, another to the tower's side, and the third on the other wing of the castle...

Ba-DOOM!! BOOM!!

The three electrified creepers exploded almost at the same time!

Their explosions, charged by lightning, were the *biggest* creeper explosions I had ever seen! Of course, I hadn't seen many ... but I was amazed! Stone bricks showered in all directions, and the castle was *ripped open* in three different places, showing the edges of walls, upper floors, and all manner of destruction...

Skeleton Steve and I were both awestruck.

"Next three ssspecial attack team! In posssition!" C'Thor shouted, seemingly unimpressed. "Attack! Adjussst for maximum damage!"

The next three charged creepers stepped forward. I could see that C'Scorp was still waiting for his turn. As the next trio of attackers moved forth, I could tell that they were aiming to hit areas of wall that were in between the last explosions. If they hit the right places, the entire front half of the castle would be gone! After that, any hits further in from the remaining four charged creepers would likely collapse the *entire structure!*

A coughing fit came out of nowhere, and I was spitting up green junk.

When the three charged creepers were halfway to their targets, I suddenly saw *the Steve* appear on his balcony again. This time, he was decked out in the full suit of iron armor I'd seen him wear multiple times now, shining in the morning sunlight...

The Steve pulled out a bow.

"Ssskeleton Sssteve!" I exclaimed, motioning my friend's attention to the balcony.

"I'm on it!" Skeleton Steve said, pulling out his *own* bow. He pulled an arrow from his quiver. I recognized it as one of the magical arrows he scavenged from the *Strays* up in the icy mountains.

The Steve fired his first shot, and I watched as a flaming arrow streaked through the sky and struck one of the charged creepers approaching the castle. The creeper staggered back, then *caught on fire!*

Oh man—I had to *do* something!

Skeleton Steve fired his first shot, and I watched the magical arrow fly across the field toward the balcony...

The Steve sidestepped it with ease, and my friend missed.

Taking aim once more, the Minecraftian hero fired again at the *second* attacking creeper, and his flaming arrow found its mark! The first creeper that was on fire already was wandering around, blinded by the flames, then fell to the ground and burned up.

Now, a second charged creeper was on fire!

"Ssstop!!" I cried to the third charged creeper. "Ssskeleton Sssteve, *distract* him!!"

When the third charged creeper stopped its attack and turned toward me, I put my stronghold block down onto the grass, and reached out with my powers to feel the grassy dirt under its feet.

My bony friend fired at *the Steve* again, who once again dodged out of the way of the magical arrow.

Suddenly, I lifted the dirt block straight out of the field under the charged creeper's feet. The glowing and electrified soldier staggered as his balance was tested, but he *stayed on the block*.

"Hold on!!" I shouted at him, and flew the lightning-wrapped creeper *straight toward* the balcony...

The Steve stood still for a moment, shocked. Or, at least I *think* he was shocked, but his face never changed expression, so I couldn't tell! Skeleton Steve shot at him again, distracting the Minecraftian from shooting down the incoming creeper.

"Firssst sssquad, normal creepersss," C'Thor yelled. "Attack! Target inssside sssupportsss!"

I delivered the charged creeper toward the balcony, through the air, as he clutched tightly onto the dirt block. *The Steve* must have determined that it was too late to stop the attack, because he disappeared back inside. The charged creeper, flying through the air, getting closer and closer, began to hiss and sputter. The lightning crackled around him. He began to stretch and shake...

Several normal creepers passed me, heading straight into the holes ripped into the castle by the last attack...

BOOM!!

My flying charged creeper exploded next to the balcony, shattering the entire area of the tower and leaving a gaping hole in the wall! Cobblestone, shards of glass, and stone bricks flew every which way, along with splinters of wood, furniture, and other debris I couldn't identify. On the ruined piece of a high cobblestone floor I still saw clutching to what was left of the tower wall, I saw a *single bed* with red blankets...

So it *was* his bedroom.

I coughed and spit.

Boom! Boom!

I heard the creepers inside start exploding in the interior of the castle.

Both of the charged creepers that had been set on fire were gone now, dead and burned up.

"C'Thor!" I called. "Resssume your attack, but keep sssome ssspecial unitsss in ressserve!" I climbed onto my stronghold block and lifted myself up into the air.

"Yesss sssir!" he called, then started shouting for more squads.

"Where are you going?!" Skeleton Steve asked, nocking another arrow.

"I'm going to finish thisss," I said. "You should go to the back door to ssstop *the Sssteve* if he triesss to sssneak away!"

Skeleton Steve made a face like he was annoyed at me for rushing off without him again, but turned, and started running, bow in hand, to the back of the castle. "Be careful!" he shouted as he ran.

But I was already flying through the air toward where the balcony used to be…

Boom! Boom! … Boom!

Creepers on the inside of the castle continued to wreak havoc, taking apart the building one explosion at a time.

As I approached the open, ruined tower where the top floor used to be, I peered into the darkness.

Boom! Boom!

Explosions below me rocked the building, and cobblestone dust shook down all around.

Approaching what was left of the upper floor, I stepped down into the ruins of *the Steve's* bedroom, then swung my stronghold stone around to act as a shield as I stepped further inside...

Boom!

The walls shook all around me as I peered deeper into the room, now dark with smoke and dust. *The Steve's* bedroom was large and open, now broken up by areas of the floor being missing, and chunks of stone and wood scattered all around. I suddenly suffered a coughing fit, and spat green gunk out onto the floor.

Just then, out of the corner of my eye, I saw the flash of fire and an arrow streaking toward me! I had just enough time to swing my stone block, and deflected the flaming arrow!

Thunk!

It was *the Steve*.

Sneaky, sneaky…

As soon as I could see around my stronghold block again, I heard the *thump thump thump* of *the Stcve's* armored feet, and saw him charging at me with his sword and shield! His armor was marred from the smoke and flames, but he looked *quite* healthy and dangerous…

So I threw my block at him.

The stronghold stone launched through the air like sudden death, and just before impact, *the Steve* braced himself and raised his shield to block the attack.

Smash!!

My weapon collided with the Minecraftian's shield, which shattered into pieces of metal and splintered wood, and *the Steve* staggered back under the blow ... but stayed on his feet...

As I tugged my *stronghold block* back to hit him again, *the Steve* shook off the shattered remains of his shield, and pulled out *dirt blocks*. Before I managed to squash him, he threw several dirt blocks down in front of him, creating a *wall* out of thin air!

Then he pulled his bow as he ducked for cover behind the new defensive wall...

I dropped my stronghold stone, then used *both* of my invisible magic hands to tear the dirt wall apart, revealing *the Steve* as he pulled out a new arrow. The dirt blocks scattered around the remains of the room, some falling through the holes in the floor to the lower levels...

Boom! Boom!

More of my soldiers exploded under us, shaking the walls. Blocks started falling from the ceiling, sending shafts of daylight piercing through the thick dust into the dark room.

The Steve stood, holding the bow ready in one hand, and pulled something out of his belt— some sort of small, blue *sphere* that looked a lot like the gem in my—

He threw it across the room.

Zip.

The Steve disappeared!

In the next instant, I saw him *reappear* in a farther area of the room, his bow ready and aiming! As the Minecraftian mob-killer released his arrow, I reached out with all of my power to snatch up my stronghold stone to shield me...

And I *blocked* the flaming missile!

The Steve looked shocked.

Then I launched my weapon at him, and *bashed* him square in the chest! His armor crunched and fell apart under the massive stone block, and *the Steve* fell over the edge of a hole in the floor, disappearing down into the unknown area below...

Catching my breath for a moment, I hurried to the edge of the hole across the room.

Boom!

Another explosion rocked the building. This tower would collapse at *any moment*...

I reached the edge, and looked down into the darkness.

Below this floor was another level, *also* with the floor destroyed. It looked like *the Steve* fell from the bedroom level, *through* the next level, through *another* hole in the ground-floor level, and now lay *under*ground, sprawled out on some sort of basement level!

My stomach felt cold looking down there, seeing *the Steve* lay, his arms and legs spread out, *three levels* below me.

Boom! Boom!

The floor under my feet moved a little, and cobblestone dust and tinkling shards of glass fell through the air.

Suddenly, Skeleton Steve appeared from out of sight on the basement level, down next to *the Steve!*

"Ssskeleton Sssteve!" I yelled down from above.

He looked up.

"Cth'ka! You'd better get out of there! Everything's about to collapse!! C'Thor's bringing in the last special units!"

"What about *the Sssteve??*"

I saw my friend approach *the Steve's* body and look him over. He looked back up at me.

"He'sss dead, Cth'ka! You *got* him!"

My heart choked up a little.

It was done.

I was a killer.

Again.

And I killed *the Steve*, who was *dangerous*, yes, and had even tried to kill *me* a couple of times, but this felt ... so ... *wrong*.

Here he was, living in his castle, doing whatever he was doing, and I swooped in, blew up his awesome place, and bashed him to death...

I would never feel right about this...

Boom! Boom!

"Cth'ka!" Skeleton Steve called up. "Get *out* of there! Here they come!!"

I shook my head and snapped back to reality—I had been staring at the dead *Steve*. Looking back to the hole in the tower, I started away from the edge, but took one last glance down at the fallen hero mob-killer...

He was gone.

And so was Skeleton Steve. Probably running out of the castle!

Ba DOOM!!

477

A massive explosion rocked the castle. That must have been one of the charged creepers! Daylight spilled into the room as an entire section of wall fell away!

Uh oh...

I hurried to my stronghold stone and climbed aboard, immediately lifting myself off of the shaking cobblestone floor.

Ba DOOM!!

There went another! The next one would be following close behind...

As the castle shook with the last huge blow, the *entire floor* of the upper level crumbled away, except for the tiny piece of floor, attached to the wall, that held *the Steve's* bed...

I saw *movement*...

What was that? I thought, then, I realized that it was a *Vex*, flying around next to *the Steve's* bed, passing in and out of the wall.

What?!

478

What was *that thing* doing here??

I flew across what remained of the room, intent to get out before the ceiling finished caving in, and got a better view of the impish creature.

Where would I—I looked around for a place to land so that I could capture the creature, but the entire building was collapsing! I'd have to...

Reaching out with my *second* magical hand, as my first hand held the block I was flying on, I cast that invisible net around the little creature and squeezed...

It squeaked.

I had him!

The Vex cried out in an otherworldly voice of surprise as I caught it and held its small body in the air with my power, pulling the creature to me as I flew out into the open air on my block.

"What the—*let me go!!*" it shrieked with a tiny voice.

I could feel the pores of my power's 'net' slipping open around the creature, but I had enough focus to keep *tightening*, and I kept him bound in front of me.

"Sss ... what are you *doing* here?!" I asked. "Do you work for the witch?!"

It struggled, straining its tiny bluish-silver arms and legs against my invisible hold. Its white bat-like wings were stuck together behind its back.

"*Let me go!!*" it shrieked in a small voice.

"Why are you here?!" I demanded again, shaking the Vex from side to side.

Ba DOOM!!

Another charged creeper hit the castle, and I looked away for a moment as half of the building collapsed to the ground in a huge plume of smoke and dust!

"She sent us to capture *the Steve!* Release me, *please!!*"

"But *the Steve* is *dead!*" I shouted back at it, over the noise of the collapsing building. Other normal creepers exploded here and there down below. I could see the vast majority of my army standing by, spread around the building. Far off, I heard more explosions, and watched as the river house fell to pieces into the water. "Who *are* you??"

"My name is Volux!" the Vex responded, still struggling against my hold. "I was told to wait by the bed!"

"*MY KING!!*" I heard a familiar voice cry from down below. "SSSEE ME, MY KING!! I SSSEE YOU UP THERE!! SSSEE ME!!"

Looking down, I saw C'Scorp beaming up at me from the front lines. He was the *last* charged creeper. When he saw me notice him, the soldier leaped into the air!

"I WASSS HAPPY TO SSSERVE YOU, MIGHTY CTH'KA!! I WILL DELIVER THE LASSST BLOW TO THE CASSSTLE FOR *YOU,* SSSIRE!! *FOR DARKWOOD FORTRESSS!!*"

With that, C'Scorp charged at the remains of the castle—the last section of the tower that still stood—the lightning surrounding him crackling and arcing! A huge smile spread across his face, and I could see, even from up here, the electricity jumping and sparking around in his eyes, in his huge grin…

C'Scorp hissed and sputtered as he ran. The lightning zapped the ground all around him as he flashed, his skin stretched…

Ba DOOM!!

The last charged creeper blew up, taking the remainder of *the Steve's* castle down with him. What remained of the main tower, and the small pieces of other walls still standing, shook and shrugged, then *everything* collapsed to the ground, throwing up stone and sand and dust…

The castle was no more.

"Goodbye, C'Ssscorp," I said, then turned my attention back to Volux the Vex.

But the Vex now had its wings free, and the moment I focused on the creature, it slipped out of my magical hold, and flew away from me at great speed!

I flew back down to the field to rejoin C'Thor and Skeleton Steve, who was also approaching from the ruins on foot.

"My king!" C'Thor exclaimed as I descended to the ground.

"C'Thor, my general," I responded, swooping down and stepping off of my stronghold stone. "*Good work*, my friend! You did a great job directing the ssspecial attack team and the other sssoldiersss to take down the cassstle."

"Thank you, sssire. Did you fight *the Sssteve?*"

"Yesss," I responded. "*The Sssteve* is dead."

"Yep," said Skeleton Steve, approaching and clapping me on the back. "*Definitely* dead! Must have been quite a battle up there, I expect?"

"Sss ... yeah. *The Sssteve* was very tricky and resssourceful."

"Very good, sssir," C'Thor said. "What do you want usss to do now?"

I looked around at the farm, the fenced in area full of animals...

"We need to tear it all down. Every lassst bit. There can be no tracesss of *the Sssteve'sss* cassstle left over. But no more explosionsss! No more *death* today."

"Yesss sssir!" C'Thor responded, then turned and started shouting orders at the squads. My creeper army proceeded to do whatever they *could* without actually blowing up to raze the rest of the property, which mostly meant kicking over the hundreds of torches spread throughout the area.

"Ssskeleton Sssteve," I said.

"Yeah, buddy?"

"*The Sssteve'sss* body disssapeared when I wasss ssstill there. I'm worried he *got away*..."

Skeleton Steve smirked, but there was something odd about the expression. "Cth'ka," he said, "have you ever seen a Minecraftian *die* before?"

"No..."

I coughed a few times, and spat out more green stuff.

"When they die, their body disappears in a puff of smoke!"

"Oh," I said, looking down. "Okay..."

For the remainder of the day, I helped the army raze the rest of *the Steve's* land. Without blowing themselves up, there wasn't much my soldiers could do. They couldn't tear up crops, or knock down fences, or even open the gates to the animals' pens!

But with my blob of lava, I made short work of the farm plots and the wooden fences.

Don't worry! I *did* release the animals first.

I'm not a monster...

The closer I came to seeing the entire property dismantled to the ground, the better I felt. And by the time night rolled around, I realized that I wasn't *coughing* anymore.

With the job done, did the sickness go away?

Was I *already* free from Worla's magical Geas, since I finished the third task? Or did she still have to *release* me somehow?

When the job was done, I decided to camp my army for the night in the huge, open plateau that used to be *the Steve's* castle and surrounding grounds.

Now, it was just a field again.

A huge, open field.

It seemed like a great place to build a home!

My stomach suddenly felt cold. I'm sure that's exactly what *the Steve* thought when he first found this place...

After giving a half-hearted speech of thanks to the remainder of my army (which was still well over a hundred creepers), we settled in to rest for the night.

I couldn't wait to return to Worla and get Zarek back.

My mood was dark, though. I couldn't help but get the feeling that my difficulty with the witch wasn't over yet...

Day 49

In the morning, we marched back.

Riding at the head of the creeper army with my flying platform, which held a blob of lava and my main weapon, felt just as dramatic as when we marched here initially. Except now, C'Scorp and the other charged creepers were gone, as well as several other normal creeper soldiers.

All in all, we didn't lose many. After rearranging the squads, C'Thor's final count was a hundred and fifty, which meant that we also picked up several more creepers *on the way*.

"You're gonna have to stay sharp, Cth'ka," Skeleton Steve said. "Don't trust Worla…"

"Oh, don't worry, Ssskeleton Sssteve," I replied. "I won't!"

We passed through Ahimsa village again on the way back, and flowed through the town in the same way, sending the villagers screaming and squawking back into their homes. The odd creatures locked their doors and probably stayed inside *all day* after we were gone...

I don't know why it was so funny, but making those villagers run in fear made me chuckle. Not that we posed them any danger— maybe it was funny because they were such cowards, already.

One of the villagers didn't scream and hide in fear, though.

As I flew over and through the town, I caught a glimpse of the village's blacksmith, standing firm at his forge, watching the multitude of creeper soldiers pass by with his arms crossed and his brow furrowed. The blacksmith waved at Skeleton Steve, and my bony friend waved back.

We reached Lurkmire Swamp in the late afternoon.

"What are we to do, sssir?" C'Thor asked. "We should go *with* you! The witch won't dare messs with you when *we* are all there..."

"No, C'Thor," I replied. "If she feelsss threatened, she may hurt or kill Zarek!" I thought about it. "Ssstay clossse, but out of sssight. Sssurround Worla'sss area, and ssstand by. If I need you, and the sssoldiersss, you'll sssee, or I'll call for you."

"Yesss sssir."

Skeleton Steve and I went on alone.

I knew that I could trust the creeper army to stay quiet and hidden. We *were* creepers, after all...

When we arrived, past the crooked rock landmark and through swamp, I saw that the vindicators had been very busy working on the 'mansion' in the last two days. It occurred to me that with my creeper army, I could destroy Worla's hut and the mansion far more easily than I did with *the Steve's* castle.

But not that Nether Portal—it was made of obsidian, and *creeper-proof*.

She'd probably just call up more otherworldly creatures from there.

The mansion now had walls all around the first level of the building, and the vindicators were steadily building a second floor!

Worla stood in the swampy field outside, watching and directing.

The obsidian Nether Portal was now fully enclosed inside the massive structure.

And *Zarek* was in there ... somewhere.

As Skeleton Steve and I made our way down into the swampy clearing where Worla's hut sat on the muddy shore, all of the vindicators working on the mansion stopped their construction without a word, and ran outside, quick and eerily.

I looked over at the circle of logs with a dead torch sticking out of the ground in between. It was amazing to think that just under ... *two months ago* ... Skeleton Steve, Worla, and I stood around that torch in the darkness of night—back when Skeleton Steve was worried about burning up in the sunlight—talking about using *three Ender Eyes* to find the stronghold and the *Crown of Ender*...

Now, just like Darkwood Forest, Worla's home had evolved. The hut was still there, but now, her skeleton horse was always tied up underneath. There was also a *perfect grid* of eighteen holes (once filled by lava) nearby in the field, and most notably, a huge and imposing structure of dark oak, birch, and cobblestone, being built around a Nether Portal *I helped* to create...

The witch turned to face us, smiling like a wolf with her sharp teeth. Her black eyes glittered in the late afternoon sun.

How did I ever *trust* this creature? She was a vicious predator, through and through. I could see it so clearly now...

And how have I grown as a creeper?

Was I still as innocent and naive as I was back then? Back when I was afraid of being attacked by ocelots?

"Mighty Cth'ka *returns*," Worla said, approaching with a dangerous grace. At least two dozen vindicators walked with her, hanging back, looming darkly like a bunch of troublemakers...

"Hello, Worla," I said. "*The Sssteve* is dead. His land isss dessstroyed. Everything isss rubble and burned to the ground."

"Yes..." she said. "I can sense that your *binding magic* has been released! You must be feeling better already, eh?"

"Our busssinesss isss done, yesss? Bring Zarek back to me."

"Not *quite* done, young creeper," Worla said. "Now that your three tasks are complete, your use for me is at its end, and you have *something* I want..."

The crown, I thought. *Now, she wants the crown...*

"Worla," I said, slowly, "wasss it you? Did *you* dessstroy my houssse? Kill my friendsss? Sssteal my ssstuff? To make me kill Witherynn for you?"

"Clever creeper," she replied, her voice smooth but sharp. "But no—I didn't steal your ore. *The Steve* actually did that. But that's what Minecraftians *do*."

494

"How did you kill my friendsss? How did you get them to blow up?"

"With *these*," she said, and snapped her long fingers.

With a familiar sound that reminded me of the fight on Bald Mountain, I saw two fire creatures from another world rise up behind Worla and her vindicators. Skeleton Steve would later tell me that they were called *blazes*. The odd creatures made breathing sounds that made me think of metal scraping against metal, and smoke poured from them into the sky as their strange bodies of rotating, glowing rods spun around and around. Their faces burned and flared as they regarded me, floating up closer to the witch...

"You tricked them into blowing up??" I asked. "Attacking them with thessse onesss' fireballsss?"

"Cth'ka, you continue to surprise me," Worla said. "You're *very* smart for a stupid creeper. Now," she said, holding out one clawed hand. "Give me the *Crown of Ender*..."

"My friendsss had *namesss* you know. We're more than jussst a *bunch of creepersss*. One of them, Cho'thosss, traveled *far* to find me in Darkwood. He had a ssscar on his body from fighting *the Sssteve* once long ago. One of thossse charged creepersss wasss named C'Ssscorp. He wasss very dedicated, and died to finish *your* dirty work! And *I am Cth'ka*—Mighty Cth'ka, the creeper king, and I will bring creeperking together! We have *livesss!* Hissstory! We are more than jussst—"

"Yeah, yeah," she said, her voice dripping with sarcasm. "Just hand the crown over, creeper, *or die...*"

I scowled.

The vindicators were starting to produce their axes, and I could see the iron blades shimmering in front of their dark clothes.

Looking up at the blazes, I contemplated their faces—passive, unreadable faces and eyes of fire. Did they *feel?* Did they care? Were those two best friends? More tools for Worla?

496

Reaching out with my power, I cast the invisible nets of *both* of my magic hands over them, just like I did with Volux the Vex, one for each of them. And just like with the strange impish creature, I felt my magical nets slipping around them, but I could *also* feel the pores, and tightened them up!

The blazes each made a weird, surprised sound when I grabbed them tightly, and gasped in shock with their metallic voices as I *threw* them together, against each other, and *shattered* their fiery bodies in my powerful magic hands!

Pieces of the blazes' glowing rod bodies, sparks and flames, and other strange, alien material exploded in a huge fireball above Worla and the vindicators, and the shards and pieces of the two creatures rained down upon them.

Worla gasped, her eyes wide and fearful for maybe the first time I've ever seen! She held her hands above her head and fended away the burning pieces of blazes showering down...

Skeleton Steve pulled his bow, and nocked a magical arrow.

"Now *you* lisssten, witch," I said. "We are *done*. Go and get my friend, and you'd better hope for *your* sssake that he'sss not hurt any more than when you took him..."

Worla cackled, shaking out her hands.

"Foolish creeper. You've got some tricks, but can you defeat us *all?*"

As she spoke, the vindicators stared at me with hateful eyes, each raising their axes. The dark villagers, as a group, were truly terrifying to behold!

"Don't do it, Worla," Skeleton Steve said. "We can *all* walk away from this peacefully."

"Oh, Skeleton Steve," the witch said. "The mob who doesn't even remember who he is and where he came from! When will you get tired of this *creeper project* and move on to helping *another* down and out mob, huh? What's next? Going to befriend another chicken? Help another zombie find his parents? Go make friends with a *cow* next time?? Why don't you—"

She stopped. Cocked her head to listen.

I opened my mouth to speak, but then I heard it too.

From all around.

Hissing.

There was a faint, steady hissing, building ... all around us.

Eventually, the vindicators heard it too, and their black, evil eyes started darting around.

Ssssssssssssssssssssssssssss...

"What *is* that?!" Worla asked.

Ssssssssssssssssssssssssssss...

Skeleton Steve smirked. "*So* dramatic," he said, with a low chuckle.

And then we saw them.

Ssssssssssssssssssssssssssss...

Coming in from all directions was a multitude of green bodies. Crackly-skinned, green faces with sad eyes and frowny black mouths approached with quiet footfalls from all around us...

"My army..." I said.

A hundred and fifty creepers approached like a huge green *trap* closing in around Worla and her group of vindicators, hissing continuously as they drew in closer.

I began to relax.

Ssssssssssssssssssssssssssssss...

The army came in tighter, scores and scores of creepers, some appearing quite angry, all glaring at the witch, all hissing louder and louder, until they were finally all surrounding the immediately area—close enough to advance and *destroy the entire place* if Worla and her brutes didn't back down...

Ssssssssssssssssssssssssssssss...

And then the hissing stopped.

I looked around at my army in admiration.

Skeleton Steve smirked.

The witch's eyes darted around the massive group of creepers. I could see the wheels turning in her brain. Was she *seriously* thinking of how she could fight an entire army of creepers?? She sure wouldn't be able to use her *lightning* as a weapon against us...

Even the two dozen vindicators behind her looked a little uncomfortable...

Everything was quiet for a while until I finally spoke again.

"Worla," I said. Her eyes snapped back to me, her face unsure, and perhaps a little more submissive now. "Sssend your people to go and get my friend."

She laughed a nervous laugh.

"Well, Cth'ka," she stammered, then regained her composure. "It seems your army is a little larger ... than I thought. We are at a ... stalemate??"

"This isssn't a ssstalemate, witch," I said, narrowing my eyes. "You return Zarek to me, or I will dessstroy everything, *and* you."

501

Worla made a gesture to the nearest couple of vindicators back to the mansion. They nodded silently, and moved away, into the building.

"Of *course*, creeper. I was *always* planning on delivering him back to you unharmed! I just needed to make sure you would do the task—that's all. I'm sure you can understand?"

"And you won't be getting the crown," I said. "I'm pretty sure I've *earned it*, wouldn't you sssay?"

She nodded and gave me a disarming smile.

"And now," I went on, "asss the leader of Darkwood Foressst, I declare that *you* and … *your people* … are not to ssstep foot into our woodsss. *Ever*. Or I will *finish* thisss, do you undersssstand, witch?!"

"It's fine," she said. "You have what you want—you're done with the tasks. I have … *something* I want. A girl can't have *everything*, can she??"

The two vindicators returned to the door of the mansion with Zarek walking in between them.

502

The zombie warrior was adjusting the golden armor on his shoulders, then turned to the vindicator holding his katana. When the dark villager offered the weapon back to him, Zarek took it without bitterness, and made his way over to me.

"Welcome back, my king. It is good to see you," he said, in his low, dull voice. "I see you brought your army?"

"Are you okay, Zarek?" I asked.

"I am okay *now*, sire."

"Goodbye, Cth'ka," Worla said, with a sincere smile. She shooed her vindicators off, and they all migrated back to the mansion to resume construction. "Maybe we'll talk again."

"Let'sss hope not, witch," I said.

When she turned back to her building project, trying to act like she wasn't surrounded by a ring of a hundred and fifty creepers, my friends and I turned to leave, walking back to where I left my flying platform. My army, my *people*, all filed

503

along behind me, gradually clustering back into their squads.

I never pointed him out during the confrontation, but I made my way straight back to my general, who looked like *all the other* creepers to anyone who couldn't tell the difference.

"Good work, C'Thor," I said. "The hisssing wasss a nice touch."

"Thank you, sssir. What now?"

I looked at Skeleton Steve, who smiled back at me. "Well, my questsss, the price of thisss crown, it'sss all done! Time to finish building Darkwood Fortresss, and expand our people sssome more!"

"Why didn't you kill her?" Skeleton Steve asked. "You *totally* could have! You would have been *right* to. It might have also saved you some trouble one day..."

"I know," I replied. "But I wasss tired of killing. I think the witch hasss to ressspect us, ressspect our ssstrength. I'm not jussst her tool anymore. We're *bigger* than that now, and can *defend* ourssselvesss—even from her. She mussst realize that."

"Smarter to kill her," Zarek said, walking along behind me.

Day 50

When we returned home later that night, C'Thor was approached by the squad we left behind while the army was away on *the Steve* mission.

Did I mention that?

After all, *someone* needed to stay to look after the clearing, at least just a squad. And more importantly, with more creepers coming in every day, there needed to be some soldiers back there to take them in and tell them what was going on.

C'Thor and the squad leader were talking about something very dramatic.

I put down my flying platform, and walked over.

"What isss it?" I asked.

C'Thor looked at me. "It'sss *the Sssteve*. He'sss not dead! And there'sss ... well..." He turned to the squad leader. "Tell *him* what you told me!"

The creeper spoke up after giving me a quick nod of respect. "Well, sssire," he said in a gravelly voice, "*the Sssteve* came *here*. He wasss looking pretty torn up, sssir, hisss armor all burnt and broken, and he wasss sssaying sssomething, but I didn't undersssstand of course. He ran away from usss, but after a while of him looking around, going into your mine and sssuch, he wasss attacked by ssstrange mobsss, and a *witch!*"

"Ssstrange mobsss?" I asked. "What kind of ssstrange mobsss? And why wasss he ssstill alive??" I said, looking at Skeleton Steve.

What was going on??

"Sssire," the squad leader continued. "There were two creaturesss that flew and ssspit fireballsss at *the Sssteve*. And more flying creaturesss that were sssmall, and had ssswords."

"Blazesss … vexessss…" I said.

"And when they almosssst killed him, the witch came out, and they captured him and took him to the *north*. To where you *came from*, jussst now!"

508

Worla had *the Steve. But how?* Didn't I kill him?

"Thank you, sssquad leader," I said, and turned away. C'Thor continued debriefing the creepers behind me as I walked with Skeleton Steve. "What'sss going on, my friend? I killed *the Sssteve*—you were there. You sssaid ssso!"

"Something about Minecraftians, Cth'ka ... they never die. They just come back. On their *bed* or somewhere else..."

I suddenly remember Volux the Vex. *He was told to wait for the Steve at his bed...*

"Ssso he died and came back to life, then came here??" I asked.

Skeleton Steve looked over at me, then, put a bony hand on my back.

"Not *exactly*, buddy," he said. "I *lied*."

"What?!"

"I lied to you—about *the Steve* being dead. After all of our talk about him maybe not being such a monster, and putting all the pieces together—not like you did about Worla blowing up your house, that was *brilliant*—I realized that *the Steve* didn't deserve our *vengeance*."

"But ... but I killed him! I sssmashed him and he fell three ssstories to the basssement!"

"Yeah, that was *crazy!* But, he was still alive. And I bet he *sure was confused* when a skeleton like me came at him and gave him a *potion of healing...*"

"Ssso he didn't die and disssappear in a puff of sssmoke?"

"Nope," he said, smirking. "He healed up, jumped to his feet, and ran away through a basement tunnel that probably led to one of his *mines* or something."

"But why did you *lie* to me??" I asked.

"To end the *Geas curse*, of course!" he exclaimed. "I told you I'd do my best to think of a way to get out of that—a way that was good for *everyone*. Or, at least I *hoped* I would. And then the opportunity *presented itself!* I remembered that Worla said that the only way you'd be free of the

510

magic is to *truly believe* that you were done with your task! Once you thought *the Steve* was dead, and you carried through her ridiculous demands of razing the whole place to the ground ... *poof!* The *Geas* was gone! At least, I *hoped* so, and then the witch confirmed it for us!"

I smiled.

"Thanksss, Ssskeleton Sssteve. I feel ssso much better! Thanksss for lying to me!"

"Oh come on," he said, and shrugged. "I won't lie to you again. That is, unless you're hit with *another* curse, and I have to lie to you to get the magic off of you while faking some more deaths..."

I gasped.

"But ... we have to sssave *the Sssteve!*" I stared at Skeleton Steve, and he stared back. "If he didn't kill Cho'thosss and the othersss, and blow up my houssse, then he hasssn't really done anything *wrong*—other than treating usss like invadersss! What on Diamodia do you think Worla'sss going to *do* to him??" I gasped again. "And there wasss a

511

Vex, *Volux*, back at the cassstle, by *the Sssteve'sss* bed! It wasss ssseparated from the othersss, but they were sssuppossssed to *capture the Sssteve* after I killed him! Oh no!" I looked at my friend. "Worla wasss intending to capture *the Sssteve* all along—not kill him. I wasss only sssuppossssed to kill him to make him easssier to capture! And now she'sss got him!"

Was it too late??

Worla mentioned that she got something she wanted. *The Steve* must have been the *something!* He was there, captured already, all along! Probably held prisoner in the mansion, just like Zarek was, while we all talked outside!

"Yeah," Skeleton Steve said. "That's probably the right thing to do. Heck—*the Steve* probably came here looking for *me* after I helped him, and got *himself* captured instead."

"I can't imagine what sssort of nasssty ssstuff she hasss planned for him!" I said.

"*That* must have been why she was so upset with you when you interfered with their fight on Bald Mountain, remember?"

It was all starting to make sense now.

For some reason, Worla was killing witches and doing something dark and weird with creatures from another dimension. And for quite a while now, she's been trying to catch *the Steve*.

"Everything'sss making more sssenssse now! The Geasss, the manipulation! What'sss sssome of the other weird ssstuff Witherynn sssaid?"

"Wele..." Skeleton Steve said.

"Wele..." I repeated, trying to remember.

"Wele'Gumali," Skeleton Steve said.

"Yesss—that'sss it. What'sss that?"

"I don't know," said Skeleton Steve. "No idea."

"Well," I said, looking at Skeleton Steve, looking at Zarek, passing my eyes over my massive creeper army. "Let'sss go asssk Worla..."

"And rescue *the Steve*," my bony friend said.

"I'm with you, my king," Zarek said.

"Another adventure already?" Skeleton Steve asked.

"I sssuppossse ssso ... *another adventure.*"

Want More Cth'ka?

Can you *help me*, please?
Please REVIEW
this book!

1. Please go to where you bought this book and *leave a review!* It just takes a minute and it really helps!

2. Join my free *Skeleton Steve Club* and get an email when the next book comes out!

3. Look for your name under my *"Amazing Readers List"* at the end of the book, where I list my *all-star reviewers*. Heck—maybe I'll even use your name in a story if you want me to! (*Let me know in the review!*)

About the Author - Skeleton Steve

I am *Skeleton Steve*, author of *epic* unofficial Minecraft books. *Thanks for reading this book!*

My stories aren't your typical Minecraft junkfood for the brain. I work hard to design great plots and complex characters to take you for a roller coaster ride in their shoes! Er … claws. Monster feet, maybe?

All of my stories written by (just) me are designed for all ages—kind of like the Harry Potter series—and they're twisting journeys of epic adventure! For something more light-hearted, check out my "Fan Series" books, which are collaborations between myself and my fans.

Smart kids will love these books! Teenagers and nerdy grown-ups will have a great time relating with the characters and the stories, getting swept up in the struggles of, say, a novice Enderman ninja (Elias), or the young and naïve creeper king

(Cth'ka), and even a chicken who refuses to be a zombie knight's battle steed!

I've been *all over* the Minecraft world of Diamodia (and others). As an adventurer and a writer at heart, I *always* chronicle my journeys, and I ask all of the friends I meet along the way to do the same.

Make sure to keep up with my books whenever I publish something new! If you want to know when new books come out, sign up for my mailing list and the *Skeleton Steve Club*. ***It's free!***

Here's my website:

www.SkeletonSteve.com

You can also 'like' me on **Facebook**: Facebook.com/SkeletonSteveMinecraft

And 'follow' me on **Twitter**: Twitter.com/SkeletonSteveCo

And watch me on **Youtube**: (Check my website.)

"Subscribe" to my Mailing List and Get Free Updates!

I *love* bringing my Minecraft stories to readers like you, and I hope to one day put out over 100 stories! If you have a cool idea for a Minecraft story, please send me an email at Steve@SkeletonSteve.com, and I might make your idea into a real book. I promise I'll write back. :)

Other Books by Skeleton Steve

The "Noob Mob" Books

Books about individual mobs and their adventures becoming heroes of Diamodia.

Diary of a Creeper King

Book 1
Book 2
Book 3
Book 4

Diary of a Lone Wolf
Book 1
Book 2
Book 3
Book 4

Diary of an Enderman Ninja
Book 1 – *FREE!!*
Book 2
Book 3

Diary of a Separated Slime – Book 1

Diary of an Iron Golem Guardian – Book 1

The "Skull Kids" Books

A Continuing Diary about the Skull Kids, a group of world-hopping players

Diary of the Skull Kids
Book 1 – *FREE!!*
Book 2
Book 3

The "Fan Series" Books

Continuing Diary Series written by Skeleton Steve *and his fans!* Which one is your favorite?

 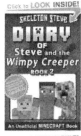 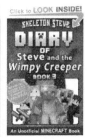

Diary of Steve and the Wimpy Creeper
Book 1
Book 2
Book 3

Diary of Zombie Steve and Wimpy the Wolf
Book 1 *COMING SOON*

SKELETON STEVE

The "Tips and Tricks" Books

Handbooks for Serious Minecraft Players, revealing Secrets and Advice

Skeleton Steve's Secret Tricks and Tips

Skeleton Steve's Top 10 List of Rare Tips

Skeleton Steve's Guide to the
First 12 Things I Do in a New Game

Get these books as for FREE!

(**Visit www.SkeletonSteve.com to *learn more***)

Series Collections and Box Sets

Bundles of Skeleton Steve books from the Minecraft Universe. Entire Series in ONE BOOK.

Great Values! Usually 3-4 Books (sometimes more) for almost the price of one!

Skeleton Steve – The Noob Years – Season 1
Skeleton Steve – The Noob Years – Season 2

Diary of a Creeper King – Box Set 1

Diary of a Lone Wolf – Box Set 1

Diary of an Enderman NINJA – Box Set 1

Diary of the Skull Kids – Box Set 1

Steve and the Wimpy Creeper – Box Set 1

Diary of a Teenage Zombie Villager – Box Set 1

Diary of a Chicken Battle Steed – Box Set 1

Sample Pack Bundles

Bundles of Skeleton Steve books from multiple series! New to Skeleton Steve? Check this out!

Great Values! Usually 3-4 Books (sometimes more) for almost the price of one!

Skeleton Steve and the Noob Mobs Sampler Bundle
Book 1 Collection
Book 2 Collection
Book 3 Collection
Book 4 Collection

-

Check out the website

www.SkeletonSteve.com

for more!

Enjoy this Excerpt from...

"Diary of a **Zombie Hunter Player Team –** *The Skull Kids*" Book 1

About the book:

Meet the **Skull Kids**.

They're three Minecraft players who hop from world to world, hunting zombies and searching for the elusive *Herobrine*--the ghost in the machine.

Teleporting down into a new world, the group is surprised to find that the game has changed once again, rendering almost ALL of their technology and mods useless. And when two of the Skull Kids are starving and distracted by exploring a desert village on Day 1 of their new adventure, the whole group is in danger when the sun goes down. Will the Skull Kids survive?

Love Minecraft adventure??

Read on for an Excerpt for the book!

The Skull Kids Ka-tet

Renzor51

Renzor51 is the warrior-scribe of the group, and always documents the party's adventures and excursions into game worlds. He's a sneaky fighter, and often takes the role of a sniper, but can go head to head with the Skull Kids' enemies when needed. A natural artist, Renzor51 tends to design and build many of the group's fortresses and structures, and keeps things organized. He also focuses a lot on weapon-smithing and enchanting, always seeking out ways to improve his gear.

Molly

Molly is the group's fiery and independent free spirit, and is a natural-born miner at heart. She loves to go for the diamonds, and will happily create vast, safe, and highly-organized mining networks. The most efficient of the group at resource gathering, Molly always has the most *stuff*. Stone, wood, iron, diamonds—she can get her hands on any of it faster than the others. She also loves to fish, farm, manage large ranches of animals, and is an expert Minecraft *chef*.

quantum_steve

As the group's *techno-wizard*, quantum_steve is the developer of the group's technology, acquires and adapts the excursion's *mod* tech, and controls the Destiny Net—the unique equipment that allows the group to hop between worlds. He's a brave fighter and a fearless explorer, and will often charge into battle head-on. With his interest in the technical aspects of the game, quantum_steve is a master of Redstone and Nether portals.

Day 1 - Morning

I was the first one into the new world.

This is the first entry of Renzor51 of the Skull Kids Ka-tet, documenting our excursion into this particular Minecraft universe.

When I finally got my bearings, I realized that it was morning. Mid-morning. The sun shone high in the sky, but there was still plenty of time for us to figure out how we were going to hole up and protect ourselves before dark.

Standing in the shadow of an oak tree, I looked around. It had been a long time since I set foot in a Minecraft world. Molly, quantum_steve and I had been exploring other games for so long that I was worried about how much this game had changed.

There was grass under my feet, but not far away, the grass gave way to sand, and the sand continued *forever*. Behind and around me was a forest of oak trees, gradually changing to tall, thick, dark oak.

"Okay," I said into the comm. "I've appeared on the edge of a desert … and a forest."

I heard the chatter of quantum_steve and Molly in my earpiece, but couldn't make them out. They must have still been in the *Destinal Net*.

The *Destinal Net* was the teleportation technology quantum_steve built for us to travel from world to world.

I was *first feet on the ground*.

A group of chickens clucked nearby, and I saw a pool of water surrounded by the plump, white birds just inside the trees.

Molly's voice garbled in my ear. I caught a moment of "…you have to…" from quantum_steve. They were having trouble with the Destinal Net.

I wasn't hungry yet, but it was good to know that there was a flock right next to our landing zone. Of course, I wouldn't be able to do anything about hunger anyway—at least not until I crafted some weapons and tools. It was very difficult to catch and kill a chicken by hand.

Looking around, I saw that the desert extended far into ... whatever direction. I would look into directions later. The sun was opposite the desert, and the sun always rose in the east. I guess the desert went west...

In the hazy distance of the barren landscape, I saw several light, sandy-colored building on the horizon.

"Oh, there's a village!" I said.

"Nice!" said quantum_steve's voice over the comm.

"It's not letting me …" Molly's voice garbled and faded out in my ear. What if they couldn't get through? Would I be stuck here all alone? I took several steps out into the sand toward the village, but hung back at the landing zone.

I turned around to face the spawn point, and saw quantum_steve standing in the sand not far from me. His light blue, checkered polo shirt was bright in the sun, and several pieces of small electronics equipment hung from his belt.

"Oh, there you are," I said.

Quantum_steve ran over to me distracted, holding his comm piece to his ear, and typing something on his arm console. He must have still been trying to help Molly transport. He stood next to me in the desert, hardly paying attention to the new world around us.

He and Molly chatted back and forth as he helped her through the Destinal net.

Most of the time, we were able to hop from world to world without a problem. But sometimes the worlds *changed*. And whenever the worlds changed, quantum_steve's Destinal Net technology—as well as our mods—had to be *adapted*.

Once, back in our earlier days of *planeswalking* (as quantum_steve calls it), we were stuck on a world without technology for quite a long time!

But we survived. That's what we do. We're the Skull Kids. We survive.

When we learned, long ago, about the myth of *Herobrine*, the ghost in the machine, we decided to travel from world to world to see if we could get a glimpse of the elusive creature amidst our adventures. I suspect that quantum_steve wanted to study him, to learn about the *code* he had inside that allowed the ghost to bend the laws of the game.

Although, to this date, we've never seen it. We've been on worlds where other players have reported sightings of the ghost, but after setting up extensive bases and exploring the worlds for miles across terrain and down to the bedrock, we never found anything outside of the normal Minecraft universe.

Universe.

Multiverse.

I don't know ... quantum_steve talks about the 'multiverse'. I guess it's not like traveling from world to world—not really. It's more like 'universe hopping' according to my more technical friend. Each Minecraft *universe* has a world, a *Nether*, and an *End*. So going from Minecraft world to Minecraft world is actually shifting back and forth between totally different universes!

Or ... a *Multiverse*.

I've always called it 'world hopping' for simplicity. But that's too simple of a term for it.

Heck, maybe there are other planets out there too, outside the atmosphere of this world, past the square moon, even past the square sun. But we've never gone off planet before. I've heard of some other players visiting space, but we never have.

Looking down at my own arm console, I could see that the directionals and coordinates were working, as they always did, but my *JourneyMap mod* did not. My mapping software was *gone*.

While quantum_steve talked with Molly over the comm, I made a mental note of where we spawned on this world, and decided to explore *just a bit* into the desert. My feet hissed through the sand, as I sprinted across the distance to get a closer look at the far-off village.

Approaching the large, bright-green cacti that grew here and there, I broke up a few cactus blocks to carry with me. Ever since my first exploration into these Minecraft worlds, I learned that *cacti* can be valuable as an obstacle for the mobs.

Who knows where we'd end up?

Maybe it would be a good idea to make a *cactus fence* around the front of whatever home we built.

It passed the time, anyway...

My friends were still having problems with the Destinal Net by the time I was halfway to the village. I broke up more cacti, looked around from the top of a sand dune, then headed back.

Returning to the spawn point, our landing zone, I saw a single cow standing at the edge of the sand and forest among the group of chickens.

I *was* a little hungry, so I approached with a piece of cactus in my hand and hit it with the spikey, green block. It *mooed* in protest and tried to run, so I chased it through the sand swinging my piece of cactus whenever I was close enough. Man, that cow was *fast* on open ground!

"Moo!" it cried. "Moo! Moo!"

My arm console told me that Molly arrived, and I saw quantum_steve approaching.

"I'm killing a cow," I said over the comm, and my friend joined me in chasing the animal, hitting it with his fists. Eventually, we cornered it, and obtained our first pieces of food on this new world.

"Yay!" I laughed.

Quantum_steve laughed too, and we turned to join up with Molly.

"Okay, let's go to that village!" I said. "I now have *three steaks* to start us off with."

"Cool," quantum_steve said, and we began running through the desert to the cluster of sandstone huts in the distance.

I hadn't heard from Molly yet since she arrived on the world, and couldn't see her on my map since my *map mod* wasn't working, but before I said anything, I saw her in the distance, running ahead of us to the village.

She knew *exactly* where to go first.

I laughed.

Day 1 - Afternoon

Sprinting across the desert, I tried to catch up to Molly, and reached the outlying farms just behind her. The hot sun made her blonde hair glow, and she stood out distinctly from the villagers in her pink shirt and green shorts. I passed all of the green stalks of plants sprouting from the tilled dirt, the colorful crops and blue water a stark contrast against all of the sand-based blocks that made up the village.

"Hurrr…" a villager said, as I ran past, catching up to Molly.

I ran past the small homes and into the center of town, and saw desert bunnies hopping around in the streets as I approached the village's well.

Multiple villagers bustled around us, talking in their weird, squawking *villager* language.

"Where did you guys go?" quantum_steve asked over the comm.

"Village," I said. I ran through a bunch of villagers and bunnies, rapidly exploring the different buildings to see what this small desert town had for us. "There are rabbits!"

"Okay," quantum_steve said. "Are the buildings built with *sand*? Can *we* build with sand?"

I climbed a ladder inside a small building without a door.

"It's like 'sand-block' and stuff," I said. "Sand stone ... and bricks."

"I'm just wondering," quantum_steve said. "It's going to get dark. We're going to *die*..."

He said that with drama. He was kidding, of course. But it had a grain of truth to it. Was it late afternoon already? I wasn't worried yet, but we would have to figure out a way to secure our safety before dark.

"No, not necessarily," I said. "We can easily just hole up in a building here." I descended the ladder after taking a quick look over the town from the roof, then ran through the rest of town.

Man, all of this running was making me hungry!

"Oh man," I said, "I'm *super* hungry all of a sudden!"

Molly's voice came in over the comm. "But all of the villagers will die," she said, "if we just stay here."

"Maybe not," quantum_steve said. "The world is different now. They might be able to get away better?"

I opened a door and went into one of the larger houses. A table, and some sort of structure made from stone slabs. Maybe I could find a chest somewhere with food so I wouldn't have to eat one of these raw beef steaks.

Nothing useful in here, I thought. I left, closed the door, and went into the smaller house across the street. Also nothing. Closed the door behind me as I left.

Suddenly I was too hungry and tired to run. Walking through town, I entered another larger building. It was the village library. Scores of books lined the walls, and I approached a crafting table in the corner, but stepped away when I realized that all I was holding was raw meat and cactus blocks.

Enjoy this Excerpt from...

"Diary of a **Lone Wolf**" Book 1

About the book:

Dakota was a young wolf, happy with his life in a wolf pack in the taiga forest where he was born.

Almost fully-grown, Dakota was fast and loved to run. He had friends, loved his mother, respected his alpha, and had a crush on a young female pack-mate.

But his life was about to change forever when his pack was attacked by *the Glitch*, a mysterious and invincible horde of mobs that appeared and started killing everything in their path!

Now, he was a **lone wolf**. With the help of Skeleton Steve, would he ever belong to another pack again? Would they escape *the Glitch* and warn the rest of Diamodia?

Love Minecraft adventure??

Read on for an Excerpt for the book!

SKELETON STEVE

DIARY

OF A

LONE WOLF

BOOK 1

An Unofficial MINECRAFT Book

Day 1

So how does a *wolf* tell a story? What should I say, Skeleton Steve?

Oh? Where should I start?

Okay.

So, I guess, my name is *Dakota*. I'm a wolf.

Heh ... I already said that. I guess, technically, I'm a *dog* now. No? Doesn't matter?

Skeleton Steve is telling me that I'm a wolf. *Steve* calls me a dog. But I don't understand much about what *Steve* says.

Is this confusing? I'm sorry. Where was I?

Just from ... okay, right before.

Well, I guess I can start by telling you about my old pack. My family.

Just a few days before the attack, it was a day like any other.

559

I woke up in the forest and leapt to my feet! It was a *beautiful* morning. The forest was in shadows of the rising sun, a cool breeze was crisp on my face, and I could smell the woods come alive! Approaching a tall pine tree, I scratched my shoulders on its bark.

All of my pack was waking up around me.

What a great life!

I ran down to the creek, and drank some water. Splashed my face into it. *Cold!* And shook my fur, sending drops of cold mountain water all over before bounding back up the hill.

I guess it's a good time to introduce *the pack*.

My eyes went first to the alpha and his mate. Logan and Moon. Logan was a huge wolf, and he was really nice. He and Moon didn't talk with us very much, but he was a good leader. Logan mostly kept to himself, quiet and strong, and he led us through the mountains day by day whenever we moved.

Right now, we'd spent the last several days hanging out *here*. There were fields full of sheep nearby, and with this nice, flat area, a mountain creek down the hill a bit, and plenty of shade, it was a good clearing to stay in for a while. I was sure we'd move on soon. We always did.

My belly rumbled. We didn't eat yesterday. Today, I knew the alpha would probably send Archie and me to scout out another herd of sheep for the pack to hunt. I was so *fast*, one of the fastest wolves in the pack, and Archie was pretty fast too, so Logan usually sent us out to find the food.

I loved my job! It was great, roaming around with my best bud, running as fast as we could, exploring the mountains all around the clearing where the pack lived. It was only last year when I was finally old enough to be given a job to do. I loved being able to help my family so well.

Taking a big breath of fresh air, I looked around at the rest of the pack waking up and frolicking in the brisk morning.

Over at the edge of the forest were Colin and Arnou. They were the *warriors*, really. We all help each other, and we all have shared tasks given to us by the alpha, but the big and muscular brothers, Colin and Arnou, were really great at fighting, and they were always the first to defend the pack against any mobs that attacked us—the first aside from *Logan the alpha*, that is.

There was my mother, Minsi, one of the older female wolves. I loved my mother. She sat on her own this morning, watching the birds and chewing on a bone.

Running and playing together was the mated pair, Boris and Leloo. Leloo helped raise the cubs (all of the females did, really), and Boris, along with his brother Rolf, were very good at hunting and taking down our prey. The two hunter brothers were very skilled at circling a herd of sheep or other food, and making the animals run whichever way they wanted.

Sitting in the shadow of a couple of pine trees were Maya, and her daughter, Lupe.

Lupe was my age.

She was a beautiful wolf. And smart too. And funny.

I dunno. For some reason, I had a really hard time *talking* to her. Archie joked with me a lot that I should make her my mate, but whenever I walked up to her, whenever I tried to talk to her, my tongue became stupid, I forgot was I wanted to say, and I just embarrassed myself whenever I tried.

It was terrible! Yes, I guess, I really, really liked her. It should have been easy!

Easy just like with Logan and Moon. Logan has been alpha since before I was born, but my mother told me that before he was alpha, when he was younger, he just walked up to Moon one day and *decided* that they were going to be mates.

I don't really understand how that works. Maybe one day I will.

"Hey, dude!" said Archie, running up to see me.

"Oh, hey! Good morning!" I said, sitting in the dirt.

Archie was a year older than me, and my best friend. When we were growing up, we always did everything together. And now that we were practically adult wolves (almost), we worked together whenever Logan gave us an assignment.

"You ready?" he said, wagging his tail.

"Ready for what?" I asked.

"Going to look for a herd, of course!" he replied.

"Well, yeah, but Logan hasn't told us to yet."

"I bet he will," Archie said.

Not an hour went by before the massive alpha called on us.

"Dakota! Archie!" he said, his deep voice clear above the rest of the pack, chatting in the morning. We ran up and sat before him.

"Yes, sir?" we said.

"You two explore down in the valley today, see if you can find another herd for us to hunt."

564

"Right away," I said. Archie acknowledged as well, and we departed our pack's temporary home, flying down the hill as quickly as our speedy wolf feet would take us. With the wind in my face, I dodged around trees, leapt over holes, exploded through the underbrush, and felt great!

When we emerged from the huge, pine forest, I felt the sun warm up my face, and I closed my eyes, lifting my snout up into the sky. Archie popped out of the woods next to me.

"Look at that," Archie said. "Have you ever seen anything so beautiful?"

The sunshine on our faces was very pleasant, and looking down, I could see a huge grassy field, full of red and yellow flowers. Little bunnies hopped around here and there, and in the distance was a group of sheep—mostly white, one grey, one black.

Beautiful. I thought of *Lupe*.

"Awesome," I said. "And hey—there's the sheep over there!"

We returned to the pack and led everyone through the forest back to the colorful and sunny meadow we found.

Soon, we were all working together to keep the sheep in a huddle while Logan, Boris, and Rolf, darted into the group of prey and eventually took them all down. After Logan and Moon had their fill, the rest of us were free to eat what we wanted.

I chomped down on the raw mutton and filled my belly. The sun was high, a gentle breeze blew through the meadow, and I felt warm and happy. Archie ate next to me, and I watched Lupe from afar, dreaming of a day when I would be brave enough to *decide* she was my mate.

Life was good.

Day 2

Today Archie and I went for a swim.

It wasn't necessary to go looking for more food yet, according to the alpha, so we were instructed to stay together, for the most part.

As a pack, we didn't eat every day. But sometimes, I got lucky and found a piece of rotten zombie flesh on the ground after the undead mobs burned up in the morning. Today wasn't one of those days, but it happened *sometimes*.

Anyway, it was fortunate that the mountain creek was just down the hill. Archie and I were able to run down and swim, while the rest of the pack sat around digesting all of the mutton we ate yesterday.

A section of the creek was nice and deep, so my friend and I splashed around and competed to see who could dog-paddle the longest. Archie won most of those times, but I know that I'm *faster* than him on the ground, ha ha.

567

There was a bit of a commotion around lunchtime when my mother happened upon a skeleton archer that was hiding in the shadows under a large pine tree. She gasped and back-pedaled as the undead creature raised his bow and started firing arrows into our midst.

Arnou was nearby, and responded immediately, with Colin close behind.

As the warrior wolves worked together to flank the skeleton, the mob did get *one* decent shot off, and Colin yelped as an arrow sank into his side. But the two strong wolves lashed out quickly, and were able to latch onto the skeleton's arms and legs, taking him down in no time. Only bones remained.

Colin and Arnou each took a bone, and went back to their business of lounging with the pack.

"Are you okay?" I said to my mother.

"Yes, thank you, Dakota," she said. "I'm glad you were out of the way."

"Oh come on, mom," I said. "I could have taken him."

"I know you could have, sweetie," she replied, and licked my face.

I don't know why the skeleton attacked. Sometimes the mobs attacked us. Sometimes not. Sometimes we (especially Colin and Arnou) attacked *them*. We did *love* zombie meat and skeleton bones, but I've never felt the urge to outright *attack* one of the undead to get it. I knew that if we were patient, we would always find more sheep and get plenty to eat.

Later that day, Archie caught me staring at Lupe, and decided to give me a hard time.

"You should go and *talk* to her, man!" he said, nudging me with his snout in her direction. Lupe noticed the movement, and looked over at us. I saw her beautiful, dark eyes for an instant, and then I turned away.

"Cut it out, man! Jeez!" I shoved him back with my body. "You made her look!"

"So what?" he said. "What's wrong with looking?" He laughed. "Maybe she *should* look. Then something will finally *happen*!"

I stole a glance back to her from the corner of my eye. She had looked away, and was laying in the grass again, looking at the clouds as they rolled by. Usually she hung out around her mother, Leloo, but she was by herself for the moment.

Could I? Did I dare?

"Look, dude," Archie said. "She's by herself. *Go for it!*"

I gulped, and looked back at my friend. I looked around at all of the other pack members. They weren't paying any attention. Just going about their own things.

Padding silently through the grass, I approached. Quiet. Well, not *too* quiet. Didn't want to look like I was sneaking up on her! I just didn't want to look *loud*. Okay, I needed to be a *little* louder.

Snap. Crunch. I made some random noises on the ground as I approached.

570

Jeez, I thought. *I'm being a total weirdo! What am I doing?*

Lupe turned her head to my approach, and when I saw her face, my heart fluttered.

"Hi, Dakota!" she said.

She was happy. Good. I wanted to see her happy. Make her happy. Umm ... if she *wanted* to be happy. Then I'd help her be happy. *What?*

"Oh ... hi," I said. Gulped.

She watched. Smiled. Waited patiently. What would I say? I couldn't really think of anything.

"How's it going?" she asked.

"Good. *Great!*" I said. "*Really* great!"

"That's cool," she replied.

I looked back, and saw Archie watching. He nudged at me with his nose from far away. *Go on*, he said without words.

"Uh," I said, "How are you?"

Lupe smiled and looked back at the clouds.

"Oh, I'm fine, thanks." Her tail gave a little wag.

"So, uh," I said, trying to think of something to talk about. "Did you get plenty of mutton yesterday? Lots to eat? I hope you ate a lot! *I mean*—not that it looks like you eat a lot, or too much. I mean—you're not *fat* or anything; I didn't think you look fat—"

Her face contorted in confusion.

Holy heck! What was I doing?

"Um ... I'm sorry! I'm not calling you fat I just ... uh ..."

Lupe laughed a nervous laugh.

"Ah ... yeah," she said. "I got plenty to eat. Thanks to *you*."

"Um ... me, and *Archie*. We found the sheep."

"Yeah, she said. "I know." She smiled, then watched the clouds.

"Yeah," I responded. I watched her, trying to think of something to say that wasn't completely *boneheaded*. After a few moments, she noticed me *staring*, and looked back at me. I looked up to the sky.

Her tail gave a small wag.

"Okay, well," I said, "I guess I'll go see how Archie is doing."

"Oh, really?" she asked. "Well, okay, I guess..."

"Okay," I said. "Well, bye."

"Bye," she said, gave me a smile, then looked back to the clouds she was watching.

I walked back to my friend feeling like an idiot, being careful not to walk like a weirdo.

Later that night, I laid in the grass, watching the stars. As the square moon moved across the sky, I looked at a thousand little pinpricks of light, shining and twinkling far, far away, drifting through space.

Most of the pack was already asleep. I could see Lupe sleeping next to her mom. Archie was sleeping near me, and the rest of the pack kept close together—my mother, the warriors and hunters, Leloo. The alphas slept away from us, a little ways up the hill.

The night was quiet, aside from the occasional zombie moan far in the distance, or the hissing of spiders climbing the trees. I was a little hungry, but tried to ignore my belly.

The stars all looked down at me from the vast, black sky, watching over all of us. So pretty.

Day 3

The morning started like all others.

We woke up and the pack was abuzz with hunger. It would be another scouting day for Archie and me. I ran down to the creek to splash cold water on my face, and found a piece of zombie flesh.

Even though I was hungry, I decided not to eat it. I took the delicious piece of meat in my mouth, careful not to sink my teeth into its sweet and smelly goodness, and brought it to my mom.

"Aw, *thanks*, honey!" she said. "Do you want to split it with me?"

"No, that's okay, mom. You have it," I said.

"But you're probably going to go looking for a herd with Archie today, right? You should take some and have the energy."

"That's alright, mom. I'll eat later."

"Okay, but I'll hang onto half of it in case you change your mind, okay?" She started to eat the zombie meat.

As we expected, Logan called on Archie and I to go out and find another herd of sheep. We happily complied, and ran through the forest for the better part of an hour, seeking out prey for the pack.

It was a warm day, and the breeze in my face felt great! My feet were fast, and the forest smelled good, and I ran like the wind. After a while, I caught the scent of mutton, and led Archie to a small herd of sheep wandering around in dense trees.

"There's our meal ticket!" Archie said. "Let's go back!"

"Let's *do it!*" I said, and we laughed as we sprinted through the woods back to the pack.

After dodging through the trees, leaping over boulders, and running silently through the straights like grey ghosts, we approached the forest clearing where the pack was living.

But something was *wrong*.

As we came down the hill, past enough trees to see the clearing, I smelled a weird smell. Something different that I hadn't smelled before. Something *alien*. And as we approached closer, I heard the sounds of battle!

Zombies moaned and growled. Skeletons clattered. Bows twanged, and arrows whistled through the air. I heard growls and scratches, thumps and crashes. Yelps and cries and raw wolf snarls!

"What the—?" Archie cried, as we ran down to the clearing.

Our pack was *fighting for their lives* against a group of zombies and skeletons!

I couldn't count how many of the undead were down there—the scene was confusing. For some reason, the battle was taking place in *broad daylight*, and the mobs weren't burning up in the sun!

In the chaos before us, I had a very hard time making out who was alive and who was already dead. The alpha was obviously still alive, running to and fro between the undead, striking with power and mainly pulling the attackers off of the other wolves. Moon, I think, was doing the same. Several wolves lay dead. My stomach suddenly turned cold...

CHECK OUT
SKELETONSTEVE.COM
... to CONTINUE READING!

The Amazing Reader List

Thank you SO MUCH to these Readers and Reviewers! Your help in leaving reviews and spreading the word about my books is SO appreciated!

Awesome Reviewers:

MantisFang887 EpicDrago887

ScorpCraft SnailMMS WolfDFang

LegoWarrior70

Liam Burroughs

Ryan / Sean Gallagher

Habblie

Nirupam Bhagawati

Ethan MJC

Jacky6410 and Oscar

MasterMaker / Kale Aker

Cole

Kelly Nguyen

Ellesea & Ogmoe

K Mc / AlfieMcM

JenaLuv & Boogie

Han-Seon Choi

Danielle M

Oomab

So Cal Family

Daniel Geary Roberts

Jjtaup

Addidks / Creeperking987

D Guz / UltimateSword5

TJ

Diary of a Creeper King
Full Quadrilogy

Xavier Edwards

DrTNT04

UltimateSword5

Mavslam

Ian / CKPA / BlazePlayz

Dana Hartley

Shaojing Li

Mitchell Adam Keith

Emmanuel Bellon

Melissa and Jacob Cross

Wyatt D and daughter

Jung Joo Lee

Dwduck and daughter

Yonael Yonas, the Creeper Tamer (Jesse)

Sarah Levy / shadowslayer1818

Pan

Phillip Wang / Jonathan55123

Ddudeboss

Hartley

Mitchell Adam Keith

L Stoltzman and sons

D4imond minc4rt

Bookworm_29

Tracie / Johnathan

Jeremyee49

Endra07 / Samuel Clemens

And, of course ... Herobrine

(More are added all the time! Since this is a print version of this book, check the eBook version of the latest books—or the website—to see if your name is in there!)